The Psychology
of Alcoholism

Hindsfoot Foundation Series
on Alcoholics Anonymous History

The Psychology of Alcoholism

William E. Swegan

with Glenn F. Chesnut, Ph.D.

iUniverse, Inc.
Bloomington

The Psychology of Alcoholism

Originally published © 2003 as
On the Military Firing Line in the Alcoholism Treatment Program
by Sgt. Bill S. with Glenn F. Chesnut

iUniverse books may be ordered through booksellers or by contacting:

iUniverse
1663 Liberty Drive
Bloomington, IN 47403
www.iuniverse.com
1-800-Authors (1-800-288-4677)

ISBN: 978-1-4502-8598-8 (sc)
ISBN: 978-1-4502-8599-5 (ebk)

Printed in the United States of America

iUniverse rev. date: 11/15/2011

Dedication

This book is dedicated to my friends who were either killed or wounded on 7 December 1941, in the attack on Pearl Harbor and Hickam Army Air Base. As one of the first people subjected to the horrors of that war, the loss of my comrades and fellow airmen was devastating. The destruction wrought during the first three hours of the attack at the air base defied description. Many of the casualties were very close friends of mine, for we were a much closer unit during those years, and very few members of the Army Air Corps were teetotalers. Five of us in particular drank together constantly at the NCO Club and a local beer garden which we had dubbed "the Snake Ranch." The other four were all killed that day, and I, the only survivor, was left with an indelible impression of the horrors of war. Because of the security measures which were immediately clamped down, my own family did not know whether I had lived or died for several days afterward. Although many Americans are unaware of this, the casualty rate that day among the Air Corps personnel at Hickam exceeded even that among the Navy people at Pearl Harbor next door to us. In addition to the dead, two hundred and eighty-two individuals who survived received either Purple Hearts or Silver Stars. No one who was not there that morning could ever imagine what we felt when we heard the sound of the airplane engines overhead and heard the thump of the exploding bombs, and realized instantly that one of the deadliest wars our country would ever be involved in had just broken out over our heads. So this book is dedicated to the memory of my buddies: those grievously wounded, and those who did not make it. I will never forget you.

DISCLAIMER

The following interpretations of the A.A. program and its therapeutic benefits do not represent the official position of Alcoholics Anonymous. They are the opinions of the authors and in no way are meant to infer or imply that they have been endorsed by or empowered to represent Alcoholics Anonymous as such. We also make brief mention of problems with drug addiction in a few places in this book: Narcotics Anonymous is a program of recovery with principles and activities which are patterned closely after A.A., but we wish to stress that it is a separate program which is in no way organizationally linked to Alcoholics Anonymous. The A.A. principle of "singleness of purpose" requires their groups to confine their discussions and suggestions to alcohol problems alone.

— Bill S. and Glenn C.

A SPECIAL NOTE OF THANKS

I am deeply indebted to Glenn Chesnut, the co-author of this book, for his dedication and writing skill, and insisted on including this note of thanks. Those who have reviewed this volume prior to publication include both professional and lay people who have a profound knowledge of the problem of alcoholism and the workings of Alcoholics Anonymous. Their response has been overwhelming, both in their endorsement of the contents and their compliments on the skills which he contributed to the clarity and strength of their presentation. I am most grateful to you, Glenn, for your interest, your dedication, and your ability to turn ideas and feelings into words that communicate with the heart. Thank you for your humble and skillful devotion, which turned the publication of this book into a reality.

— Bill S.

Table of Contents

1. Introduction 1
2. Childhood in Niles, Ohio 16
3. From Lindbergh to the Depression Years 32
4. High School Years 47
5. Discovering Alcohol. 63
6. Joining the Army Air Corps. 76
7. The Attack on Pearl Harbor. 93
8. Sabotaging Every Success 101
9. First Tragic Marriage 116
10. My First Encounter with A.A. 128
11. The Blonde in the Merry Circle. 142
12. Getting Sober: July 5, 1948 155
13. The Road to Maturity 169
14. Beginning the First Military Alcoholism Treatment Program 193
15. The Effects of Alcohol on Our Emotional Development 213
16. Kent State University and Sister Ignatia 230
17. Lackland: the Fully Developed Treatment Program 246
18. Recovery through the Twelve Steps .267
19. Another Generation and Another War. 288
20. The Silver Dollar 297
    Afterword 309
    Notes 311
    Index 319
    About the Authors 323

CHAPTER 1

Introduction

Veterans Hospitals did not take alcoholics: 1945

I would like to begin this book by telling two stories about things that happened to me during the 1940's. The first story took place during the latter part of 1945. I had been discharged from the Army Air Force in August. During my period in the service, I had somehow lived through the bullets fired by the airplanes which were strafing Hickam Army Air Base in Hawaii on December 7, 1941, as part of the Pearl Harbor attack, and then had sweated in the jungles of New Guinea and the equatorial island of Biak as part of the war against Japan. I had contracted dengue fever, from which I had recovered, but also malaria, from which I was still suffering. I was also drinking uncontrollably, and had quickly lost my first civilian job after my discharge because I kept showing up for work drunk.

The Second World War was over, and I had somehow escaped death by enemy bullets during those years, but I was now in the local town hospital, in bad shape. I was only twenty-seven years old but already a doomed man. A friend I had known for many years tried to gain admission to a Veterans Hospital for me. They refused to admit me—the V.A. Hospital would have been willing to treat the malaria, but the fact that I was also a drunk meant that I was barred from all medical aid.

This had been the doom of alcoholics in the United States since the founding of the republic. Hospitals refused them admittance, and no one really knew how to treat them. There were a few expensive private facilities where drunks whose families had money would send them periodically for "drying out," but there were almost no lasting cures. Many alcoholics died in alleys, others were sent off to long imprisonments in state and federal penitentiaries for things they had done while they were drunk and out of control, while others were labeled "dipsomaniacs" and sent off to rot in mental institutions with the other maniacs. Drunks and lushes like myself—the term "alcoholic" had only recently been developed, and was still not in common usage—were regarded either as morally defective people who were to be scorned and cast out by all decent folk, or as simply insane. Most medical doctors regarded us as hopeless and doomed, and refused even to treat us at all, even when we were clearly dying. In all fairness, they did not really know anything to do anyway: if they kept us from dying this time, we would simply go right back out and start drinking again. We were going to die, and nothing could be done to save us from eventual death. And we embarrassed people and made them feel uncomfortable, and some of us were argumentative and violent, and caused trouble.

After the end of the ill-fated experiment of National Prohibition (1920-1933), the federal government had abandoned practically any national attempt at alcohol treatment and awareness, and the military dealt with alcoholism by purely punitive measures: when drunks like me got too far out of hand, we suffered reductions in pay, demotion, imprisonment, or were kicked out of the service. As far as most decent folk were concerned, there was no help for people like me, and we were simply abandoned to our fates.

So there I was in the hospital. I was sick, very sick. A judge granted my wife a divorce. My beautiful little daughter I was not to see again for forty years. I was a veteran of the Pacific campaign, but the United States government had cast me off. The Veterans Hospital refused to admit me on any grounds. This was America in 1945, if you were an alcoholic.

Three years later, my talk on alcoholism
at a military base: 1948

But a revolution was taking place—in fact had already begun quietly in the latter 1930's among a small group of recovered alcoholics—and three years after being refused admittance to that Veterans Hospital, I found myself on the forefront of this revolution.

I had reenlisted in the Air Force, because I had not found any civilian job I could handle. I was eventually sent to Mitchel Air Force Base on Long Island, New York. My drinking had continued. But on July 5, 1948, I was able to stop drinking for good after I began attending the meetings of an Alcoholics Anonymous group on Long Island and actually taking the program seriously. That was almost fifty-five years ago, and for that entire half century—more than half century—I have remained continuously sober.

Back in 1948, Alcoholics Anonymous was still almost brand new. A stockbroker from New York city and a surgeon from Akron, Ohio had begun working together in the summer of 1935 on a new method of treating alcoholism. Recovered alcoholics helped one another to stay sober: that was an essential ingredient in its success. Within a relatively short period, they had enough alcoholics staying sober on the basis of their new approach, that they decided to write a book about it. The description of their method was published in 1939 under the simple title *Alcoholics Anonymous*. It was printed in fairly large type (for the benefit of blurry-eyed drunks who stumbled into their meetings) on very thick paper, so from the size of the volume it quickly became known simply as the "Big Book."

Small A.A. groups began to be established here and there across the United States (and even abroad) during the early 1940's, but even in 1948, it was still a very small and struggling organization. Nevertheless, by that time they had amply proven their point: almost anyone who took their program seriously, and was capable of self-honesty, and was willing to actually carry out the principles and steps in his or her everyday life, could get sober and stay sober. The discoveries made by the A.A. people, coupled with new understandings of alcoholism being developed by alcohol researchers like Dr. E. M. Jellinek at Yale (with whom I later studied), were revolutionizing the whole concept of alcoholism and its treatment.

And there I was in July of 1948, an alcoholic who had certainly been doomed to an early death, joining this quiet revolution and staying sober for the first time in almost twelve years. I had just turned thirty. And after just a short period of sobriety, impassioned with zeal, I asked my Squadron Commander if I could give a talk on alcoholism to the members of my Squadron. At first he looked at me as though my sanity had left me, but finally gave his permission.

I stood up before the other 159 members of my Squadron and said, "My name is Bill, and I'm an alcoholic." And they laughed uproariously, because they certainly already knew that. I had been the Squadron drunk. I saw them laughing at me, and for the first thirty years of my life, I had been the kind of person who would have slunk away feeling totally humiliated. Even the slightest thing—things that would not have bothered a normal person—would send me running, feeling totally rejected and shamed. But some enormous change had taken place inside me, and I just plunged on:

"I am an alcoholic and have found a way to live a useful life without having to drink alcoholic beverages." I kept on talking, and tried to explain to them what I had learned. After my talk, two people came up and asked for my help. I started taking them with me to the little civilian A.A. meeting there on Long Island. Two people became four, and four people became eight, and finally I had so many who wanted to go to the meeting that I could no longer find a vehicle large enough to hold them all. So I started an A.A. meeting there on the base.

Marty Mann and Senator Hughes

A.A. was still small enough in those days that news could travel fast, all across the country. What I had been doing on my own at Mitchel Air Force Base on Long Island came to the attention of Mrs. Marty Mann. She was the first woman to get continuously sober in A.A., and her story, "Women Suffer Too," began to be included in the Big Book from the time of the second edition in 1955. It has remained in the Big Book ever since, and is the third story (beginning on page 200) in the current fourth edition, which came out in 2001. She founded the National Council on Alcoholism, and teamed up with Senator Harold E. Hughes from Iowa (another A.A. member) to help produce massive changes in the way alcoholics were treated at the federal and national level. Marty was also one of the most impressive women I have ever known, and had a spontaneous, instant generosity and compassion unlike anything I have ever seen. I owe a good deal to her for the help she gave to me at many points in my life.

Marty had numerous connections with society people, major educators, government figures, authors, and people in the publishing business in New York City and Washington D.C., and in fact the entire east coast. She brought my work on the military base to the attention of several key people, and the next thing I knew, I was accepted at Yale University's School of Alcohol Studies and invited to study in their summer program. They granted me a nice scholarship as well. I got to study with Dr. E. M. Jellinek and other Yale experts, and learn about the latest developments in the medical and psychiatric field, and eventually was able to combine forces with Dr. Louis Jolyon West at Lackland Air Force Base to establish a treatment center for alcoholic rehabilitation to which airmen and officers from bases all over the world were sent.

Marty Mann was the inspiration for a good many of the things going on in alcoholism treatment and awareness programs during this period, all across the nation. Senator Harold E. Hughes eventually joined in the cause at the national legislative level, and he was one of the people who backed me too.[1] Among other things, the senator got Congress to pass a law stopping hospitals in the United States from refusing to admit sick alcoholics: he opened up the closed hospital doors I had found back in 1945, when I was so very ill.

Marty Mann, Senator Hughes, and I were part of the activist wing of A.A., a side of the movement which has had an enormous impact on government at all levels (federal, state, and local), the military, large national institutions, and even local communities all across the country over the course of the last sixty years. There are now treatment centers and alcohol awareness programs in place. Americans in general still use the old words on many occasions—he's a drunk, a lush, a sot, and other similar terms of abuse—but the technical term alcoholic is now also used, and most people in this country are now aware, to some degree, that it refers to a kind of illness and that it is treatable.

We who belonged to the activist wing of Alcoholics Anonymous followed the Twelve Traditions: we did not mention in public that we were A.A. members, but we did say openly that we were recovered alcoholics. We went out into the public domain to carry out the spirit, as we saw it, of the Twelfth Step: having been awakened, "we tried to carry this message to alcoholics" and also to those who had to deal with them, by creating structures and institutions which were not part of A.A., but were nevertheless working toward program-inspired goals. We never mentioned in public speeches or in anything we wrote that we were A.A. members ourselves, so that if we failed or disgraced ourselves or became over-zealous in inappropriate ways—or went out and got drunk again, although I did not personally know many of us who were genuinely deeply committed who actually did this—then it would not reflect harshly on the A.A. organization itself. If I failed, I did not want the general public to think that this meant that the Twelve Steps and the meetings did not work, because they certainly did. If I inadvertently said something inappropriate, I did not want to drag my fellow A.A. members into any bitter public disputes my remarks might have caused, nor could I ever appear to be speaking as an official representative for the groups as a whole.

The purpose of this book

Marty and Senator Hughes were activists at the national level, dealing with large foundations and the U.S. Congress. I was "on the firing line," so to speak, during those same years, trying to implement these goals and ideals through work on military and later naval bases with enlisted people and officers who had themselves fallen prey to the disease of alcoholism. So my book actually tells two stories which are linked together: one is the story of my own troubled youth and fall into compulsive alcoholism, together with an account of what early A.A. was like back in the 1940's, back in the days of the good old-timers, and how these good and caring men and women totally transformed my life. The other story is the one of my life "on the firing line" during the 1950's and afterwards, which I hope will complement Sally and David Brown's recent book on Marty Mann, the first detailed account of that great social reformer's life and work, and the book by Nancy Olson which has just come out, on Senator Hughes and his friends and supporters in the U.S. Congress during the 1970's.[2]

Of necessity, people who are talking about alcoholism treatment and awareness to national foundations, congressmen, and generals and admirals, have to speak about broad ideals and goals, and national statistics. The ideals, the goals, and the statistics are all necessary, but they can sometimes seem bloodless and lifeless. My job, I believe, is to complement what they said by speaking of the thousands of real faces I myself have seen. I have seen all these individual human beings dragging in one by one, their faces filled with hopelessness and despair. They have blurted out the sad stories of their lives to me: the blighted hopes, the ruin of their lives, the harm they did to their spouses and innocent children. And I have also seen their faces eventually brighten with a new light: they suddenly started to look people in the eye, they began speaking with a new confidence, they were able to relax and smile, and they demonstrated that they could now handle major responsibilities with efficiency and new-found skill. No one works harder, or smiles more, or acts with greater wisdom and compassion, than a recovered alcoholic who has really caught the spirit of the program. There on the firing line, I saw the individuals who were actually being helped by what we were doing, and it was a vision that made me continually work all the harder. We were actually accomplishing something real!

There on the firing line, I also had to confront the power which the old attitudes still had over many people. My attempts to help alcoholics were on occasion undercut by military people who still had the old punitive attitudes, or who could not fit us into their preconceived versions of the military system, or who simply totally failed to understand what it was that we were really trying to do. Even worse were the officers and ranking noncoms who felt that publicly admitting that anyone in their unit was an alcoholic would make them look bad, and who wanted to deal with this widespread and costly problem by simply denying that it existed. No matter how much heavy drinking was going on—and anyone who has been in the military knows how much it goes on—they would protest, "What do you mean, drunks in my squadron? I don't run that kind of outfit. I don't allow that. If I had a drunk, I'd get him out of my outfit and out of the service instantly."

Because of this lingering presence of the old attitudes and beliefs, we not only had successes, we also had some dismal failures, and my book has to talk about that honestly too. There is no way that we can create systems at higher governmental and command levels which will supply real help to alcoholics, until we understand what the forces are which will attempt to thwart these systems lower down at the applied level. I very much hope that some of the people who work on the problems of alcoholism and drug addiction at the community and national level, and within the upper levels of our military forces, will read my book and heed some of my warnings.

The impact of alcoholism on society

This is a problem that our nation must take seriously. Alcoholism is one of the most devastating diseases known. It not only destroys the individual who contracts it, it does harm to everyone who comes in contact with that man or woman. Alcoholics cause accidents on the highways, in the work place, and in the military. Their actions destroy both property and human lives. At the very best, a work place or military unit filled with alcoholics is going to lose most of the good they would obtain from these potentially quite talented people, who are unable to function satisfactorily on the job because of the effects of the alcohol that they are drinking or have drunk the night before.

And the most adversely affected are the most innocent of all, namely the alcoholics' children. They can end up going without food and clothes and other material needs because the alcoholic parent is unable to hold a job, or is spending all the money he or she earns on drink.

These little children are traumatized for life by seeing and becoming victims of what their parents do while they are drunk. You can show the terrible statistics of the rate of suicide and debilitating mental disorders in later life among men and women who were raised in a home where one or both parents were active alcoholics. The combination of genetics and environment makes the adult children of alcoholics many times more likely to become alcoholics themselves.

Alcohol awareness

Creating greater alcohol awareness is just as important as treatment itself. Unlike other diseases, the initial symptoms are still usually ignored until there is a truly major disruption in the individual's ability to function. Even where programs are already available to assist the alcoholic, problem drinkers all too often balk at taking advantage of them until massive catastrophes have occurred.

In a work situation, supervisors and fellow employees usually become aware that the alcoholic has a problem long before the sufferer is willing to concede that he or she is in trouble. Mixed emotions usually prevail at that point: should the alcoholic be dismissed or retained? In most incidences, many attempts are made to salvage the once productive worker. Americans do in fact have often extraordinary compassion for those who suffer from alcoholism, and will frequently "carry" a worker for an unbelievably long time. But alcoholism is a progressive disease, and supervisors finally get pushed beyond their level of tolerance. An important part of the problem here is that bosses and co-workers simply do not know what to do with the alcoholic. Non-alcoholics know too little about the disease, which is why alcohol awareness programs are so important.

Alcohol awareness information is equally vital to the families of alcoholics, who usually act in ways that simply make the alcoholic's problems worse. First, the other family members are apt to begin by trying to ignore the existence of the problem. Second, they then go on to over-protect the person for too long, while the alcoholic's problems keep on mounting. Third, they eventually end up rejecting the alcoholic and casting him out, scolding him moralistically and heaping shame and scorn on his head because (in their minds) in spite of everything they have done for him, he still cannot control his intake of alcohol. Neither ignoring, nor over-protecting, nor moralistic scolding deal with the real inner dynamic of the disease.

Every segment of our society is negatively affected by alcoholism. At least five other family members on the average will be harmed in some way by the alcoholic's behavior. Although alcoholics tend to become more and more isolated from others after the disease has progressed far enough, during the early stages of the disease they have friends. The alcoholic often hurts these other people deeply: he makes them weep (because in fact they like him), he insults them, and may even damage their property or steal from them. Alcoholism has a very negative impact on our nation's economy. At many levels of society, when the drinker can no longer hold a job, his family has to go on public assistance, and every taxpayer has to dip into his own pocket to help pay for this.

I should add here however, that alcoholism is equally prevalent at all economic levels of our society. It is important to counter the stereotype which still exists in some people's minds, that all alcoholics are shabby derelicts dressed in dirty trench coats with a bottle of cheap fortified wine in a brown paper bag stuck in one pocket. If you enter a typical present-day A.A. meeting, what you will in fact see is a perfect cross-section of modern Americans, from the highest to the lowest. There may be one or two doctors or lawyers, a scientist or a psychotherapist, a priest or nun or pastor. The majority however will be typical ordinary working folks and middle-class people, men and women of all ages, dressed just like the people you would see walking down the halls at a community's shopping center. And just as in any American community, you may also see a few tough-looking "street people" as we call them now, or some of the down-and-out who refused to come into A.A. until they had finally lost everything. Even when they come in wearing tattered blue jeans or shabby hand-me-down clothes, the A.A. people treat every member with the same respect and kindness.

Greater awareness of how the disease of alcoholism actually affects people is important, because nowadays, due to the revolution in knowledge which occurred back in the 1930's and 40's, there are in fact answers to the problem. In spite of that, it is still the case that the majority of alcoholics do not seek assistance until they have first lost many of the things they once had. As one hears people talking in an A.A. meeting, the most striking thing one notices is that it is not usually the material things they lost which still make them grieve, but the loss of the love of those other people with whom they once were close. There is nothing more painful than being rejected and cast out, if you are a person who was once an acceptable member of your community and family.

The program of Alcoholics Anonymous

The most successful program for bringing about recovery from alcoholism is Alcoholics Anonymous. If we look at the percentage of people who will actually accept a recovery program and commit themselves to it, or the number who continue to stay sober for any great length of time thereafter (say by carrying out a three-year or five-year follow-up on who is still staying sober and out of trouble), there is no other program which can boast of much appreciable success at all compared to A.A.

During the past almost seventy years now, A.A. has been responsible for providing recovery to untold numbers of alcoholics because of its unique and non-evasive approach to coping with the disease. And this is accomplished without imposing any financial burden on the individual who is afflicted or that person's family, because Alcoholics Anonymous people refuse on principle to accept payment. They own no property as a group, and they rely almost totally on volunteers who pay their own way.

People in all walks of life have found the solution to this disease through participation in A.A. Now that more and more people are coming into the program early enough in the progression of the disease, we are finding that long-term hospitalization, loss of work, and loss of loved ones is beginning to become the exception rather than the rule.

But this only happens when people not only start coming to meetings, but also practice the principles of the A.A. program in their daily lives.

My own descent into alcoholism and recovery

As I mentioned earlier, one of the two stories I will be telling in this book, is the tale of what I experienced in my own troubled childhood and youth, and what happened to me as my own drinking became worse and worse. There are many variables on the road to alcoholism, so that some of the points which I emphasize in my own personal history may not be applicable to everyone who becomes an alcoholic. If I say that I myself did X and you never did X, or if I say that I felt Y, and you yourself never remember feeling that way, that does not automatically mean that you are not an alcoholic.

You need to read my own story, not in terms of specific things that happened, but in terms of the general pattern of progression. A very large number of the people who ultimately become addicted to alcohol fit into one version or another of that general pattern of progression. That was one of the things which my old teacher, Dr. E. M. Jellinek of Yale University, proved so conclusively. But perhaps even that does not fit you.

There is one condition however which is common to all who become alcoholic. They inflict great pain on themselves, their friends, and their relatives while they are actively engaged in using alcohol. They find that the only answer to this problem is total abstinence. If you yourself are presently involved in that kind of pain and are nevertheless still actively drinking, I hope that you will find, from hearing my story, some help in resolving whatever individual conflicts or compulsion exist within you, in your own struggle to feel good about yourself, and function in a positive and stable manner.

Alcoholism is not a behavior problem, but a very complex disease

In the past half century, more has been accomplished to recognize, define, and eliminate the stigma associated with alcoholism than had been brought about in any previous era. At the heart of this change has been the partial removal of the old principle of defining alcoholism by the behavior it produces, and the progress that has been made in solving many of the mysteries surrounding the disease. It is an illness, and this is now recognized by most health agencies, medical treatment facilities, and therapists.

Some resistance to the disease concept still remains however among law enforcement people, who often still wish to regard it completely as a behavior problem. And this is also usually true among the members of the alcoholic's family. We must not forget that parents, brothers and sisters, spouses and children, are the ones who are constantly exposed to the negative consequences of the alcoholic behavior. It is difficult indeed for families to think of alcoholism as a disease, when they are the ones who are most immediately subjected to all of the financial and social pressures caused by the alcoholic family member, and they are the ones most likely to suffer physically from the alcoholic's rages and tantrums and automobile accidents.

Normal social drinkers are totally mystified by the alcoholic's problem. "Why can't this person drink like I do?" Their lack of understanding creates a breach between them and the alcoholic. In fact, alcoholism is a quite complex disease, so that there is no one single, simple answer to that question: There can be a genetic component; there will be both social and emotional factors; and there is also a physical component involved. The complexity of their interweaving is in fact often difficult to understand by those who are free of any chemical dependence themselves. But some degree of greater comprehension is possible, for those who are willing to study and learn, on the basis of modern scientific research.

I am very grateful for the increased interest which has appeared during my lifetime in solving the problems of this disease. Extensive research has been carried out, and some of the secrets associated with this illness have been uncovered.

Despite this, however—let the reader take warning—many mysteries still remain, because of the extreme individuality exhibited by those who become addicted. My own response to alcoholism contained unique elements. Most other alcoholics display certain unique responses. This complicates the recovery process: something that will work for me may not work for you, and vice versa. Because even the major components of behavior differ widely from alcoholic to alcoholic, it is easy for someone who is an alcoholic to pretend to himself that he is not. I certainly did that to myself when I was in my twenties: convincing me that I was in fact an alcoholic was a very difficult process, even though when you read my story, this may seem preposterous. How could I conceivably not have known, quite early on, that I was an alcoholic? It was because people would point at so-and-so, and say that he was an alcoholic, and I seemed to myself to be totally different from that person, in numerous essential ways. Therefore—I would try to convince myself—if he is an alcoholic, then I am not, because I am not the same as him.

Since alcoholism produces guilt and destroys the alcoholic's feelings of self-worth, this produces even greater barriers to responding in any kind of positive way. If I had to admit that I had become an alcoholic, then I would feel even guiltier than I already did back when I was in my twenties (which was overwhelmingly great), and my almost totally-demolished sense of self-worth would have been even further destroyed. So I fought any attempt by others to try to convince me that I had a problem with drinking.

We must continue working to educate people about the true nature of alcoholism. It is not a behavior problem, and the kind of guilt I felt about my compulsive drinking was inappropriate. I had to do something about it, and I had to do it before I was totally destroyed by it. But becoming ill is not a matter for which one should feel guilt, nor is contracting an illness something which should shatter one's sense of self-worth. We do not blame sick people in a civilized society, but help them to get well again. And if I myself fall prey to some treatable disease, from which I could recover by taking appropriate steps, the intelligent response is not to feel that I have become worthless, but to take those steps which I must take to bring about my recovery.

Hope

Above all I want to stress that this book is about hope—real hope, thoroughly proven hope. The story of my own life demonstrates how concrete this hope is, and the extraordinary benefits that are gained through recovery from alcoholism. Treatment in my own case not only dealt with the internal and external effects of the heavy drinking itself (which had gone on for almost twelve years), but also involved the healing and modifying of deeply ingrained attitudes and feelings and perceptions that had been ruining my life and my happiness since I was a small child.

And I also demonstrated that proper alcohol awareness and treatment programs in the military could produce impressive concrete results. No, we could not save all the alcoholics we attempted to treat, but we did in fact rescue a significant number of them. Even for a very cold-blooded financial accountant, the costs saved the military by our successes far more than paid for our program. We proved that it was in fact a profit-making venture in the purely business sense.

But I worked with the incoming patients myself, and I cannot exaggerate the human sense of joy that came from seeing enlisted persons or officers who were destroying themselves, overcome with guilt and despair, learn how to turn their lives around. I saw them as real individuals, learning to work productively and reestablish meaningful relationships with other human beings, and learning how to experience real happiness and a deep sense of simply feeling good about themselves. This is a book about concrete hope based on what has actually been proven and demonstrated repeatedly. I am now in my eighties, one of the generation that fought in New Guinea and Iwo Jima, North Africa and the mountains of Italy, on the beaches of Normandy and at the Battle of the Bulge. I have seen this hope fulfilled during my lifetime, of producing real recovery from alcoholism, and I want to pass this hope on to the next generation. It can be done, because we showed it could be done.

CHAPTER 2

Childhood in Niles, Ohio

Writing about my childhood was not an easy task. Of course, as I frequently explain when I am talking before groups, I have the advantage of having a photographic memory. The problem is that there is often no film in the camera!

People usually laugh when I say that, and that is good. The initial reaction many people have when they go to their first A.A. meeting is sheer amazement at all the smiles and the easy laughter throughout the meeting. In recent years, I have had more than one young person admit to me, that when they first started going to A.A. meetings, they were absolutely convinced for the first several weeks that all these people must be on drugs. One young man, who has several years in the program now, told me that he said to himself at first, "There is *no way* that all these people can be that relaxed unless they're on *something*!" And as he told me that, he laughed heartily, at himself and at his own hilariously funny initial reaction, because he had learned better now. Those people in the meeting were not on mind-numbing drugs, but had learned how to smile and laugh at themselves, and see the humorous side of life. This is the world's greatest medicine for washing away stress, and making us more relaxed. This is one of the best antidotes for the pervasive negativism that most of us alcoholics had when we first came into the program.

When I was a child, we used to get the old *Farmer's Almanac*, and one of the trite sayings in it was:

> The thing that goes the furthest
> Toward making life worthwhile,
> That costs the least and does the most
> Is just a pleasant smile.

And the little poem was simple-minded and corny, but it was true. When I was a child, I did not know how to laugh at myself. I did not know how to get up in front of a group, and recite a silly little poem, and get everybody laughing, and get a simple-minded kick out of it myself. I took myself too seriously, and continually fell deeper and deeper into negativism.

Let me give you an example of the way I used to react to things back then. In high school, my favorite teacher for a long time was my homeroom teacher. But then one day, two dogs (a male and a female) somehow got into our classroom, and took up their position right next to my desk, and started trying to have sex. The teacher, all embarrassed, looked the opposite direction and cried out in a strangled voice, "Take them out, Bill!" It quickly turned out that I was no hero to the two dogs. They promptly turned on me and tried to attack me for interrupting their fun. Somehow, in spite of that, I finally managed to carry out the mission successfully, while all the rest of the kids in the classroom were laughing hysterically at the sight of me and the two dogs bouncing off the desks and knocking the chairs over.

Well, I think that even for present-day films, there was a bit too much raw sex in that scene to put it in the movie theaters, but other than that, it was a marvelous piece of slapstick comedy that would have had almost any audience rolling in the aisles with laughter before it was over. What was my reaction at the time though? I was so embarrassed by it all, that I hightailed it for home and refused to go back to school that day. When I crept into school the next day, some of the other kids made comments that I regarded as snide and derogatory. I held a resentment against the teacher for the remainder of my high school days.

What would have happened if I had reacted a different way? I could have laughed with the other students at the absolutely crazy and chaotic scene, and poked a little fun at myself the next day. And I would have remembered it as a great tale to tell later on, when I wanted to entertain people and make them laugh. Everything lies in our perceptions of events. Unfortunately however, back when I was a child, if there were two ways of perceiving a situation, a positive way and a negative way, I would pick the negative one every time.

I was also programmed from the beginning to feel a lot of guilt before I was out of my teens. Part of this guilt centered around drinking alcohol. My life seemed destined to be a guaranteed catastrophe, almost from the very start. Or better put, that was my perception of my life for many years. Perceptions are funny things that way: what you perceive, all too often ends up coming true.

In my family when I was growing up, my father tried to impress upon us his own negative attitude toward alcohol. This arose from the fact that his own father had had very serious problems with liquor. So he was contemptuous of those who drank alcohol, preached against its use, and did his best to teach all of us children to feel the same kind of aversion which he did. As a child, I automatically despised people who drank, and regarded them as bad people. Little did I think that I would eventually become addicted to alcohol myself, and experience twelve years of severely alcoholic behavior.

Later on of course, when I was in my thirties, I learned at the Yale School of Alcohol Studies and in my other researches that alcoholism runs in families, but can often skip a generation before it reappears once again. This was what happened in my case. After I began setting up alcoholism treatment programs and helping other alcoholics to recover, I would listen to them tell their family histories and see this same skipping of one generation occurring in some of their stories also.

But I did not learn that until much later on. When I first started drinking heavily myself, which was when I was eighteen, at some deep level I still continued to believe exactly what I had been taught as a child: people who drank were bad people, and alcoholics were to be totally condemned. So I felt an enormous sense of guilt down deep inside, no matter what I was saying to other people up at the surface level. There are only two diseases which invariably have a sense of guilt associated with them: alcoholism and venereal disease. During my twenties, I did not want to admit to anyone else that I was an alcoholic, and fought as hard as I could to keep from admitting it to myself, because I felt so guilty about it.

My mother died when I was very small. That was another of the defining issues of my childhood. I cannot recall any memories of her when she was alive, but I have very vivid memories of the day she passed away. At the heart of the trauma which was produced in me, was an overwhelming sense of having lost something huge which could never, ever be replaced. From that point on, I felt different from the other children. When they skinned their knees, they had mothers to run home to. She would hug her child, and wash and bandage the child's knee. This sounds so simple, but when you were a small child who did not have that, it was everything in the world. In my case, an older sister gave me a good deal of love and protection and tried to fill this void. I am very grateful to her for this, but the hole inside me could never be totally filled by anyone else.

Another memory I have, from later on, was of the time I hurt myself on the pump in the kitchen. We lived in an older house without modern conveniences. There was no running water, so water was drawn from a well located next to the house, with a hand pump by the side of the kitchen sink. I can recall my dad and my older brother digging that well, with everybody in the neighborhood coming over to watch. When they finally got deep enough to strike water, there was a big celebration with everyone involved.

When the water level got too low in the pipe leading up to the kitchen, the pump had to be primed before it would start functioning again. Since it worked on a vacuum principle, the column of water in the pipe had to extend unbroken all the way from the pump mechanism itself down to the place many feet below, where the other end of the pipe dipped down below the water level at the bottom of the well. This required pouring water from someplace else into the top of the pump until the entire pipe was full again. And then it had to be pumped very vigorously to get the water flowing again.

One time the counter-pressure in the pump was very strong, when I was trying to pump the handle as hard as I could with soapy hands, and the handle flew out of my grasp and rebounded back up at me, breaking my nose. No one comforted me in my pain; in fact I was severely scolded and blamed. In those days, doctors were rarely summoned to such a minor event, so my nose was left to heal on its own, with no medical care.

Now this is just one event which got stuck in my memory, but as you can see, my perception as a child was that if I got hurt no one really cared. I was on my own, and had to take care of myself, completely by myself, when real problems came. Even as a teenager later on, I was enormously afraid of being hurt, which was why I played on the high school baseball team but did not go out for football. In high school football we would have been tackling and blocking one another as hard and violently as boys our age could.

The loss of my mother was an event which had a devastating impact on my life. It not only made me feel that no one really cared what happened to me, it was also responsible for many of my other emotional problems later on. I was overcome with envy of the other children who had the benefit of a mother's love. One boy in particular was the focus of my frustrations: since I was older than he was, I could take advantage of him and bully him and physically abuse him. I would pick a fight with him, but then feel guilty afterwards because I knew deep inside that there was no real justification for my mistreatment of him. To make the guilt worse, this boy's mother was always good to me in spite of the way I treated her son. I spent many a night at their house, and she showed me a lot of compassion.

In the Big Book of Alcoholics Anonymous, one of the twelve promises says that "we will not regret the past nor wish to shut the door on it." In order to tell the truthful story of my life, I had to open the doors of my mind to a lot of memories like these, and look at them fully and honestly. I can still recall all the pain that I felt then, but I have learned how to live differently now. The program enabled me to learn how to live today so that I do not have to keep repeating the way I thought and acted back then. There is no longer any reason why I have to keep bringing fresh pain down upon myself today, which means that I can feel happiness today, and can feel good about myself here in the present. And there is no reason why I need to bring that kind of pain down upon myself in the future either. I just have to keep remembering what I have learned about myself.

The pain of my mother's death was unavoidable of course, just like the pain of losing my wife, who died three and a half years ago, and for whom I am still grieving. But it was the way I reacted as a child to that natural and inescapable pain which set me on a course where I compounded the original pain over and over again by my own attitudes and behavior, and dug myself deeper and deeper into an inner world inside my mind where no happiness would ever be possible.

A medical doctor tries to treat a person with a broken arm so that the natural healing processes of the person's own body will make the arm get well again. A broken arm which was mistreated over and over again would never ever set, and the person would be in pain all the rest of his or her life. After I began setting up alcoholism treatment programs later on in my adult years, many suffering alcoholics came to me who had been trapped in misery and torment by memories of the past. My job, I felt, was to help them to learn how to start healing the inner mental pain, instead of acting in ways that just made the pain grow worse and worse. There are natural healing forces in the universe; we have to learn how to relax and let them work.

There were enormous conflicts inside my mind when I was a child, which eventually contributed to my alcoholism. I longed to feel accepted, loved, and wanted, but this eluded me. At the forefront of my thoughts was a feeling of not belonging to any of the groups in which I participated. When I first started school, I instantly felt rejected by the other children. When I was forced to participate in some kind of group, I often became withdrawn or deliberately disruptive. I thought that I did not and could not measure up to their standards. There was no notion at all of ever becoming a leader in any kind of group activities, because of my deeply ingrained feelings of personal unworthiness.

There was a great irony here of course, because the year I turned thirty, I started working the A.A. program seriously, and was propelled into a whole series of major leadership roles during the years that followed. My childhood perception of myself had been false, and that false perception kept me from fulfilling my own true potential during those early years. I withdrew and I avoided, and I felt totally isolated, and I ended up totally betraying myself—all because of the way I perceived things.

Some people can develop a sense of belonging by developing hobbies and identifying with others who have similar interests. I did not have many hobbies. I liked fishing, but that was a solitary sport, which at the time suited me just fine. There was no desire to be a boy scout, go to church, or become involved in groups which might evaluate my achievements or lack thereof. My constant fear of rejection or failure was so great that it totally outweighed any sense of personal reward I might have gotten from feeling like I belonged to some group. I had also developed a very negative attitude toward authority, which made me rebel against anything the group leaders asked me to do.

The only place where I was able to get out of this feeling of total isolation was in playing baseball. I was never good enough to make it onto the professional level, but I was certainly much better than average and drove myself to become even better. Whenever I was playing with the baseball team, I did everything in my power to win praise from my fellow players. Driven by this constant need to be praised or rewarded for my efforts, I was motivated to excel at any cost. Later on in the service, when I was stationed in Hawaii, I developed a local island reputation as an outstanding pitcher, and could hear the crowds cheering for me as I wound up to throw the ball. No matter how well I did though, either during my school days or later on in the service, it never seemed to overcome my underlying sense of unworthiness and isolation.

Human beings have to feel loved and wanted, and have a sense of security. The satisfaction of these needs seemed to elude me during my path to maturity. My mission in life most of the time could be best described as "just existing." There were no higher goals, no desire to prepare for meeting life's challenges, nor any thought of what the future might hold for me. I lived from day to day, and the only motive for my existence was whether I liked or did not like what was going on right now.

At any point in our lives, what we think happened is a matter of perception. Two people standing on the same street corner can see the same automobile accident, and give two totally different accounts afterward of what happened. My seven brothers and sisters were brought up in the same family that I was, and their memories were that they had had a happy childhood. My own mind, on the contrary, focused on the negative experiences and disregarded the positive ones. At the conscious level, my mind obliterated the memories of the good things which were part of growing up.

In fact, when I make myself think about my childhood from a more balanced perspective, I can tell a series of tales of the wholesome pleasures and enjoyments of an earlier, simpler era. Descriptions of life in small-town America during those days can easily make it sound like an absolutely idyllic existence. Many older people look back on those times with enormous nostalgia.

After my mother died, my father, God bless him, had his hands full raising the five children who were left at home but did his best to give us some enjoyment and fun. (The three older children had left the roost and married by then.) Until he remarried, which happened when I was eight, he would take us on camping trips, for example. We would go to a place called the Fifth Bridge. It was the fifth crossing point, going upstream from the Mahoning river, along one of its smaller tributaries called Mosquito Creek. The earliest settlers had given the stream its name because it was stagnant most of the time, except when a good rain had just flushed it out, so that mosquito larvae swarmed by the thousands in its shallows, and hatched out into tiny winged attackers who began honing in on our bare skins with insatiable blood-lust the minute we arrived.

We drove there in my dad's Model T Ford. I can still see dad cranking the engine by hand to get the old flivver started. This was during the early 1920's, and automobiles had no electrical self-starters in those days. It took muscle and sometimes multiple attempts, to get the engine to finally kick over and start running. We ran at an average speed of around twenty-five miles an hour, chugging along down country roads and making an enormous racket. I was so little that it seemed to take an eternity to get there, even though it was only ten or fifteen miles from our house.

My two older sisters and I would ride sitting on the floorboard in back, leaning against the back of the front seat and propping our feet up on the back seat—a strange position, but we thought it was a grand experience to ride backwards like this. There was a small place called JB's Grocery Store which we had to pass on the way there, and as we approached we would hint that Dad might stop and get us some candy at the little store. If he failed to stop, we would start singing mournfully, "Bye-bye JB's candy." This usually eventually worked, because he would often end up stopping on the way back to ease his guilty conscience.

As we approached closer and closer to our traditional family fishing spot, we three kids would get more and more excited. When we finally arrived and piled out of the car, I was so impatient that it seemed like we were just wasting time when my father insisted that we do so many boring things first, like setting up our tent and getting all our supplies in order. All my thoughts were on getting my fishing hook in the water as quickly as possible, with dreams of "catching the big one" and getting praise and glory.

My dad loved fishing so much, he would spend hours in just one spot, hoping that a big one would finally grab his bait. You could not get him to put his pole down even for a moment, because he was convinced that, at exactly that moment, a big one would seize the barbed fishhook and make off at full speed, dragging the fishing pole into the water and down the creek, to be lost forever. He always fished with a cane pole, and instructed us not to refer to it as a rod. Rods and reels were for the big-time sportsmen, and that was not our style. But I knew he had his dreams, just like mine, because every time he lost a fish, he would always insist that this had been the biggest one he had had on his line in a long time. I have to laugh when I remember the intense look on his face while he was telling us how big that fish was, the one that got away. I think he actually believed it!

With our cane poles, we did not in fact get sports fish very often. Most of the fish we caught were catfish, the kind called bullheads. Every once in a while, though, Dad would put on a crayfish for bait (we called them crabs, but they were just tiny little freshwater crawdads), and would sometimes hook a bass. Getting a bass was an earth-shaking event: when we finally got back home, I was appointed as the "town crier" to carry the fish all around the whole neighborhood, to display our trophy for everyone's admiration. Again, looking back at that today, the image of the terribly serious little boy lugging the big fish around to all the surrounding houses, just bursting with pride, must have been delightfully funny to see, and I am sure that the neighbors all smiled when they saw me coming.

We also fished for what were called grass pike. These were the small pike which stayed in the water weeds close to shore. We would walk the banks of the creek, and when a pike was spotted, we would dangle our bait right in front of its nose. Sharp eyes were required to spot them down under the water, but we became adept at the sport. Most of the time the fish would charge the bait, get hooked, and we could then pull them out of the water. We had gunny sacks over our shoulders (old brown burlap bags), and the pike we caught were tossed into the sacks.

Many times we would catch thirty or forty of these small fish before we were done, ranging in size from twelve to eighteen inches long. We would cut them up and fry them in deep fat, and eat the fried pieces stuck between two pieces of white bread. I can still remember how delicious they tasted, better in fact than the finest and most expensive gourmet meals I have had in years since.

I do remember one time when we pitched our tent right next to the creek, and a cloudburst almost wiped us out, and Dad said we had to go home. But otherwise, we always stuck it out, even if the weather turned rainy. Dad liked to fish right after a storm, because he said the rain always washed food into the water, and brought all the fish out to feed. We did in fact seem to catch more after a rainstorm.

This was the good life in small-town and rural America during the early 1920's, the kind of nostalgic picture we see painted in novels and art and movies set back in that era. But how we remember things, as I have said, is a matter of perception. What I perceived in my mind was always steered away from the positive and towards the negative. So in fact, my being the youngest caused me to imagine that I received less attention than some of my older brothers and sisters. I realize now that, if it happened at all, it was completely unintentional. But I did feel very strongly that I could not really communicate with my dad about matters which had upset me. We could go fishing together, and talk about who caught the largest fish, and the best place to dangle our hooks in the water, and "the big one that got away," but I could not talk with him about important things.

Dad had to work for a living, so after the death of my mother we went through five years where he hired a series of live-in housekeepers. Some were very kind and others were crude. I recall one who made me sit under the apple tree on a warm summer day, wearing an overcoat, because I had a cold and she was convinced that this was the proper remedy. I could never figure out her logic on this issue. I will tell you that no love was lost on my part when she eventually left and went her way.

Dad remarried when I was eight years old, and my whole life changed from that day forward. I never felt close to my new stepmother, and now I had a stepbrother also, a young man who made my life miserable. I deeply disliked him from the beginning, because he seemed to do everything in his power to create chaos within the family. Sometimes he went off to stay with his sister, and I would heave a sigh of relief, because things seemed to go back to *almost* normal during his absence. My stepbrother had a lot of personality problems, and was a cruel, hostile person, who took pleasure in mistreating me. He even tried (unsuccessfully) to engage me in sexual acts. I can understand just a little bit of the tremendous fear and anger which must exist in the minds of A.A. people who were grossly sexually abused as children. I still think of my stepbrother with total repugnance. We had many fights, and since he was older, I always came out the loser.

I also resented my father, because he would never defend me during these quarrels and altercations. I wanted my stepbrother to be punished, and punished severely. In fact, I was very angry at Dad for not forcefully bringing that young man into line, and stopping him from doing what he was doing to me, and what he was doing to our family's reputation in the community. Even though our family was fairly poor, we were nevertheless regarded with respect by the neighbors and town folks. My stepbrother was causing troubles not only inside the home, but outside too, which jeopardized our family's basic standing in the community.

I can still remember the Sunday morning when the police came to our house looking for him, because he had stolen the family doctor's car. This was acutely embarrassing to all the rest of us, because in those days the family doctor was looked up to by everyone, and was one of the most highly respected and venerated people in town. My stepbrother had humiliated our entire family. According to the laws of the state of Ohio at that time, this was grand theft, but somehow he got off without serving any jail time. This made me even angrier, because I thought he should have been sent off to prison—I wanted some vengeance, some real vengeance, for that and everything else he had done. I still think he should have been locked up for a good long period at that time.

My stepbrother was in the military, like me, during World War II, and ended up being highly decorated for his actions. Although I only saw him briefly after the war, it was very strange, because it seemed to have had a positive effect on his character, and he had become calmer and gentler. After his release from the military however, he soon died a horrible death from cancer. When alcoholics come into A.A. like I did, if we live long enough, we discover that even the worst things in our lives were all of them—or almost all of them—eventually washed away in the flow of time. I doubt that there are many people left alive now who ever knew my stepbrother, and even fewer who actually remember him.

My negative childhood attitude toward my stepmother was also mellowed by the passage of time in later years. How we remember things is just a matter of perception. I can now look back on that period of my life, and recognize what a tall order it was for a woman to marry a man with eight orphaned children. Most women would have refused to take on such a task. I can now appreciate the sacrifices which she had to make. She died about three years before I finally got sober, and I feel badly now that I could never tell her that in person. When it came time to do my eighth and ninth steps in A.A., I realized that I owed her some kind of amends for my unrelentingly negative attitude toward her during my early years—I needed just to tell her thank you, for the kind and caring things she did do for me—but it was now too late.

She was a good cook, and creative. Although we had less than average means in those days, she could make a satisfying meal out of just about anything. I still remember the fresh, yeasty aroma of the excellent homemade bread baking, and how good it tasted, especially when it was still warm and fresh from the oven. She was a meticulous housekeeper. She tried to take care of us, and it was an awesome responsibility which she took on when she married my dad. Why did I not appreciate that back then? I suppose because I refused to accept her as a replacement for my mother, and I remained locked in the belief that if my real mother had lived, I myself would not have been so miserably unhappy so much of the time.

We lived in an older house without modern conveniences, as I have already mentioned, where all of our water had to be hand pumped in the kitchen from a well dug right outside the house. Each time we needed any large amount of hot water, we had to pump away over and over again. We would fill an old kettle, heat that up on the stove, dump the contents into whatever kind of container we were going to use, and then repeat the process as many times as necessary. I can still hear the kettle whistling when the water finally reached the boiling point. It took several kettles full to fill the large round galvanized steel tub which we used both for washing clothes and for bathing. This was another of my many resentments: how I resented the people in town who had running water inside their homes, hooked up to the city water mains, where all one had to do was turn on a faucet. And they had real bath tubs too, which could be filled with marvelous hot water with the mere twist of a wrist.

It was on Saturdays that we took our baths. During cold weather, the galvanized steel tub was shoved into the dining room right next to the potbellied stove, which at least kept us from freezing to death while we bathed. I discovered that if I stood up in the tub and continually rotated while I washed, I could keep one side or the other of my chilled, wet body at least a little bit warm. Whichever side of my body was warm of course, the other side was simultaneously painfully cold. I have learned now to see the humor in that scene: the little naked kid dancing the bath time three-step in an old wash tub, and wondering in his little head why adults were so obsessive-compulsive about personal hygiene, making him take a bath once a week, "whether he needed it or not." Later on in high school, I thought I did not know how to dance, but I am telling you that I sure knew how to dance on Saturday's back then.

The original kitchen stove was called a "Kalamazoo Direct to You," but we eventually replaced this with a contraption which burned unleaded gasoline. It had to be pumped up before it was used, because it was compressed air which sprayed the gasoline out the tiny nozzles of the burners. Looking back at it now, I have to laugh with sheer amazement that we never had an explosion which blew the whole kitchen up and burned the house down to the ground. Later on, when I was in the Army Air Force in the Pacific, we could have dropped stoves like that from airplanes and wiped out whole enemy regiments.

With no running water, our home also of course lacked indoor toilet facilities. During an Ohio winter, it could drop down to twenty or thirty degrees below freezing outside the house. There would be a lot of careful deliberation inside our minds before we went out to that unheated outhouse many yards away! For that matter, it was not always that much warmer inside the house. We had no central furnace. The stoves we used to heat individual rooms would go out during the night, so when we had the real subzero temperatures, the house itself would become so cold that a glass of water left in a bedroom overnight would be found frozen solid the next morning. I can still remember the enormous weight of the piles of blankets I had to have on top of me, pressing down on me in my bed at night.

One Christmas my dad got us a little pool table, about four feet long, which became one of our greatest pleasures. It was not a present to this individual child or that one, but a kind of group present to all of us. We all took turns when we started playing. On Sunday mornings in particular, when it was cold outside, we would stoke up the stove in the living room, and all of us would spend the morning playing pool. I got to play a lot, because I became fairly good at hitting the balls where I wanted them to go, and the rules were that the one who won the present game got to play the next game against the next contender.

I suppose you could call this one of my hobbies or pastimes too. A major part of my social life during my later adolescent years was spent playing down at the local pool hall and gambling on the games. I got reasonably adept at it: we played Nine Ball, and I had my share of winnings. Later on, in my serious drinking days, I won many a much-needed drink by my pool shooting. This was not the kind of thing you put on a job application, of course: "good enough at shooting pool to get very drunk indeed on very little pocket cash."

Ice skating was also very popular in the wintertime. In those days, shoe skates were a luxury which we could not afford. We had the kind of skates that clamped on your regular shoes, and the soles of my shoes were usually so thin that they would buckle when all that pressure was applied to the sides. It made a big lump in the soles, which often made my feet begin to hurt very badly before the day was over, but there was no quitting just because of pain. We would sometimes play ice hockey, and in fact I remember having had some very good times out on the ice, in spite of the cold weather and the way my feet would finally start to hurt. It was also nice to come home and gather around the potbellied stove to get warm again. Dad usually had some popcorn waiting for us, which would satisfy our hunger until dinner was ready. Although I did not appreciate it enough at the time, there was an elemental kindness in his heart, and this was one of the ways he tried to express it.

In the summer, we kids were not allowed to play all the time. The most distasteful task for me was working in the family garden. We always had at least half an acre which required continual weeding and hoeing. To a small child, one of those rows could appear absolutely endless. I can still remember the hot sun beating down on us, and the painful regimen of hoe, hoe, hoe. To this day, I find working with plants unpleasant—lawns, flower beds, any kind of green plants—so one of my wife's tasks for many years was to keep reminding me that this kind of thing was my family responsibility, not hers!

I must also talk about my great love, a dog named Sport whom my father gave me when I was only one year old. We had so much fun together. He was a gentle dog, and my constant companion. He was also very protective, and would attack anyone who threatened me. Sport lived to be sixteen. It was the saddest of days when we finally had to end his life: his back legs had become paralyzed, and the only way he could walk was to pull himself forward with his front legs, and just drag the rear ones along. In those days most people could not afford a veterinarian, so even if anything could have been done for him, we did not have that kind of money. When your family pets got too sick, you had no choice but to either drown them or shoot them, to spare them any further misery. The whole neighborhood cried when Sport was put to rest.

I must have been around seventeen by then. It happened about a year before I graduated from high school and first started the destructive drinking that was going to completely ruin my life. Sport's death—the death of my constant childhood friend—was symbolic, in a way, of the end of that first major period of my life. I was thrown into the adult world all alone, or so I perceived it, feeling that I no longer had a single living creature who cared what happened to me.

Before I move on to describing my drinking years however, I need to talk a little more about my childhood and early teens. I want to give a fuller picture of my family life and what was going on in the world around us, because modern young people live in a very different kind of world. What seemed the good life of the 1920's was followed by the Great Depression and the violence-ridden labor strikes of the 1930's, which created enormous tensions and fears in the little town of Niles, Ohio. This atmosphere affected even those who were still children, like myself. I was a deeply troubled child living in a society that had already been thrown into its own deep troubles by the time I was eleven years old.

CHAPTER 3

From Lindbergh to the Depression Years

Those were the days before television. When I was a child we sat around and listened to the radio instead, the old programs like Amos and Andy, Ma Perkins, Jack Benny, the Lone Ranger, and the Shadow. I do not know why—there was certainly no picture showing on it like a modern television, just knobs and dials—but we sat with our eyes glued to the front of the radio set while we listened, just like modern kids watching the television screen, totally mesmerized. Why did we stare at the front of the radio? Because I never once saw the Lone Ranger's masked face looking back at me from the window over the dial! We had fun "watching radio," if you want to put it that way, but there was one unbreakable rule. When one of my dad's or my stepmother's favorite programs was on, we children had to be absolutely quiet, and were not allowed to make any kind of conversation or comments at all. Both of them took "watching radio" very seriously.

The first radio program I recall listening to, was the famous Dempsey-Tunney heavyweight boxing match in 1926. That first radio we owned had three different dials on the front, which all had to be synchronized to get any decent reception. It ran on three huge batteries, which took up a lot of space. When they ran down and went dead, there went our program. If the batteries gave out before the end of a boxing match or baseball game, our opportunity to hear it was gone forever. There were no replays of sports broadcasts in those days.

But the event which really riveted itself in my childhood imagination occurred the next year, shortly before my ninth birthday. The newspapers were full of the stories when Charles A. Lindbergh, "Lucky Lindy," flew a small single-seat airplane from New York to Paris on May 20-21, 1927. The plane was called the *Spirit of St. Louis*, and he made the journey across the whole width of the Atlantic, nonstop (obviously) in thirty-three hours and thirty-nine minutes. No one had ever done anything like that before, and it was headline news for days. Every time a plane flew over our house, we kids would all run out and yell, "There goes Lindbergh." One time an airplane crashed about five miles from where we lived, and everyone rushed to see if this was the mighty Lindbergh who had finally gone down. Cars came from miles around to view the wreckage, and even in those days, when not nearly so many people owned automobiles, traffic in the area was tied up for hours.

Lindbergh's famous trans-Atlantic flight made a deep and lasting impression on me. I suppose it was not surprising that it was the Army Air Force in which I chose to enlist when I was twenty-one. The idea of being close to real airplanes was incredibly glamorous and romantic in those days. There still is a romance to piloting and working on sleek military aircraft, and sensing the raw power inside their fuselages as their jets suddenly thunder out and they surge down the field and hurtle up into the air. But no one today can truly imagine how magically the sight of machines actually flying through the air affected a child like me, who was used to chugging along in his dad's Model T Ford, bumping along on dirt roads at twenty-five miles an hour.

Almost every Sunday we had to turn on the radio and listen to the Cadle's. This was a Protestant evangelical religious program, not much different from the kind of programs broadcast by the modern television evangelists.[3] Frankly, I think Dad used to respond every once in a while to their oft-repeated pleas for donations and send them a dollar or two to help support the program. This was my only exposure, while I was growing up, to religion or spirituality. It did not give me much help later on when I was in my thirties, and I finally started taking the A.A. program seriously.

I still feel deficient in my understanding of God. I was not required nor encouraged to believe in God during my process to maturity, so I had no real concept of his being and felt hopelessly inadequate in even discussing anything at all which pertained to him. When I attended spiritual meetings in A.A., I sat at the back of the class, and being alcoholic and somewhat of a perfectionist, I was afraid to get fully involved in the discussion. I realize that this fear denied me the right to feel competent and knowledgeable in this area of life.

When I first began developing a military alcoholism program at Mitchel Air Force Base, back in the initial stages of my sobriety, they did not know where else to put an alcoholism counselor, so they appointed me as a Chaplain's Assistant. Unfortunately, the Chaplain's Office interpreted this posting in such a way that, in addition to working with alcoholics, I was also required to teach a children's Sunday School class every week! I felt like a phony, but did my best. These were the dependent children of parents who were stationed at the base. The only way I knew how to teach spirituality was to talk about what was in fact the A.A. program, translated into terms that non-alcoholics could understand. I did not know where anything I was teaching could be found in the Bible, which was one of the things that made me so apprehensive. But what I was telling the children about how to live a better life seemed right to me, and completely in line with what I and the other people in the A.A. meetings were discovering and experiencing. In fact, I got several calls from parents during this time, expressing profound thanks to me for what I was teaching their children. My co-author tells me that almost everything in the twelve step program can be paralleled with traditional Christian biblical teachings, especially the teachings found in the Sermon on the Mount, the Epistle of James, and 1 Corinthians 13, but I did not know how to do it then, and still do not know how to do it now. I can only talk about what I learned about spirituality in A.A., where I learned it from the Big Book and from going to meetings.

Many of the early A.A. people were knowledgeable about the Bible and Christian doctrines and dogmas in a way that I was not. Some of them were Protestants and others of them were Catholics, but they purposefully designed the program to work just as well with people from almost any religious background: Jewish, Muslim, Hindu, Buddhist,

Native American, or whatever. It was also deliberately put together in such a way that people just like me—men and women who had had no religious upbringing at all—could use A.A. just as effectively. The program was not intended to deal with formal religious doctrines and dogmas, but with universal spiritual principles and the inner life of the individual human mind: all the decent religions of the world will teach you that envy, resentment, bullying those who are weaker, fear, and guilt will eventually plunge any human being into deep inner misery. This was the way I had been living, and they told me that if I worked on those things, in whatever way made sense to me, and started figuring out a different way to live, my life would get better. Now, over fifty years later, I can tell you from my own personal experience that they were absolutely right.

But to get back to my childhood: Dad started out as a carpenter by trade, and did a lot of independent contracting. I was amazed at how much he knew about building. Sometimes he would take me with him when he was paying a call on a potential customer, and I would sit in awe while he showed them the various building plans he had drawn up for their approval. I also often went with him after he got the construction job, and while he was busy building or supervising, I would carve a boat out of a piece of scrap lumber. I also sometimes took my hand-carved toy boat with me when we went fishing, and would start playing with the boat in the water instead of fishing, until Dad would get mad at me.

He finally gave up this trade however, and started a little grocery delivery route out in the country. He began by selling cheese which he purchased from a cheese factory in our area. He later renovated an old panel truck by putting shelves and an ice box in it, and started stocking it with groceries and meat as well. He became known as the Traveling Grocery Man. There were no government regulatory measures in those days to dictate the handling of perishables, so he was never questioned about how cool or germ-free he actually kept some of these items in the truck. As far as I know though, we never actually killed any of our customers by giving them a fatal attack of food poisoning.

He fairly quickly turned this into a way to make a passable living, and then decided to expand the business by opening a little grocery store next to our house. There was a small cottage there, which he had built for his own mother and father to live in after they became elderly, but they had passed away now. The vacant building was actually ideal for a small local grocery store. My two sisters and I worked in the store after he had set up the shelves and the other things we needed, and all the neighbors came to us to buy their groceries. I was always embarrassed back then by the fact that what we sold was somewhat overpriced, in my estimation. I knew that they could have gotten their groceries more cheaply somewhere else, and I suspect that many of them knew that too. Thinking back on it now, I suppose that they appreciated the convenience of just being able to walk over and get something, and there was also a sense of neighborhood solidarity. If someone in our neighborhood could do something or provide something, it was understood that we took care of our own, and helped make sure our neighbors could stay in business.

Now Dad of course still maintained his country delivery route, so we kids had to manage the store. I employed every conceivable method to avoid working. We were never paid any kind of salary for this, and sometimes had to put in very long hours. My experiences never produced any great amount of motivation to become a grocer when I grew up. And Dad did not tolerate carelessness or accidents on the part of his youthful grocery crew. One day a produce man delivered some vegetables and fruit, including some fresh watermelons. These we were supposed to keep in the cellar, so they would be reasonably cool when they were purchased. I remember carrying a big one down the cellar steps, and struggling with the sheer weight of the huge melon, and the slick outer skin, which made it awkward to hang onto. It slipped out of my hands and splashed in wet, red fragments and sticky, sweet juice all over the cellar floor. I cleaned it up and decided to keep my mouth shut about what had happened, but my strategy of silence did not work. All hell broke loose when Dad came home and did a count, and found that one of his watermelons was missing. This was a business loss which the little grocery store business could not tolerate, he said, and I was severely punished.

Among the other items we carried in the store were what we called "grab bags," packages of candy which were supposed to have a surprise hidden inside. We kids would carefully pick all the packages open when Dad was not around, and check to see if there was anything we wanted inside. If they were not "winners" in our estimation, we would equally carefully reseal them and put them back out for sale. I did it, but I felt a lot of guilt feelings inside about doing it. There was a lot of guilt in my childish mind, some of it over fairly minor things, but it seems like I just felt guilty about something or other (which I had either done or not done) a large part of the time. When this was added to my other negative feelings, I was carrying some heavy burdens inside, and did not know any good way to deal with them.

_____

In October of 1929, when I was eleven years old, the stock market crash began the period of the Great Depression. We lived in a good neighborhood, but during the 1930's work was scarce, and many people were without jobs. There were no welfare programs in those days, and families who had no income coming in could barely survive. There was a lot of sharing and compassion in our neighborhood, particularly when sickness or some other tragedy visited one of the neighbors. Everyone came to the aid of the families that were suffering especially badly. The rest of us, who were usually struggling pretty hard ourselves, nevertheless did whatever we were able to do to help: we would drop off some groceries at their house if we could, or try to give them assistance in some other way.

Niles, Ohio, was a very small town. Our population was less than twenty thousand. Most of those who were gainfully employed worked at industrial jobs. The major portion of our economy was dependent on the local steel mills, the tool and die plants, and the other small factory operations in town. The onset of the Great Depression had a devastating effect on these industrial operations, which in turn affected almost everyone in Niles. The steel mills had to cut back their operations to a very low level, because people in other parts of the country did not have the money to purchase the finished products which would be made out of the steel we produced.

When Franklin D. Roosevelt took over as president in 1933, one of his first actions was to issue a proclamation on March 6 closing all the few remaining banks which had not yet shut their doors. I was fourteen then, old enough to be aware of the full dimensions of the enormous suffering all over the United States caused by this catastrophic event. Roosevelt prodded Congress into action, and within a week, the sound banks were allowed to reopen, but the insolvent ones had to be put under government control and handed over to the comptroller of the currency to do the best he could. Billions of dollars in supposedly safe accounts had gone down the drain irrecoverably; many of the most prudent and hardworking American families found their life savings wiped out. Panic was seen everywhere, and many people took their own lives. This was truly a dark spot in American history.

Roosevelt began to assert his power in various ways however to give ordinary people like my family a little help and a lot more hope than we had been feeling. Government programs were established, for example, to create jobs for some of those who were out of work. The WPA (Works Progress Administration), which was authorized by Congress in 1935, was assigned the task of repairing roads and buildings, beautifying forests and parks, and so on. Over the following eight-year period, nearly nine million people were given jobs by that one program alone. Many families in our town, who had been plunged into total hopelessness by that point, were greatly assisted by that particular program. Even if the boost it gave us was partly psychological, that was what we needed most: some signal that there were men and women in the government who cared and were concerned, a signal which also gave a call to the ordinary people of this country to start looking for solutions instead of just quitting in despair. I saw it happening, and I saw it with my own eyes. It taught me as a child, by firsthand experience, that the right kind of government and national programs could give enormous assistance to people who were suffering, and could help turn a whole society around even when the magnitude of the problems we faced seemed enormous.

I remembered this later on, when I began to become involved with the national alcoholism programs which good people like Mrs. Marty Mann and Senator Harold E. Hughes were establishing, and started taking a leadership role myself in the military alcoholism program which was being started. If we could lick the Great Depression, we should be able to devise similar tactics for dealing with what had become America's number one public health problem by the 1940's and 50's, the destruction wrought by alcoholism.

Roosevelt's initial efforts, back when I was in my early teens, did a lot of good, but the country was not to return to full health instantly. In Niles as in many other places, a big move began to get the labor unions recognized in all the factories. Many companies became victims of long strikes. I recall that many of the steel mills voted to continue working, which created a major calamity because pickets outside the mills would block any workers from entering or leaving. Violence erupted as workers and strikers confronted one another. Those who decided to stay on the job in the mills were branded as scabs, and their families were threatened with violence.

The National Guard had to be called up to patrol the streets near the manufacturing plants. Some acts of violence continued to occur however. A deep division arose among the people of my town, where some sided with those who wanted to continue to work, and some sided with the union members who were on strike. People who had been close friends became bitter enemies, and tension pervaded our community for months. I was still too young to understand how friends and relatives could become so unrelentingly hostile to one another over such issues. Aircraft were then called in to drop supplies to those who stayed in the steel mills working. There were reports that some of these planes had been shot at, rumors which were never confirmed, but which caused the bitterness in Niles to escalate even further.

Union contracts were finally negotiated and ratified, and the strikes finally ended. The town went back to work. But those who had stayed on and worked in the mills and plants during the strikes were never accepted by the people who had been union members. Some of the individual anger and resentment continued for years to come, even after calm had prevailed again on the surface.

I had been a troubled child to begin with, with many deep inner fears and insecurities tied into all my close personal relationships. The onset of the Great Depression, the bank closings, and the labor strife made me fear the larger outside world too. That world did not appear to me to necessarily be a friendly place, nor did it seem a place where I could ever feel much real security.

Almost every American family suffered from the cruel tricks which the economy played on us during that period, and my own family was no exception. During the dead of winter, we had to walk to school even in subzero temperatures. One winter the family could not afford to buy me a real winter coat which would fit, so I trudged my way to school and back through the ice and snow with nothing to protect me but a thin baseball jersey. It had the words King's News Stand lettered on the front—they had sponsored the local team which wore those jerseys one summer, and had donated the jerseys in return for the advertising they got when the team walked out on the field. Nowadays, wearing clothing with the names of sports teams on them and various other logos is a status symbol—children beg their parents to spend excessive amounts of money to buy them these clothes—but that was not what it meant back then. It meant, to everyone who saw me coming, that my family was too poor to afford anything else. I already had an inferiority complex, and this just added to it. It is interesting, you know: we had food to eat, and my father managed to keep his little grocery business going, and I should have counted myself lucky, but it was this status thing, of not having stylish clothes to wear, which ate into me and made me feel even worse about myself. It was also true that the jersey was too thin to keep me warm—in fact I was freezing cold by the time I finished my journey—nevertheless, it was not that but those words "King's News Stand" lettered across the front, that got to me.

Those were hard times. Nevertheless, during those lean employment years, I can also recall the neighbors getting together and clearing an empty lot and making a baseball field. Everyone participated when we played, both men and women, and some were very good ball players. Our men's team had all four of my brothers and myself on the roster. We were all on the first team, so when the local newspaper wrote a story about our game, our names would be listed on the box score. When people looked at the paper they would see five team members with the same last name, three of them with first names beginning with R.

I feel a little sad today that, in our present-day society, there are so many fewer common bonds. We hardly know our next-door neighbors any more. In those long-ago days, caring and sharing was what life was all about. It seemed that the same neighbors lived in the same house forever, so I can still remember everyone who lived on the two streets in our semi-rural setting. Only two families in our little neighborhood community were regarded as representing any kind of negative presence, and they were isolated and did not mingle with the rest of us.

Several of the neighbors were especially kind to me and my brothers and sisters because of the tragic loss of our mother. One person in particular acted as almost a surrogate mother. She was a marvelous baker, and always made sure I got some when she made doughnuts or pies or other special treats. I was in her house getting fed and fussed over almost daily. Her husband often took me fishing with him. I can still hear the swish in the air when he threw his line out. He used a long cane pole just like my dad, and felt that the more limber it was the better it would work. One special treat of going fishing with him was that he brought lunch along with him, enough for both of us, and there would always be some of his wife's baked goods packed in there with the rest of the food.

Another neighbor went up to Canada fishing every year. It was a big event for the neighborhood when we saw him and his wife start preparing for the trip. Some of us kids helped by going out at night with flashlights and walking through the dewy grass looking for earthworms that had come up to surface, night crawlers we called them. We wanted to make sure the fishermen had plenty of bait, because when they returned they would hold a big fish fry, and all the neighborhood would be invited. The pickerel and muskies they were able to catch up in those cold northern waters were especially delicious eating. The filleted fish crackled as they were placed in the hot fat and the mouth-watering aroma of the cooking drifted through the air, luring everyone in to join in the festivities.

––––––––––––––––––––

Why is it that alcoholics can recover in A.A., when they cannot stop drinking on their own? One major reason is because an A.A. group is composed of fellow alcoholics all helping one another. Human beings need to feel a real part of a group or community in order to achieve the fullest psychological health. It is an absolute necessity. We need to know that there are other human beings who actually care what happens to us. A.A. provides not only formal meetings, but dances and baseball teams and picnics and people going fishing together, and all the other things that make up a warm, close human community. People feeling isolated in a huge urban metropolis, or lost on a large military base, rediscover something much like small town or village life once again. No one is forced to participate in these things in A.A., but those who do, find that it is deeply healing, and helps restore their wounded inner psyches.

Some people who come into A.A. are totally cut off from their families. I have heard many of these men and women say, as they looked around at the other people seated around the meeting table, "This is my family now," and say it with real gratitude in their voices. Feeling wanted, feeling secure, and feeling that there are other people who care what happens to us, is necessary for full mental health. That is a basic psychological truth.[4] It heals the inner wounds to our souls, and enables us to experience real happiness and feel good about ourselves once again. It is such a simple thing, but it is one of the most important A.A. recovery tools.

In the A.A. fellowship, I have learned how to handle this kind of closeness much better. That has been another thing that has helped me enormously. I can enjoy things like this so much better now, because the program showed me how to think more positively.

As you have seen, I can remember a lot about "the Good Old Days" when I was a child in small-town America, and many of my memories are pleasant ones. But whenever someone uses that phrase, and makes me start talking about my childhood and youth, the unhappy memories used to begin flooding in too, and I would quickly start becoming very defensive. I am still not completely over that, even now. In writing all this down, I still felt some of the old pain—it does not make me turn self-destructive now, but I can still feel it sharply when I relate these events.

Let me give you an example of the way negativism would inevitably contaminate and destroy what should have been some of my most pleasant memories. We had general neighborhood picnics every summer when I was young, in a place called the Sixty Acres along the banks of Mosquito Creek, but close to home, not way up along the creek where my dad had taken us fishing. We played games and everyone enjoyed themselves. I made a discovery at these picnics, that I was addicted to potato salad! I do not know why we hardly ever had that at home, but this was my downfall at these get-togethers. I would go back to the picnic table over and over until I had stuffed myself. At one of these parties, my dear sister noticed how much potato salad I was putting away, and scolded me and called me a pig. It is strange the kind of things that stick in your mind. But back in those days, it did not take much to make me feel acutely guilty, and that I must be some kind of a basically bad person. I had a truly enormous guilt complex. Getting caught going back for too many helpings of potato salad, silly and trivial as it was, was enough to make me feel worthless and a general failure as a human being. I can still remember that "pig" was the word she used when she was chastising me. And so, the way my mind worked, what should have been an extremely pleasant memory would get turned into something that tormented me whenever I recalled it.

As a child and youth, I was over-sensitive and could not stand to have people laughing at me. I had been traumatized by the death of my mother, felt abandoned and rejected, and was filled with envy. I was capable of being a real bully, and in school I was either withdrawn, or acting disruptively and causing trouble. Everything I was involved in seemed to leave me feeling guilty in one way or another. It was extremely deep guilt, an "I'm no good at all" kind of guilt. Those of you reading this who are in a twelve-step program can see that some of the things I have been writing about are part of doing a Fourth Step. In that step, we are asked to look at our lives, and see where we feel the great, persistent resentments and fear. Guilt and shame come in here as well. And then I have to stop looking at the external events for the answers, and instead have to start asking what there was in me which made me feel so much resentment and fear, and so much guilt and shame, and why it was able to get its hooks in my mind so deeply that I could not get rid of the painful feelings. I worked with some very good psychiatrists and psychologists when I was helping set up military alcoholism programs, and they helped me to see even more deeply into myself than I had done in my Fourth Step. Many people in the A.A. program get a skilled professional to help them at some point along the line, because the A.A. people do not claim to be professional psychiatrists, and they will tell beginners when they appear to have problems that run deeper than the twelve step program is designed to handle.

Both in doing my Fourth Step, and in talking to the psychiatrists I worked with, I was told that I had to look for the repeating patterns. Envy ran like a thread through many of my experiences for example. This envy turned me into a bully in some kinds of situations, and when I acted like a bully I ended up feeling guilt. When I learned what was actually happening in my mind, and why I was doing these things, it gave me the power to slowly develop different and more positive ways of dealing with situations of that sort. It changed my perception here in the present, and when my perceptions changed, my feelings and actions changed. I learned how to quit betraying myself and destroying myself over and over again. I started actually becoming a productive member of society for a change.

Even as a child, I somehow knew that what I needed most was just someone I could really discuss things with, and I yearned for that. We were not very good at that kind of communication in my childhood family, so there was no way of resolving what I was feeling. All I knew was my loneliness and despair. I did not know why I was feeling that way, so I did not know how to get out of it.

And my own family were probably too close to the situation anyway, to talk productively about things like this. I would have given anything to have been able to discuss my problems with someone outside the family. But there were no counselors in schools in those days: teachers were paid to teach, not to counsel. Corporal punishment was not only allowed in the schools, but frequently practiced. The cops would sometimes beat confessions out of criminals with stiff, thick rubber garden hoses in those days. The school system in my part of Ohio felt that misbehaving students should get a healthy taste of the same, so I received my share of lashes with a rubber hose.

Perhaps this is just a case of hindsight being better than foresight, but I still cannot help but wonder if someone who could have responded to my need to talk about what I was actually feeling back in those days, might not have meant the difference between the misery I actually suffered inside, and the happiness that a boy should have felt during his childhood. But I had to grow up, and learn a lot about myself in A.A., and then combine that with everything I then began learning about psychology and psychiatry once I was involved in the Air Force alcoholism treatment program, before I could penetrate some of these mysteries within myself. Until I learned the reasons for my internal responses to external events, I could not start learning how to free myself from those old patterns.

When we come into the A.A. program, we can find people with whom we can finally start talking about these feelings. Ideally, each newcomer will choose a person with more time in the program to serve as his or her sponsor. A good sponsor is someone you can talk to about anything, literally anything at all, no matter how embarrassed and frightened it may make you feel the first time. Good sponsors will usually begin their response by telling you something they once did or felt, which is often worse or more embarrassing than anything you ever did. That usually makes you feel a little better right away, as you suddenly discover that you are not the only person in the world who ever felt or acted that way. That helps get us out of our feeling of being totally "different" and "flawed" as people, and pathologically isolated. Even if you cannot find an ideal sponsor at first, some of these things can be talked about at meetings, or over coffee and pie after a meeting. Going to hear A.A. people give talks about themselves at open meetings or A.A. conferences can also be eye-opening.

An alcoholic cannot quit drinking or get well by himself. If you the reader think you may have a drinking problem, just ask yourself: have you ever yearned for someone who would really listen to you, where you could really talk these things over without fear, in a positive way? I am willing to bet that you have. You need to listen to what your mind is telling you here. The positive part of your mind is very wisely telling you what you will have to do in order to start feeling better about life and about yourself: you need to find someone to talk to, the right kind of person who will listen and genuinely understand.

I was at Hickam Army Air Base in Hawaii on the day Pearl Harbor was bombed, running for my life in my underwear through a hail of strafer bullets from the enemy airplanes and then trying to shelter behind a palm tree as flying shrapnel simply tore off the top of the tree as though it were made of paper. There were five of us who were drinking buddies, and the other four were all killed. I do not know why the hail of bullets missed hitting me, because I was running right through the incoming gunfire. If you are a civilian, you cannot ever know how that actually felt. It is literally indescribable to someone who has never experienced it. Only someone who has been in the military, and has actually been in combat, can truly know what it is like to be in combat, and everyone in the military knows that. Civilians can never really understand what it felt like, and why we did some of the things we had to do, because they have never been there.

A man can never really understand what it feels like to a woman when she is giving birth to a child. People who have served sentences in the penitentiary tell me that this too is an experience which can only truly be understood by another ex-con. They can tell the difference instantly between somebody who has just read books and magazine articles about it, and somebody who has actually been there.

What we have found in A.A. is that only another alcoholic can ever really understand down deep, the way an alcoholic hurts inside, or why we did some of the things we did. That is because we fellow alcoholics have been there ourselves. It was in A.A. that I first found people whom I could talk to about what my childhood had been like. At the beginning, the most I could do was to make myself blurt out a few words, expecting to be put down or derided, but then I began to realize that I did not need to fear that any longer: they understood exactly what I was trying to say from the moment I started talking. They knew because they had been there too.

CHAPTER 4

High School Years

Back in the mid-1930's when I was in high school, everyday life in the small cities and towns of the Midwest was for the most part quiet and law-abiding. There was very little crime compared to the present. Rarely did we lock our doors, and when we were working outside, we could walk off and leave our tools unattended. The biggest criminal in our neighborhood was a chicken thief who began a rash of stealing at one point. One family after another started noticing that the number of chickens in their chicken yards was going down, and that other property was sometimes missing as well. My family was exempted from these losses, because we had a goose which acted as a watchdog: if a stranger came around at night, the goose would begin honking loudly and sound the alert, and anyone up to no good would leave to seek easier pickings.

But other families were not so lucky, and feelings began to rise. What I call my neighborhood, by the way, was just a little community established on two dirt roads in a rural setting outside of the town of Niles itself. A midnight patrol was established to put a halt to the thievery, and it turned into a real adventure for people whose lives were otherwise fairly quiet and boring most of the time. We had all watched cowboy movies, we knew how this kind of frontier justice was carried out, and it was a chance for a little drama and excitement for a change.

My cousin got deeply caught up in the whole thing and began carrying a big shotgun around at night like an old-time cowboy vigilante, convinced that he personally was going to play the role of the hero in this drama, and bring the dastardly thief to instant justice. In his case, I think his bloodthirstiness was all in his mind, and if he had actually stumbled across the thief in the night, I doubt seriously if he would have used the gun. In fact, I suspect he would have dropped the gun and run, right there on the spot! But there were others in the midnight patrol who were more aggressive, and who were also vowing to shoot the thief in the act if they caught him out stealing during their nightly tour of duty.

Eventually the criminal was in fact caught, and it turned out to be a local character called Sneaky Pete. Most of the other stolen goods were recovered, but the chickens of course were all long gone: Sneaky Pete had killed and eaten those the minute he got them back home. It is strange that he had not been the prime suspect from the beginning, because he had a long criminal history. Perhaps no one thought about him at first because he did not live on our two roads, but over in an area called the Allotment, where a number of immigrant families had their homes. So, the criminal having been apprehended, life went back to normal again, which was fairly sleepy and uneventful.

I believe that one reason we had so little theft in most of the United States in those days, was because there were so few people hooked on drugs. Addicts can quickly get to the point where they absolutely have to obtain large amounts of money in order to maintain their habit. In fact we know that a major portion of present day crime of this variety—robbery and small-scale burglary and theft—is produced by addicts stealing money or goods in order to pay for drugs.

I cannot recall anyone in our town back in the 1930's who was a drug addict, so we had very little crime of that sort. I do not know what would have happened to me if the world back then had been like the modern age, where illegal drugs are easily available even in small towns, and where many teenagers experiment with them while they are growing up. Given all the conflicts and misery in my mind back then, I would have been hideously vulnerable. Could I have resisted peer pressure from other adolescents who were "trying out" some of these substances on a lark? Could I have pulled back in time when I began feeling the fatal lure of this particular drug or that?

That I will never know, but I did learn, from my work in treatment programs when military people from the Vietnam era started coming in as patients, that anyone who is on the path to chronic alcoholism is also very susceptible to drug addiction. Although there are differences, we found that we could adapt alcoholism treatment methods to help drug addicts successfully too, even though their attitudes and behaviors tended often to be more self-destructive, totally despairing, closed off, and antisocial. But the twelve step program works for them too.

I only remember one person in our neighborhood, a man named Ham, who was obviously an alcoholic. He was a good friend when he was sober, but he would go on binges where he drank constantly for two or three weeks at a time. While he was actively drinking, he would stagger around canvassing the neighborhood, begging from door to door for money to feed his habit. He was a very likable person, as I said, when he was off the booze. He could remain abstinent for two or three months at a stretch, and then for some reason would feel the need to punish himself by going off on another binge. When he finally drank himself to death, the entire neighborhood mourned his passing.

He completely changed personalities once he began to drink. I do not know what the underlying problems were, but you could tell when he was getting ready to go off the wagon again, because he would start getting very irritable and unfriendly. You knew that the nice, likable Ham was starting to disappear. Then, in a short time, he would be back on the bottle again for another two or three week spree.

When I was in high school, I could not understand how anyone's mind could work that way, and I made a solemn vow that I myself would never indulge in such a practice. Unfortunately, making solemn vows and promises never keeps an alcoholic from drinking, and by this time I was at one level already an alcoholic too—I just had not started the actual drinking yet. Ham and I were brothers under the skin, even though I did not realize it.

Later on, after I was in my thirties and started to study psychology and psychiatry, I came to realize that part of "the nice Ham" was a layer of inhibitions set up in his mind: "don't do this, don't act like that, always do such-and-such, nice people don't get angry over that sort of thing." As long as the inhibitions were in control, Ham acted in a likable and friendly fashion. This layer of inhibitions was trying to hold down, by sheer brute force, a bubbling cauldron of negative forces down in his subconscious mind: fears, dark and frightening desires, feelings of inadequacy, and so on. I never got to know him well enough to guess exactly what those inner pressures were and where they had come from. It is clear that there has to have been some real anger buried deep inside his mind, because some of this would start breaking through in the form of irritability and unfriendliness shortly before he actually picked up the bottle.

The important thing is that when the forces down in his subconscious became too strong, the only way he knew to relieve the terrible pressure was to drink. The inhibitions would be dissolved away, and he would spend two or three weeks acting out all those repressed subconscious urges. That would finally relieve the pressure enough that he could put the bottle down and let the inhibitions settle back into place for another two or three months. But the pressure down below that layer of inhibitions would finally grow too great once again, and the cycle would be repeated for yet another round. Finally one of these drunken binges did him in, and he died.

I want to talk more about this in a later chapter, where I will explain in greater detail how this particular psychological and psychiatric process can become a major cause of chronic alcoholism. Knowing more about what was going on in my own mind when I felt a craving for alcohol helped me in staying sober, and also aided me in helping other alcoholics who came into treatment programs I was running.

Knowing more about these kinds of mental processes also made it clear why no alcoholic could get sober and stay sober just by exercising more will-power. How could the conscious mind control subconscious pressures when it did not even know they existed, let alone what they were? And usually trying to stay off alcohol by will-power alone also involves trying to strengthen the level of inhibitions, so that the alcoholic becomes even more inhibited. At the end of each binge, a remorseful Ham would try even harder to be "a nice guy" all the time, and to stay off the booze completely by white-knuckling it. All this meant was that the subconscious pressures would have to build up even higher before they could explode through the layer of inhibitions, which meant that the resultant binge or spree would be even more destructive.

Knowing something about these psychological processes also helped me to understand why alcoholics who come into the twelve step program cannot stay sober forever on just the first three steps. The alcoholic eventually has to take a real fourth step, which calls for an inner inventory of some of these fears and resentments and guilts he has been blocking out of his conscious mind. This step, and the ones which follow, provide positive ways to deal with these deep, pent-up pressures. Until the alcoholic gets down below the surface and starts dealing with the real inner problems, he will still remain a time bomb: when external events finally create a great enough inner pressure, he will drink. The only path to dependable long term sobriety is through working all twelve steps.

This also explains why preaching at alcoholics and lecturing them on the errors of their ways will never permanently keep them off the alcohol. Moralistic preaching and lecturing and scolding can at best make a person more inhibited, and strengthen the barrier of inhibitions which hold down the subconscious forces. Now there are people who fall into the habit of drinking more than they should, who are *not* real alcoholics, who can in fact sometimes stop drinking when someone really lays down the law to them. Not everyone who drinks too much is a true alcoholic. That is why preachers can sometimes delude themselves into thinking that they can cure real alcoholics by just preaching sermons filled with images of threats and guilt and punishment: this may in fact sometimes work on ordinary people who have fallen into the habit of drinking a little too much, so these preachers mistakenly think that it would work on everyone if they just put a little more hellfire into their sermons, or more doctrines and dogmas, or more bible verses.

With a genuine alcoholic however, trying to do it this way will never work in the long run: trying to lock down the inner subconscious forces more tightly by making the alcoholic even more inhibited will just make the next explosion more destructive. That is why A.A. refuses to preach at people, and why it welcomes alcoholics in with unconditional love and acceptance. In the Big Book, the twelve steps are introduced as suggestions, not orders or commands. On the other hand, the people in an A.A. meeting who have some continuous long term sobriety will explain to newcomers that they themselves were unable to defeat the compulsion to drink until they began working all twelve steps, including the self-inventory in the fourth step, where we privately, and entirely on our own, start looking down into the parts of our minds where the real problems are coming from.

I have already talked in the two previous chapters about some of the things I found when I did that: deep feelings of inferiority, envy, feelings of being rejected or judged all the time, other kinds of fear, and in particular, an enormous amount of guilt. I felt like I was a failure, and that whenever anything went wrong in my life, I was the one who was at fault. Everyone in A.A. who does a fourth step finds a different mix of things. If poor Ham, our neighborhood alcoholic, had gotten into A.A. and eventually done a fourth step, his inner inventory would have been different from mine. That is why no one in A.A. will sit over you and give you a list of detailed rules to use in your fourth-step inventory: only you know what the ideas and feelings were, down in your own mind, which drove you to despair, so only you can make that list.

My seven brothers and sisters were brought up in the same family as I, and we all went through a lot of the same external things together, and yet none of them became alcoholics like I did. At one level, alcoholism often functions as a disease of perception. It was my own unique perception of these events which created the subconscious conflicts and disturbances within myself, and only I had access within my mind to what I had actually felt and thought. So none of my brothers or sisters could have done my fourth step for me. Likewise, a wife cannot do her husband's fourth-step inventory for him, and a husband cannot do his wife's inventory—although husbands and wives often try! Even a good A.A. sponsor or a highly skilled psychiatrist could do no more, most of the time, than make suggestions about the kinds of questions we should be asking ourselves.

But we need to wait until a later chapter to start talking more about the subconscious and the layer of inhibitions which holds it down. For now, I need to talk a little more about what life was like for a teenager in Niles, Ohio, in the mid 1930's.

We lived outside of town, in the county. There were many unpaved roads in those days. Walking back and forth to the school in town, my brothers and sisters and I had to go along North Road, as it was called. It was paved within the city limits, but where it extended out into the county, it was just ten miles of untended dirt road. Although it had a lot of automobile traffic, the county either had no money to pave it, or did not choose to do so. When there had been a recent rainstorm, we children would often be splashed with muddy water from passing cars as we trudged our way back home. The road was also full of deep pot holes and there were no street lights. When we were little, we were scared to walk it at night, because the pitch blackness made everything so eerie and foreboding.

The two roads that made up our local neighborhood were also simply dirt, and continually developed pot holes. We had to empty the ashes every day from the coal stoves that we used to heat our house in the winter, so we tried to take care of two problems at once by shoveling the ashes from the stove into a scuttle or bucket and then carrying them out and dumping them in one of the potholes in front of our house, or in the muddy driveway to make it a little bit firmer.

Most teenagers did not have access to cars in those days, so "joy riding" around town just to pass time was not a normal part of teenage life. There were only a very few students in my high school who did have cars they could use. Their parents were very well off financially, and I (along with all the rest of us who were on foot) really envied these kids. I did not learn how to drive myself until I was almost finished with high school. I never would have wanted to take a girl out riding anyway in my dad's old Model T Ford with homemade windows. It would have been just too embarrassing.

The Model T only had a maximum speed of 35 miles per hour, but in spite of that, my dad once managed to get two tickets in one day. He was doing his top speed of 35 in a 25 mile per hour zone, when Niles' only motorcycle cop pulled him over for speeding. Dad was really mad, and after grabbing the ticket out of the cop's hand, drove off at only 5 miles per hour to show that cop what he thought. So then the cop gave him the second ticket, this time for "blocking traffic"!

Nevertheless, Dad was not a speed demon in the modern sense. I remember when my brother-in-law bought a new 1932 Ford V-8 (this would have been the year I turned fourteen) and took Dad and me with him while he put it to a road test. Dad was really enjoying it as we cruised along at a moderate speed. Those were sturdy automobiles in those days, built to last, with bodies made of heavy duty steel, and real bumpers made out of thick chrome-plated steel instead of the modern flimsy rubber and plastic contraptions. And those old V-8 engines could produce a lot of horsepower. So things were going along nicely until my brother-in-law suddenly decided to push the gas pedal all the way to the floor, "to see what it'll really do." We were up to 80 miles per hour in a flash, when my dad, terrified, cried out in an anxiety-laden voice, "Slow down or I'll jump!"

This is the way the human mind jumps around when we are trying to remember and talk about our pasts. I have deliberately left these three chapters about my childhood and youth partly disorganized, because that is the way it comes out in the office of a psychiatrist or psychotherapist, and that is the way the images will also come into our minds when we are working on the fourth step in the twelve-step program. Pleasant memories, and humorous memories, pop out side by side with very unpleasant things which we also recall. They cannot be made to fit smoothly together, because that is what we mean by subconscious conflict. There was a good deal of conflict going on in my mind during my high school years, and the various parts of my life did not seem to fit together in my mind because in fact they did not fit with one another.

I held bitter feelings toward some of my fellow high school students because their families had not suffered like mine had during the lean years of the depression. I felt rejected and unimportant. I would try to put forth an enormous effort to somehow feel accepted by the other students, but always ended up feeling "like an object" rather than a human being. I longed to be part of school activities, but never could feel as though I really belonged. I had very few close friends in high school. Most of my experiences were negative. The problem was that I could not stand looking at these kinds of feelings, so I shoved them down into my subconscious. "Out of sight, out of mind," as people are apt to think, but it is not so.

And unfortunately, it was the school teachers—not my fellow students—who mostly became the target for my hostility. That is the problem when subconscious fears and resentments are held down below a layer of rigid inhibitions: the feelings are still acted out at the conscious level, but always directed toward the wrong targets. Most of the teachers treated me with a kind of nonchalant and indifferent attitude. I totally mistrusted them, because I was convinced that none of them really cared one way or the other what I was feeling, or even doing. In retrospect, I realize that there were in fact several teachers who tried to reach out to me and enlist my trust, but I instantly rejected every one of their attempts. I had talked myself into believing, falsely, that their efforts to be friendly and caring would be jerked away again the minute they found out what kind of flawed person I really was. What I did, at every opportunity, was to try to make them aware of my presence by being disruptive and disrespectful. People who have no real self-respect cannot be respectful toward others.

My family's finances had never improved, so when I walked in the doors of the high school, my clothes were shabby and sometimes my pants were patched. I felt unbearably self-conscious and out of place. Attending school functions like dances and proms was out of the question. The subconscious feeling of being inferior and rejected by others was always present. I never learned how to dance, because I was too afraid of not measuring up to the other people who would be out on the dance floor. They would judge me, and that was a thought

I could not stand. If I asked a girl to dance with me, she might say no, and I could not stand any more feelings of rejection.

So what did I do? I remember that whenever I heard a train whistling far off—those long, deep, lonesome moans of the old steam whistles that seemed to cry out with an elemental feeling of total heartbreak and vast distances stretching forever into nowhere—I would daydream about getting out of Niles. I just wanted out of my life there. I also went fishing or hunting, because I could do that all alone. I played hooky for days at a time. There were some other sports which I also used to substitute for real personal involvement with other people. I could do it as pure, concentrated physical activity and surface chatter without having to actually be intimately involved with any other human being.

When the baseball season began every year, you could guarantee that my seat in the classroom would be empty. When I was in eighth grade, I was of course absent from class on the opening day of the season. The next day I handed my homeroom teacher an excuse for this absence which I had in fact written myself, signing one of my parents' names at the bottom in what I thought was a very clever and undetectable forgery. He took the little excuse note from my hand, glanced at it casually, and then simply said, "What was the score?"

This man had my number, and in fact I could not fool him. The pity is, that he was actually my favorite teacher at the whole school until that incident with the two dogs coming into the classroom, which I told you about earlier. I never forgave him for that, and so one potential friend among the teaching staff was lost forever.

Baseball was my really great love, the game that I still continued playing even after I got into the military. One of the highlights of my life was the time in 1932 when my uncle took me to Cleveland to see the Cleveland Indians play, and I got to see Babe Ruth, Lou Gehrig, and the rest of that truly great New York team. My real hero however was Earl Averill, and I prayed that day that he would hit a homer every time he came to bat. But Fate was not on my side that day, nor his, and he struck out all three times when he came to bat. He did not even get a hit. I switched my loyalty later to Bob Feller, and had the privilege of seeing him pitch on several occasions. One of these was a game played after he returned from the military, where he beat the New York Yankees, the team I regarded as the arch enemy.

I also played some basketball just to keep from being bored. The game was played very differently back in that era. Many of the present day rules and plays had not been invented yet.

I also tried playing golf on the high school team. My older brother, who was a good golfer, loaned me his clubs so I could play. One of the clubs was not in good shape, although I did not know it. When we were playing another high school in the area, I teed up my ball and took a mighty swing at it, and the head of the club came loose from the shaft and flew further down the fairway than the ball did. Everyone around laughed and made jokes, and I cringed inside and felt like my world had come to an end. That was part of my subconscious makeup: I could not stand any situation where I thought I looked silly or ridiculous, or where people were laughing at me and what I was doing. This somehow opened up the ultimate abyss of terror for me down deep inside.

The academic side of my high school career was a disaster. It is difficult to become involved in any kind of learning process without motivation. I had so many internal conflicts preoccupying my mind, that none of the teachers were able to arouse my interest in their classes. I never did any homework, and no one at home encouraged me to study. In fact, no one at home even seemed interested in what grades I was making; I usually signed my own report cards, because no one seemed to care anyway. My dad and stepmother were not interested in coming to school activities like plays and exhibits of things produced in classes. In fact, the only time I can recall that they actually came to something in which I was involved was a school play from grade school, long before I went off to high school. I was made to play the part of a character called Simple Simon, and the lines I had to recite implied that I was a silly boy. Going out on that stage was total, humiliating agony to me, because the idea of being thought silly or foolish, as I have mentioned, opened up the yawning abyss of my own greatest subconscious fears.

I had no real feelings of self-worth, I was not encouraged at home to study or work hard in school, and I always compared myself with the other kids around me and invariably felt "less than" and judged by them. So I did very poorly in my classes. And in turn, I bitterly resented those students who did achieve good grades.

No one advised me when it came time to pick what subjects I would study for the year, so I automatically signed up for the ones that seemed the easiest whenever I could: shop, typing, physical education, and drawing. If I took these, I could probably avoid having to read difficult material or think or conceptualize. I was not considering what was needed to prepare for a successful career in any field, but simply trying to calculate the minimum amount of effort I would have to make in order to actually graduate. I had too many personal conflicts tying up my mind to even think about my own long term survival. What was I going to do after I became an adult? At that time, I could not stand even living in the present, let alone think about the future.

There was never any real communication with my parents at all. I was essentially left to shift for myself, so in this area as in so many other parts of my life, I frequently made bad decisions, and then the pain from the consequences of those bad decisions made life even more overwhelming. I knew that I was being torn apart inside by all my inner conflicts, but I had no tools to repair them. I wanted desperately to be an acceptable part of society, but I could barely function because of all the different conflicting desires and hatreds and fears and dreads inside my mind.

I deeply regret the fact that I never took advantage of that opportunity back in my high school days to learn something more worthwhile. From my present perspective, I think back over that period of my life, and there were several teachers I had who could have taught me some very valuable things, and would have been more than willing to. A good teacher can have an enormous positive impact on a person's later life, even many years later. They can give something important, that goes beyond the mere subject matter they teach. In later years, when I would return to Niles for a visit, there were still two of these teachers in town whom I was apt to see when I visited the grocery store. I remember now that they actually made me feel good when I was in their classes, but all I had given them in return was a gross lack of respect.

I realize now that education is in fact all-important. When the opportunity to learn presents itself, we must take full advantage of it, or that particular opportunity will be lost forever. My late brother-in-law was the only member of my family who tried to persuade me to study, without any success of course, because I was just not interested in learning anything at all. He himself struggled to get his education, against almost impossible odds, and succeeded. But when he talked to me on his theme of "education at all costs," all I felt toward him was resentment.

It borders on a miracle that I was ever given a diploma. Math in particular was extremely difficult for me. I was the only one in the history of that school who ever had to take ninth grade algebra every year until I graduated, going through the same material four years in a row until I finally got a minimally passing grade. It was required for graduation however, so I had no choice. We wore our caps and gowns to all our classes just before graduation, and a number of the other students in that ninth grade algebra class made a number of comic remarks when I walked into the room that day, all dressed up for commencement. They were so much younger than me that I thought of them as just little kids. But it made me furiously angry because it opened up my deepest inner dread: looking silly or foolish.

In terms of academic standing, my grades were so poor that I graduated next to last in my class. I mentioned this one time when I was giving a talk to a group of Air Force Reserve Officers, and made a comment about how much this had always bothered me. One of the officers spoke up and asked, "Do you know what they call the person who finishes at the bottom of his class in medical school?" I said no, and he instantly responded, "They call him Doctor." My co-author, who is a historian, also told me I was being too rough on myself: he pointed out that the average American during that period of history dropped out of school at the end of the eighth grade or very soon thereafter. Regardless of my class standing, simply sticking in there to the end of twelfth grade and actually getting the diploma was a notably significant accomplishment.

Again we see that it is not the events themselves which do us so much harm, but our perception of them. This is vitally important to remember: I cannot go back into the past and change the external event that happened. I can however learn to see the event from a different viewpoint, or in a wider perspective, and change my whole perception of its significance. If I learn how to perceive that past event in the right kind of way, I can remove its power to destroy my future.

As I skip around through these fairly disorganized memories of my past, I realize that I have been steadily avoiding talking about the most painful part. I rarely dated during my high school years. On several occasions I did get a crush on a girl, and would write her mushy notes. My sister once intercepted one of the notes that a girl wrote back to me. I had told the girl about my most recent fishing trip, and that I had not caught a single fish. In her note back to me, the girl wrote, "Imagine those silly fish laughing at you." My sister made sure that everyone else in the family heard that line, and I was teased about it for a long time afterwards.

I never had the right clothes to wear, and felt self-conscious about that. I have told you that already, and also that I was afraid to get out on a dance floor, because I was terrified that the other students would judge me or laugh at me. I was certainly not going to invite a girl to go riding with me in my dad's old outmoded Model T Ford!

Nevertheless, at the end of high school, I finally spent weeks building up the courage to ask one particular girl to go to the prom with me. I had been mesmerized by her charms for months, but I had never asked her for a date before, because I was just too afraid of being rejected. Finally I mustered up all my courage, asked her, and to my surprise she said "Sure." I was convinced at that point that prom night was going to be the absolute highlight of my young life. It would not matter that much that I did not know how to dance; there were going to be other boys there in the same predicament.

Now how was I going to actually convey her to the prom? I was in high anxiety about that for a long time, but then to my surprise, my brother not only agreed to teach me how to drive, but also offered me the use of his car for that night. Money was scraped together to buy me a suit—the first suit I ever owned. This was frosting on the cake. All my apprehensions were swept away. My mind was swimming with golden fantasies of that night.

The day before the prom, I went up to the girl and asked her what time she wanted me to pick her up. She looked at me with amazement, and said something like, "didn't you realize I was only kidding back then?" She already had a date to go to the prom, she told me, a date with someone else.

I have never seen her since. I do not know what my reaction would be now if I were to run into her. If she is still alive, she would be old now, in her mid-eighties, like me.

When I graduated from high school in June 1936, I felt like a total failure at life. I felt totally worthless inside, and rejected and abandoned by everyone. As far as I could see, all the major events of my youthful years had conclusively proved this, beyond a shadow of a doubt. I had never yet drunk a drop of alcohol. That day was not far off, but you need to see that, although out-of-control drinking was going to make things even worse, my real problems went back long before I started on the booze.

When I finally started taking the A.A. program seriously twelve years later, the first thing they told me was that I had to stop drinking, completely and totally, one day at a time. There was no hope for me at all as long as I continued drinking. But there were twelve steps in their program, and I was going to have to work my way through all of them during the months and years that followed, or I would eventually go back to the alcohol once again. Or at the very least, if I somehow or other stayed dry but refused to work all twelve steps, I would simply destroy my life some other way. I demonstrated for twelve years, from 1936 to 1948, that I could not live successfully with alcohol. But it is important to remember that, for the preceding eighteen years, I had also demonstrated that I could not live successfully without it either. I desperately needed someone to teach me how to live life successfully, because with or without alcohol, that was the one thing I had never learned.

That was the real magic of the twelve steps: they not only gave me the power to stop drinking, they also taught me how to really live. They changed all my perceptions of the world around me, and they taught me how to deal with events today, whenever they start to seem totally crushing or overwhelming, by working to modify my perceptions of them. As long as I continue to practice those steps, and live by them—even in the midst of pain and loss—I do not ever need to return to the nightmare of those high school years again. I do not ever need to feel absolutely worthless again.

CHAPTER 5

Discovering Alcohol

In June of 1936, I graduated from high school. I had my first taste of alcohol at a Christmas Eve party six months later, and got drunk enough to become very obnoxious, and disgrace myself with my boss. I thought it was the most marvelous fun I had ever had, until the alcohol wore off the next day. I was eighteen years old, but I continued to drink that way, and worse, until shortly after my thirtieth birthday. I did not have the faintest idea what was going on down in my subconscious : the envy, the anger and resentment, the guilt and terror, the feelings of being rejected and abandoned, and above all the condemning sense of being worthless and a failure. All I knew was that, when I did not have alcohol in my system, a dark mass of horrifying feelings—feelings which I could not truly put a name on or identify—would eventually begin pressing up from deep inside until I did not believe I could stand it any longer. So I had to drink again, and became willing to give up anything else I wanted or desired for the sake of alcohol.

The pressure started the minute I got out of high school. A working family like mine was not going to let me sit around and loaf. I knew that I had to find employment, and the American economy was still not in good shape. At first all I could find was a series of odd jobs that led nowhere. One was as an auto mechanic. I in fact knew very little about cars, but the owner of the garage told me he would teach me "the tricks of the trade." I was young and gullible, and simply the thought of having some sort of job gave me some peace of mind, so I immediately agreed. The amount of my salary was left rather vague, but he did say he could only pay me a very small amount until I had become proficient at carrying out automobile repairs. At the end of my first week he handed me five dollars. That was my pay. It cost me almost two dollars a week to ride the bus back and forth to work, so I was left with only three dollars in pay for all that work. After another week of that, I quit. There were no government regulated minimum wage standards in those days, so an employer could pay a worker as little as he wanted.

I finally found a more decent job with the Firestone Tire and Rubber Company, and began an "on again, off again" relationship with that company for the next three years. I started with the local Firestone Service Store in Niles doing such things as minor car repairs, and selling and installing merchandise like tires and car heaters. In those days, most cars did not have heaters installed when they came from the factory, so the owner had to buy one at a place like Firestone and have them fit the heater in the car.

Two weeks working at an auto repair shop had not turned me into a professional mechanic, and I began to see what the pressures of living in the adult world were really like. A regular customer at the Firestone Store had a 1935 LaSalle, which was a very expensive car for those days, costing over $2,000 to buy. He wanted a heater installed, and in the process I stripped the threads in the motor block. This required cutting a new thread in a fixture which fit into the block, a very time-consuming procedure. I was severely reprimanded for botching that task, and was afraid I was going to be fired right then and there. I had been judged and found wanting, scolded and made to feel like a fool. My worst subconscious fears were rising inside me.

I was also supposed to do some selling, and we had a sales quota assigned by the manager. I was much better at this part of the job, soon became one of their top salesmen, and in fact just missed a trip to the Indianapolis Auto Races as a reward for my outstanding sales record. I was nearly up at the top in this area. But being successful at this did not quiet my inner subconscious fear of failure, because I was continually beset by the silent dread that one month I might not make it. Even enormous success barely eased the real stress at all.

It was on Christmas Eve of that year, at the end of 1936, when I went to the party and had my first drink of alcohol. I felt like celebrating and taking a few hours off from my worries, the effect of the alcohol turned out to be just what I was looking for, and I proceeded to get extremely drunk. All my incredible self-consciousness was washed away, and it felt so good to be part of a crowd without having to feel inferior to everyone else. The way drunks feel inside, and the way other people perceive them, are of course two entirely different things. I myself felt like I had become the life of the party. I learned later that as I became rather bold in my approaches to the girls at the party, there was an increasing amount of resentment about my behavior. I really loved the new me, but a lot of people at the party did not like the new me at all, and found me totally obnoxious.

After leaving the party, I bought an ice cream cake to take as a present to my boss. Drunks do not do a good job of thinking about everyday common sense things. I put it in the boss' refrigerator, but did not think about the fact that ice cream had to be put in the freezer compartment. I set it down on a shelf in the regular part of the refrigerator, right on top of what was to be my boss' Christmas dinner. When they went to prepare it, the ice cream had melted all over it. This time I really came close to being fired on the spot. This time I felt even more humiliated, and like even more of a fool.

The only way I knew to cope with the feeling of being such a failure, of being so inept and careless, was to go drink some more. This is another part of the psychological process of becoming a chronic alcoholic: each drinking bout brings new and fresh humiliations and requires starting another drinking bout to escape the remorse and the feelings of failure. I became continually preoccupied with drinking, or planning my next drinking bout, or recovering from my last drinking bout.

The hangovers were unbearable. A friend who had long since passed the stage of normal social drinking recommended drinking Seven-

Up soda with salt added to it. I tried that, and several other kinds of home remedies, but none of them actually relieved the suffering. But then within a short period of time, my keen alcoholic mind discovered the tried-and-true hangover remedy that really worked: start drinking again in the morning the minute you get up. Unfortunately, this meant going to work that morning with alcohol on my breath, which was apt to be a job-threatening practice. I decided to use other strong-smelling substances as camouflage, and was delighted to discover that it seemed to work. I decided that this was the method I needed to use from that point on. Alcoholic cunning and logic had triumphed once again!

My job actually did not suffer for a long period of time, because I could not stand the thought of any criticism—my subconscious fears were too great in that area, and they drove me to work extremely hard in order to justify my employment there, and also to exercise extreme caution about anything where I might get caught. It also did not hurt that my cousin was the Service Manager there at that time. We drank together quite often (he also eventually ended up with a severe drinking problem), and he protected me. I later saw the same "buddy system" working in the military, where an alcoholic in a command position would often protect even the quite severe alcoholics under his command from having to suffer the consequences of their obviously out-of-control drinking.

I never got in difficulty with the law during those first three years of drinking, except for being held a few hours at one point as a witness in an alcohol-related automobile accident. But some of my family members began to be concerned, and they sometimes nagged and scolded me about my excessive drinking. On the other hand, there were several other family members who defended me, including the brother-in-law who was married to my oldest sister. He also drank too much himself, but he also seemed to be more aware of what I was feeling inside and what was actually going on, and he never deserted me.

During this three-year period, I came and went at Firestone three times. The first time I quit my job with them, I developed an urge to travel, and my uncle hired me to drive a truck as his helper.

Unfortunately, it turned out that he had no intention of actually paying me for being his helper, so after about a month of truck driving I went back to Firestone for the second time.

I became very close to the Store Manager, who protected me whenever my drinking was going to get me in trouble, which happened quite often. Eventually he was transferred to Portsmouth, Virginia, so I went to Virginia myself and he hired me at the store he ran there. But alcoholism is a progressive disease, and I began doing things now that went past even his tolerance level. I quickly started getting in trouble because of my drinking on the job. I went to a restaurant to get my lunch, and had a beer with my meal. He smelled it on my breath when I got back to work, and gave me a severe tongue lashing. I kept on doing it, several more strong warnings were issued, and I decided to quit.

A truck driver who bought his gas at the pump there asked me if I would like to go to Atlanta, Georgia, with him, so I decided this was a good idea. I had driven a semi there in Portsmouth, so I felt competent enough to help him drive. He left me off right when he got into Atlanta, telling me that he would be back for me as soon as he had dropped his load. I never saw him again.

I was stranded penniless in Atlanta, and soon decided I had better head back north again. While I was hitchhiking just outside of Atlanta, a highway patrolman picked me up and was going to charge me with vagrancy. This would have meant a stint on a Georgia chain gang, a truly terrifying prospect. I became totally unraveled, and pleaded with him to let me go. I told him the plight I was in, and how it had happened, and I must have struck a sympathetic chord in his heart, because he drove me over to a more likely spot for catching a ride, and gave me a dollar and wished me good luck before he drove away.

I was picked up by a man who said he was on his way to New York city. He agreed to actually pay me, if I would just help him with the driving. That sounded like a real adventure, because I had never been to any place like New York city in my life. He treated me with respect, and the trip to New York was actually very enjoyable. When we got there, he gave me money for food and two nights' lodging in the Lexington Hotel.

I was a small town Ohio boy, who had never stayed in a hotel before, let alone seen anything like the skyscrapers of New York. I got a stiff neck just walking around looking up at all the tall buildings, totally overawed. But I was also a little frightened and apprehensive, and was very much aware that I was there all alone. I was sure that everyone who passed was immediately aware that I was a rube from a small town, who had gotten in way over his head.

It turned out I wasn't far wrong. As I ambled along staring up at the huge buildings, a man came up to me and made me a marvelous proposition. He had two diamond rings, which he offered to sell me for just five dollars. How could I refuse such an amazing opportunity? Here was the magic answer to the one little problem I was wrestling with at that point. How was I going to get the money to get back to Ohio after I had seen the sights of the Big Apple? Using my keen alcoholic mind, I went back to the hotel, got my one-day deposit back, handed him the five dollars, and walked off with my treasure. I felt like both a very lucky and a very clever fellow indeed.

I headed west and boarded the subway, clutching the rings tightly in my sweaty fist to make sure these little beauties were not lost or stolen. When I got off the subway, I opened my fist once again to admire their splendor—and discovered that my hand was already turning green. I did not need to go to a jeweler to be told what the friendly stranger had palmed off on me. I had been taken by a con artist who must have specialized in rubes from places like small town Ohio. I tossed the bogus gold rings angrily over my shoulder and strode off, counting the little money I had left: twenty-five cents. It was back to hitchhiking again.

I made it out into the countryside, looking desperately for a ride. An overwhelming feeling of loneliness and despair gripped me. As nightfall descended, I became more and more afraid. For hour after hour, no one who came by would pick me up. I had not had anything to eat and felt like I was starving. Then I spotted an apple tree along the side of the road, and ran over to it, reaching out to grab an apple. Out of the dark, a horse which was standing by the tree suddenly snorted at me, and I jumped back again in terror. When I realized what it was, I went back and started picking apples off the tree and wolfing them down. I still remember them as the best apples I have ever tasted.

Eventually a man picked me up in his car, and immediately offered me a drink. I felt like I had died and gone to heaven, and it tasted like the elixir of the gods. He was enjoying it too, and in fact we both ended up getting very drunk indeed. He got so drunk that he unfortunately ran into another car. The driver of the other car was injured in the wreck, so my new drinking buddy and I were both detained by the police overnight. They ended up officially putting him under arrest, but let me go the next morning after I had given a written deposition about what had caused the accident. Now I must have been in at least a semi-blackout at the time we hit the other car, and I actually could not even remember what had happened. This required some very creative writing on my part, putting down what I hoped would look like a semi-plausible account of an event which I was actually having to create from sheer fantasy and imagination.

The full significance of what had happened never hit me: I had just been involved in my first experience of an alcohol-related automobile accident, an innocent person had been hurt, I had been under police custody, and I had totally falsified a legal deposition which was going to be used in the ensuing court case. But I totally disregarded these warnings about the possible consequences of out-of-control drinking. No matter how drunk I myself had also been, I had not been the one actually driving, the police did not in fact put me under arrest by the time it was over, and as for the falsified deposition, I had merely done what any sensible person would have done under those circumstances. This was what I would have told you at the time, if you had begun lecturing me about my own excessive drinking. This unfortunate little accident was the other guy's problem, not mine. I was careful about my drinking, and I was never going to get in any real trouble because of it.

By the time I hit western New York state, I was so hungry that I actually stood on the street in a small town and begged. I finally collected enough change to buy a sandwich. I started talking to a girl who worked in the restaurant where I bought it. She asked me where I was going, and she got an astonished look on her face. It turned out that she came from another small town only four miles from Niles. I mentioned my last name, she began asking more questions about my family, and it turned out that she knew my uncle and cousins from when she was still living there in Ohio. This coincidence turned my tiny sandwich into a big meal, for which I was extremely grateful, because I was very, very hungry. I thanked her profusely, and hit the road again.

Once safely back in Niles, I decided it was back to the Firestone Store again. This time I was given a much higher position, that of Service Manager. My pay was now enormous by my standards, eighty dollars a month. I was still drinking, but it did not seem to cause me any trouble on the job. I was convinced that, even if some people were critical, there was nothing wrong with the way I drank. I was climbing up the corporate ladder. I was sharp, and I was competent, and I had already made it to the rank of Service Manager.

I actually managed to meet Mr. Firestone himself, *the* Mr. Firestone, although I did not realize it at first. One day I had just finished dusting and rearranging the merchandise in the store. It was looking very nice. But at that point, an elderly man walked into the store and started to rearrange some of my carefully positioned displays. I was outraged inside, because I had put a lot of time into that, and now I would have to do it all over again. Several times, I politely asked him if I could help him look, like a well-trained store clerk, but he insisted that he was in no hurry to purchase anything. I got more and more irritated, tried even harder to sell him something, and started becoming somewhat aggressive.

The store manager had been temporarily out of the store while all of this was going on, running an errand someplace else in town, but at this moment he returned. As he walked in the front door, he gasped out in a very strained voice, "Good morning, Mr. Firestone." I suddenly realized that I had been getting pushier and pushier with the very founder himself of the great Firestone Tire and Rubber Company. I hastily excused myself, and headed for the back of the store, where there was another door. I took off out the back door, convinced that I had just lost this job permanently. I was in a kind of numb despair.

In fact, Mr. Firestone must have somehow approved of my behavior. Instead of being fired for being rude to him, the store manager was told to give me a five-dollar-a-month pay raise. Once again, when my actions seemed to have gotten me into a hopeless situation, either my wits or my luck came to my rescue just when I needed it most.

In the earlier stages of alcoholism, where the alcoholic is still basically "getting away with it," this makes him cocky and over-confident. He may drink a lot, but he has it "under control." That will often serve as his goal later on after things get worse: not stopping drinking totally and permanently, but getting his drinking back under control again somehow, so he can continue to drink without suffering the unpleasant consequences. The problem is that alcoholism is a progressive disease, where there is no way to turn the clock backwards like that.

And by this time, trying to hold a job while drinking as much as I was, brought on an incredible amount of tension and pressure. In order to deal with the anxiety, and "relax my nerves," I was having to drink even more. And I had not been raised to approve of drinking like this: my father had been strongly opposed to all drinking. Down in my subconscious, a sense of enormous guilt about my behavior was building up higher and higher. At that point, however, up at the level of my conscious mind I still would have been totally unwilling to admit the presence of that humiliating sense of guilt. Until alcoholics become ruthlessly honest with themselves about what they are really thinking and feeling down at the bottom of their minds, they cannot begin serious recovery.

I had been getting into a serious relationship with a girl there in Niles, and right after I returned from Georgia, we had gotten engaged. Our relationship lasted almost three years. She was a very beautiful and caring girl, but my drinking created problem after problem. She was totally opposed to the use of alcohol, but I could not stop. Because of this, she finally broke off the engagement, and I fell into a deep depression. There would have been other problems of course, if we had gotten married: my family was opposed to her because she was Catholic. In fact she never did end up getting married, and I often wondered if her life had ended up being blighted by me, simply because she and I had genuinely cared for one another so much.

The crucial thing was that alcohol had now clearly become more important to me than anything else. I would give up not only a job, but a marriage, rather than stop drinking. What was happening to me was deeply tragic.

Job pressures also kept mounting, because it turned out that there were unexpected hazards to working for the Firestone company in my kind of employment. One time a call came in, for services needed, from a truck driver who had blown a tire. I answered the call, and found that the truck was overloaded with manure, and that the load had shifted so that most of the weight had been put on that one tire, which blew under the pressure. Even getting the flattened tire off was difficult, because part of the truck body was close to the rim. I sweated and strained and finally got the tire and rim off, and took the wheel back to the station to mount a new tire on it.

When I returned to the scene, it turned out that the wet, smelly, semi-liquid load of manure had continued to shift and tip the truck over that direction, so that it was now impossible to get the tire mount back on the lug bolts. I crawled under the truck with a jack to try to lift that part of the truck body up higher, when suddenly the load shifted again, and most of it slid completely off the truck and on top of me. Almost half my body was pinned under a vast weight of manure. The truck driver had disappeared, I was there all alone, and no matter how hard I strained and struggled, I could not get out from under the weight of the truck and the huge pile of manure. My whole lower body started going numb.

I lay there and screamed for help for what seemed like an eternity. Finally a man heard me yelling, and came to my rescue. He called a tow truck which hoisted the weight of the truck body off me, and I started scraping the manure away until I had freed myself.

I went back to the Firestone store, and when I walked in, the boss' only comment was to say, "Where the hell have you been? You smell like you've been wrestling in horse manure!" The only answer I could think of was, "You are absolutely right." I had been terrified while I was trapped all alone under that load, but had somehow escaped serious injury. But I had also been put in a totally humiliating situation, where I could just imagine other people laughing at me and my accident. With my overpowering subconscious fear of ever looking silly or ridiculous, or ever making a mistake, this was even worse than the raw fear I had felt for my legs and my life.

A person could in fact get injured very seriously working on large trucks. I had another accident when I was, once again, working on a big truck tire. I had just repaired the inner tube and remounted the tire and tube, and was reinflating it, when part of the rim which was holding the tire on suddenly blew off. It hit me a glancing blow, and then went all the way through the door of the garage, leaving a big hole in it. It was later estimated, by someone who knew about these things, that at least 3,200 pounds of pressure had hit me indirectly. If I had not been fairly careful and cautious about where I was standing while I was inflating it, I would have certainly been killed when it exploded. As it was, I was taken to the hospital with a broken leg, and pieces of broken rubber tire embedded in various parts of my anatomy.

Workers injured on the job were not taken care of in those days. It required eventually passing government regulations to give workers the kind of job and pay protection they have today. Back in the 1930's, your pay stopped the minute you were injured and had to be taken off the work floor.

Very few companies gave paid vacations either. I had been planning a trip to Canada, where I would have to take a week off without pay, because I simply needed a break from the work. I decided to go to Canada anyway, money or no money, broken leg or no broken leg. Fishing in a row boat with a heavy plaster cast on your leg is not the most comfortable way to fish, but I took off for a week and did it.

In 1938, I decided to buy my own car, my first one. That would have been the year I turned twenty. I had never had the money to get anything like that before. I discovered a 1929 Model A Ford which was on sale for $49.00. It was not much, but it sure beat walking everyplace. Even then, I could not afford to pay cash for it. I did not have $49.00 saved up. I arranged to buy it for $7.00 down and $7.00 a month payments until it was finally paid off. My dad was dead set against me buying that car, because of my drinking problems—I am sure he could just see me dying in a drunken wreck—but I insisted, like all alcoholics, that this was not going to happen to me, because I was going to be very careful, and I pooh-poohed his fears. I also got a radio installed in the car for about eight dollars, which made my dad even angrier. I felt like a rich kid, driving around in my Model A Ford with the radio playing, but my father knew that this was fantasy and drunken self-delusion. I was in fact only making $85.00 a month, which had to cover all my expenses.

Liquor and beer were cheap in those days, but by this time it was taking an incredible amount of alcohol just to keep me functioning. Faced with the choice between making my monthly car payment, and buying the alcohol I absolutely had to have, there was no doubt which decision I was going to make. My prized Model A Ford was repossessed by the seller when I was only $14.00 short of paying it off, because the liquor and beer were more important to me—absolutely vital and necessary to me by this point—than the joys of driving the car. Having your car repossessed was a real disgrace for a good working family in those days: again the sense of guilt was heaped even higher down in the subconscious part of my mind, the part that I never admitted consciously, either to you or to myself.

Alcohol had cost me my engagement to a girl I loved, and now it had cost me my beloved car. I had quit a job in Portsmouth, Virginia, just because they were threatening to fire me because of drinking on the job. For an alcoholic, it is the alcohol which is his "higher power." He will sacrifice almost anything else, no matter how dear, just to keep on drinking.

———————————

My drinking had by now alienated me from most of my friends and relatives. I yearned so much to spend time with my family, just feeling comfortable, but in fact we were growing further and further apart. I loved my brothers and sisters, but when I was with them, my subconscious feelings of deep inferiority made me feel hopelessly inadequate. I was beset by constant pangs of sorrow and remorse for what I had done to myself. I tried to escape these painful feelings by turning against everything that was honorable.

When I was with my drinking buddies, I was harshly critical of my family and the way they were treating me. The truth in fact was that they were trying to help me in the only ways they knew how, and there was no real effort on my part to recover from my catastrophic behavior pattern. My life had become abysmally bad, I had no tools to cope with my personality problems or emotional conflicts, and I had just given up the fight. I turned more and more to situations and circumstances which would automatically produce even greater personal failures.

I lived with my dad for a while, but given his temperament and hostility toward drinking, this quickly became unworkable. I took my things over to the home of my oldest sister, and moved in with her family. I loved them very much, but it soon became apparent that this was not going to work either. After one of my nights on the town, I got into a drunken fight with my brother-in-law. My sister had to end the skirmish by hitting me on the knees with a rolling pin. I was totally out of control.

The final straw came a few days later. Again I went out for a massive drinking bout and came home loaded. Several of my brothers and sisters were there, and we got into a big argument. I finally quietly crept upstairs, and without telling them what I was doing, packed my bags and threw them out the upstairs window. All the dogs in the neighborhood began barking however, when they heard the bags hitting the ground below the window. I went down the stairs and walked out the front door to a taxi I had called. This sad and stormy scene was the last time I saw my family for almost four years.

I went into town and drank myself into oblivion. I do not know what I did during the next few days. I was in a total blackout, and when I finally recovered my wits, I had somehow gotten from Niles, Ohio, to Portsmouth, Virginia, with no knowledge of how I had done it. I went to my old boss at the Firestone station there, but he refused to give me a job. After about a week of just wandering around the town, I started drinking again. These were the circumstances when my life as a civilian came to an end. It was 1939, the year I turned twenty-one, and I did not know where else to go.

CHAPTER 6

Joining the Army Air Corps

I felt completely stranded in that town, many miles from home, and I did not know what to do next. My family had rejected me. My girlfriend had rejected me. My old boss there in Portsmouth, Virginia, had rejected me. My brain was still hopelessly muddled from the aftereffects of the drunken blackout that had brought me there. I was so hungover, jittery, and on edge that I could not focus my mind on figuring out how to accomplish even simple tasks. So I did what any alcoholic would do in that kind of circumstances: I just went back to drinking once again.

Wandering through town in this alcoholic haze, I saw a big sign which seemed to stick out like a sore thumb: "Uncle Sam Needs You." It seemed to shine like a beacon in the darkness. "My God," I thought to myself, "someone needs me." So I stumbled into the recruiting office, and although it was clear to them that I had been drinking, they let me enlist in the Army Air Corps.

After I had signed the contract and taken the oath, I was beginning to sober up and my mind was beginning to function a little better. At that point, the thought entered my mind that I had to get out of this enlistment. But it was too late: it was very easy to get into the military but almost impossible to get back out again once you took the oath.

In those days there were a certain number of people in the military who had enlisted because they simply could not cope with civilian life. Some of these were alcoholics like myself. Now I want to make it clear that even in those days, there were many excellent people in the military world. The ones whom I admired most were those who had come from military families: their fathers and sometimes even their grandfathers had been in the armed forces, they had learned as small children about how to function smoothly in that world, it was a family tradition, and they genuinely wanted to serve their country. And I had the privilege of working with many other truly admirable people during my long military career, where I served for over twenty years, all the way down to 1961. These were people who were committed to doing a good job, and putting their lives on the line for the sake of our country.

But in 1939, a certain percentage of the new recruits were like I was back at that time. There was an ample enough population of alcoholics in the armed forces, regardless of what the commanders reported to their superiors. And we were often a real problem to the majority of the people around us, who were trying to do things right.

We new recruits were sent to Langley Field for our training. It was December 1939, and Virginia is very cold and damp in the winter. We marched in the cold and slept in tents in the cold. The day before Christmas it started to snow, and we had to roll ourselves in our blankets as best we could in those unheated tents in an effort to avoid freezing to death. My disposition was run raw, and I thought to myself, "What a hell of a way to spend Christmas." We were awakened at sunrise to six inches of snow on the ground and the sound of a recording playing "Oh What a Beautiful Morning." It turned out that this was the Chaplain's Christmas greeting to us, to show us that he was thinking of us. I actually thought in my mind about how pleasant it would be to murder the man.

There were to be many other frustrations and things that just made everyone angry. Uniforms in those days were issued in two sizes: too small and too large. Many of us had to get our uniforms altered before we were fit to stand any really hardnosed inspection. We could on occasion end up having hot dogs for breakfast, or some other inappropriate food. Just to keep them busy, enlisted men would be set to work at meaningless tasks. I remember a time later on, on my way to Hawaii, when a general canceled a planned inspection, and we were instead assigned to the chore of carrying rocks from the shoreline up to a newly built Officers Club so they would be able to look out on a rock garden while they sat at their ease and sipped their drinks.

I had always been rebellious toward those in authority. I had played hooky, disrupted classes and been grossly disrespectful whenever I could. I had left jobs whenever I felt like it, and headed out for other places whenever I got itchy feet. Being subjected to this kind of military discipline was an absolutely hellish situation for me. I very seriously considered just taking off and forgetting about any kind of military career. Then I thought about the legal consequences, and having to live as a wanted man, and realized that I could not do that. The only real motivation I had for serving in the Army Air Corps there at the beginning came from this simple calculation, that if I did not hang in and stay, I would have to live for years in fear of arrest at any time.

I was having to live without alcohol there in the cold and wet of Langley Field, and it was almost more than I could stand. Then we were given a pass to go into Hampton one night, but warned that if anyone got in trouble, the Christmas passes would be canceled. I went into town with a brash young Irishman who liked to drink as much as I did—we alcoholics know how to sense one another, and automatically tend to gravitate together. After a few rounds in a bar, we went into a restaurant to order something to eat.

My friend, who was already well plastered, called the waitress over and asked her how much she made a week. She told him, "Five dollars per week," and this outraged his sensibilities. He demanded to talk to the owner of the restaurant, who just happened to be there at that time. The Irishman scolded the owner, and told him what a marvelously good waitress he had, and how totally unjust and shameful it was that he was paying her no more than that. The owner in turn told him to mind his own business, and get out of his restaurant, and that if he did not leave, he would call the police. This argument continued for a time, getting louder and louder, while I just sat there keeping quiet.

Eventually the cops came and started to haul my friend off to jail. In spite of the alcohol in me, my mind was still functioning well enough to realize that everyone in our unit would lose their Christmas passes if even a single member got arrested this particular evening for anything at all. We had been warned. I began pleading with the cops not to take my friend in. They responded by telling me, "Shut up, or we'll take you too." Too much was at stake to follow their orders: I kept on begging them not to do it.

As a result, we both got locked up. Once we were behind the bars in the bullpen, I was overcome with anger at it all—I was angry at the Irishman and angry about everything in my life. The Irishman and I began arguing about the arrest, this turned into fisticuffs, and I was soon getting the better of him. Suddenly he called for a time-out. I stepped back in surprise, and he threw his overcoat over his head and said, "O.K., I'm ready now." Well, I couldn't hit a man who couldn't see me, so I stopped. The next morning the Commanding Officer came and bailed us out.

We soon realized that our troubles had only begun, for this was the military in the old days. When we returned to the Squadron, all hell broke loose. A quick kangaroo court was held and we were both immediately sentenced to thirty lashes on our naked rear ends with a garrison belt. Then they decided to let my friend cover himself with a blanket during the whipping, because it was clear that I had already worked him over pretty well back in the police lockup, and they felt a little sorry for him. My own butt was beaten so raw from the flogging that I could not sit down for days afterward. At first, I was the one who was blamed because the Squadron had now gotten restricted to base for Christmas. Everyone looked at me with real hatred and disgust. It was only later that the members of the Squadron learned the whole story, and that it was the Irishman who had caused the trouble, while I was only trying to save the rest of us. At that point I turned from a villain into a little bit of a hero.

Nevertheless, alcohol was involved in my first arrest by the law. I had already had near misses, but this time my luck ran out. Trouble gravitates to alcoholics, even when they can sometimes claim that they are simply innocent people who just happened to be at the wrong place at the wrong time. People who drank the way I did ended up in too many wrong places at too many wrong times. When people push their luck too much, sooner or later it runs out.

I volunteered to go to Hawaii. I had a real love for Dorothy Lamour, a Hollywood movie star from those days. I had seen so many films set in that romantic "Land of Paradise," as they called it in the movies, and I had this image in my mind of Dorothy Lamour dressed in a sarong from one of these films. All of us who had volunteered talked and joked about our great anticipations while we waited to board ship: sandy beaches, palm trees gently swaying in the breezes, and beautiful girls strolling along in nothing but grass skirts and flowered leis draped about their necks, while the music of Hawaiian guitars and ukuleles drifted in from a distance.

We were sent to Fort Slocum, on a small island near New Rochelle, New York, to await the arrival of our troopship. On one occasion we were allowed to take the ferry over to the mainland for a brief leave. Upon return to the Fort, each GI was searched by the MP's to make sure no liquor was being smuggled in. There was a whiskey bottled in that part of New York called 1860, which was about as cheap and raw as anything ever distilled, but none of us enlisted men could afford to be choosy. One of us was caught trying to sneak in half a pint of this cheap, distasteful liquor, "for medicinal purposes," as he explained. The soldier pleaded with the MP not to take the liquor away. "Look at the label," he said, "this is rare stuff, almost seventy-five years old." The MP was gullible enough to believe that line, and let him pass through still hanging onto his bottle. I noticed that it was all the young soldier could do to keep a straight face, until he got off the pier and was safely on his way to the barracks.

This was innocent fun, but in fact alcoholics will lie to anyone if they have to, at any time or place, to get or keep their alcohol. They will promise never to drink again if cornered, and they will lie about how much they actually have been drinking. This is a way of life to them, where alcohol is the one thing they cannot live without.

We were eventually herded like cattle aboard a troopship where we slept in bunks stacked five high, thirty inches apart. You had to slither in, and turning over was almost impossible. There was no opportunity to bathe, and many GI's who got seasick did not make it out of those bunk rooms before they threw up. After a short while, the odor defied description. You could end up on kitchen police, peeling potatoes for about three thousand troops, and trying to wash dishes without smashing them or getting soaking wet with dishwater, while sailing through a heavy storm on the high seas.

We sailed down the east coast and then steered toward the Panama Canal. The slow voyage through the canal itself was in fact a picture of unforgettable beauty. Words cannot describe it to someone who has never experienced it. The Pacific side of the canal was absolutely majestic. On a moonlit night, particularly when the ocean was calm, you could look down and see phosphorescent jelly fish glimmering in the dark sea. It was like being in another world. Sailing into San Francisco Bay and going under the Golden Gate Bridge was also an awesome sight. We could gaze at a panoramic view of one of the world's most beautiful cities as we stood out on deck.

We ended up having to stay almost three months on a badly misnamed place in the bay, a place called Angel Island, because several of the GI's had come down with measles, and they wanted to quarantine us until they were sure that no more of us were going to come down with the disease.

I ended up seeing San Francisco through the eyes of a raw recruit, which meant visiting parts of the city where many of its residents did not ever go. One day for example, when we were sitting around playing poker, I hit a streak of luck and won quite a bit of money. I decided to go into town and play the big shot. I was going to go to the Fairmont Hotel and rub shoulders with the elite of our society, but quickly learned that GI's were not welcome at any of the plush hotels. In those days GI's were second-class citizens. There were some who claimed they had actually seen signs posted saying "dogs and soldiers not allowed."

Our part of town was in the lower-class bars of the tenderloin district. The atmosphere was unbelievably seedy. Most of the GI's who went there had only two things on their mind, sex and alcohol. Beer was ten cents, and liquor cost fifteen cents a shot. And there were plenty of girls to satisfy the other demands. In all honesty, I was never attracted to this type of female, so my mission there was simply to get totally anesthetized. When I came back, I would declare that I had had a good time, although to tell the truth I always drank myself into a blackout and could not recall a thing afterward.

Finally the quarantine was lifted and we were allowed to set sail for the land of enchantment. When we arrived in Hawaii in April of 1940, our first glimpse of the islands made it look like it was going to be a wonderful tour of duty indeed: we were greeted with Hawaiian music, flowered leis to drape around our necks, and cordial welcomes.

I was assigned to the Army air base, Hickam Field, and given duty as a policeman. I do not mean duty as an MP, but policing the area picking up trash off the streets and around the buildings! For an ambitious person like myself, this was not only being sentenced to the very bottom of the ladder, but created an even worse problem. I could not figure out any way of ever getting out of that job. How do you pick up trash so well that someone sees you as worthy of a promotion? That was about as likely as a snow ball's chance in the Hawaiian summer heat.

There was practically no social life as a military person. The Noncommissioned Officers Club was about the only decent place where females were in attendance. In the city of Honolulu itself, military personnel were not accepted in civic activities and other civilian organizations. We were permitted to wear civilian clothes when we went to town, and some of the GI's knew how to dress well, but the people there could still spot us as military people instantly. Something about us gave it away at once.

Our pay was extremely meager, which limited our possibilities. So when we were allowed to go into town, our major source of entertainment was the second-class bars. Most of the women who frequented those places were either alcoholics or prostitutes. They were out to strip the GI's of their cash, if they had any: some would have sex with the men, but others would ditch the GI the minute he ran out of money, and just disappear, leaving him standing there in the bar with his pockets empty.

Gambling was theoretically against military regulations, but those in charge usually turned a blind eye. So payday was a day of much activity: we immediately began playing poker and blackjack, with the dream of getting rich, but with the greater likelihood of going broke. Surely few of us were so stupid that we could not have realized that most of the time we simply blew away what little had been given us as pay. This has to have been some kind of bizarre, subconscious form of self-punishment. And there was an additional neurotic payoff: losing most of your money could then give you an excuse to go out on a really cheap drunk on the little bit you had left, "to forget your losses."

On the other hand, there were a few real slick poker and blackjack players stationed at Hickam Field, and they would win a great deal of money from the rest of us, and then head for Schofield Barracks where the big money gambling went on. Thousands of dollars changed hands in these games. I was never foolish enough to try my hand over there. Usually my money was gone in a day, but on the very few occasions when I was lucky enough to win a considerable sum, I headed into town instead. When this happened, it was "fly the warning flags in Honolulu, because I was on the loose!"

Reflecting on those days of my life is still painful. The wasted time, the meaninglessness of it all—I do not have any pleasant memories to recall. The next morning after the payday gambling and drinking, there was the hangover, and no money to minister to the misery this produced. Most of the time, the less fortunate ones did not even buy cigarettes prior to going broke, so it was either bum smokes or do odd jobs to make enough money to buy a pack. Some of us poor blokes were effectually turned into slaves, having to shine shoes, clean clothes, or take care of someone else's room just to get by the rest of the time.

There were also money lenders infiltrating the ranks. They would loan money at an exorbitant interest rate, where borrowing five dollars might mean that you had to pay back ten dollars. Although the money lending was as illegal as the gambling, rarely did anyone in charge take action against either.

The gambling was in fact as much a compulsive disease as the drinking: it was self-inflicted punishment with a predictable outcome. But we could not stop doing it. Instead of admitting that we were bringing all this misery down on ourselves by our own conscious choice, we attributed it all to "luck." Alcoholics frequently think in this distorted fashion: if any element of chance at all was involved, we refuse to take personal responsibility for the decisions we made in getting into that situation in the first place, and lay all our subsequent misfortunes down to "bad luck."

I also did things like sell my haircut allotment at a reduced rate to get money to drink if I wanted to go into town later on. I got called into the Commanding Officer's office once because I had overdrawn my haircut and canteen check allotment for the month and still obviously needed a haircut badly. As far as I was concerned though, I had to drink, and this was my first priority: alcohol was the only way I knew to survive my feelings of frustration and failure.

There was an often humiliating caste system in the military in those days. Officers for example did not have to mow their own grass around their homes. Enlisted people were sent to do those kinds of things. If I had been the one detailed to cut their grass, I was given a briefing in advance in which I was told that I could have no contact with the officers' children, nor was I even allowed to speak to them. We were servants, and servants were supposed to be silent. I have always tremendously enjoyed children, and to be told that I could not even talk to them felt particularly degrading.

Most enlisted personnel in the Army Air Corps in those days felt great hostility toward the commissioned officers. Much of the conversation at the "Snake Ranch," the beer joint we frequented, was directed toward ventilating all the anger we would build up inside. The hostility was not aimed at all of the officers of course, because there were many who were obviously compassionate and concerned about the welfare of their subordinates. And it should be said that enlisted people who acted like me, who were continually involved in discipline problems, were the most negative toward the officer ranks. Nevertheless, we enlisted people were continually made to feel subservient. One became conditioned to just following directions without resistance. This was probably essential to running a military organization, but as a result a deep inner hostility within the enlisted ranks was part of the way many of our minds worked. All anyone had to do was to sit in the Snake Ranch and listen to the GI's talk as they downed their beers to become keenly aware of that.

On modern air bases, officers, noncommissioned officers, and enlisted people all go to the same social club to drink. There are no more separate Officers Clubs or Noncoms Clubs, for financial reasons I am told. I do not know how I myself would have survived back in those days, if I had been drinking heavily in the same room as a group of commissioned officers. The alcohol would have depressed my inhibitions, the attitude of blind subservience would have ceased to impede my actions, the deep inner hostility would have begun to surface, and I would have eventually begun acting out all that rage in word and deed. I can just imagine the kind of trouble I would have gotten into. And it is difficult for me to see how the present day Air Force can put officers, noncoms, and enlisted people in the same place, many of them drinking heavily, without there being an extremely strained social atmosphere on many occasions. At any rate, I myself would not have survived that part of the modern Air Force.

The Snake Ranch and the Tale of Spot the Alcoholic Dog

The Snake Ranch, as I mentioned, was the name I and some of my closest drinking buddies gave to the cheap beer joint where we did most of our drinking. It lacked the niceties of the downtown bars: all it basically had inside was a row of picnic tables lined up on each side of the room. For entertainment we sat around listlessly in the tropical heat, sharing lies, and drinking one Primo beer after another; while those who had (or imagined they had) a talent for singing, acting, performing magic tricks or whatever, would sometimes perform for the rest of us, who were forced into becoming a sort of captive audience. That was on the evenings I remember—on many another night I simply drank myself into a blackout and could not remember anything at all the next day.

The Snake Ranch opened at three o'clock every afternoon. A line began to form outside about ten minutes in advance. At the head of the line every day was a mongrel dog named Spot, who was our special friend. "Spot the sot" we called him, because he had a severe drinking problem, as did most of the rest of us who lined up early in anticipation of a cold bottle of suds to soothe their frayed nervous systems.

Spot was never patient about having to wait. He would whine and shift his weight from one side to the other, and then begin to pace around in a small circle, absolutely desperate for a drink. The door to the beer joint would be unlocked precisely at 3:00 p.m., and Spot would charge to a position at the cash register, ready for his fix. "Here's where you go first, you dummies," he was trying to signal us. It was an unwritten law that the first human being in line for beer had the responsibility for serving Spot, regardless of his financial status. So the first man would walk to the cash register and pull out his money, and then Spot would charge over to his own dish, which was permanently stationed in one corner of the Snake Ranch, still obviously a total bundle of nerves, and very impatient to be served. The first GI would take the beer he had just bought and walk over to the dish and begin pouring it in. Spot would try to shove him aside, so he could get down to business, then plunge his muzzle down into the dish and furiously lap up the beer. When he had licked it clean, he would go around the bar frantically begging for more, and there was always someone who would buy him another drink. Then as the beer began to calm his nerves, there actually seemed to be a smile on his countenance. Life was starting to get O.K. again. After consuming two or three bottles of beer, he would then go over in the corner and pass out.

That day's drinking escapade was not over yet however. After a couple of hours lying comatose in the corner, he would come to, and go around begging for still more beer. He would only leave the bar once during this period, when the base bugler came out to blow Retreat. Spot would go out to where the bugler stood and assume a rigid position beside him, howling at the top of his voice, attempting to harmonize with the melody of the bugle tune—or I suppose this is what Spot thought, but he was too drunk to really know what he was doing, and the GI's who were standing at attention while the flag was lowered often had a difficult time keeping a straight face at the way he was totally demolishing the solemnity of the occasion with his besotted howling.

As soon as the bugler put the horn away, Spot would then head back to the Snake Ranch once again to get another refill. He would again keep on putting down the beer until he was anesthetized, and then go back to his corner and pass out. It was his daily ritual, and it never varied.

Later on, after I was in A.A., I humorously wondered whether Spot was ever successful in overcoming his alcoholism and becoming an active member of a canine A.A. group. Or if we ought to create such groups, to help poor creatures like him! We could ask all the same questions about him that we would about a human alcoholic. Was Spot's alcoholism caused by a hereditary condition? To know that, we would have to find out who his parents were, their habits, their social standing within the canine community, how many brothers and sisters he had and what they were like, and where Spot himself stood in the pecking order. Did one or both of Spot's parents also have an alcohol problem? Did they endorse the use of alcoholic beverages, or were they dead set against any drinking at all?

It becomes a joke, and we just laugh, when we try to ask these questions about an animal who had become addicted to alcohol. But asking these questions, even if only humorously, does help us to see more clearly how much more complex alcoholism is in human beings than in dogs (or white rats or other laboratory test animals). When we begin searching for the origins of alcoholic compulsions in human beings, we find that each individual is in some way uniquely different. There is no one simple theory which will define all human alcoholism, nor is there one simple treatment which can be automatically and mechanically administered, which will promptly "cure" all alcoholics.

Some human beings become physically addicted through continuing use of the beverage over a period of time. Others become alcoholic as a result of their inherited genetic traits. Others become alcoholic due to the negative results of poor parental teachings, which can be compounded by personal conflicts with siblings. The nature of our relationships to the larger society around us also deeply affects us. Now it should be said in regard to the parental factor, that it does not help at all for alcoholics to blame their fathers and mothers for all the negative circumstances that were present in the family setting. There is no way anyone can go back and change the past, so just trying to blame the past over and over again does not do any good at all in changing the quality of our lives now. We ourselves must take responsibility for making our lives better now, which means we have to stop the blaming game and start looking for positive directions in which to grow.

There are families where one or both parents are clearly alcoholic, and yet their child never becomes more than an ordinary social drinker. There are families where the parents only drink in moderation, and yet one of their children goes well past that point and becomes an out-of-control alcoholic. I myself became an alcoholic, but my seven brothers and sisters were brought up in exactly the same family, and none of them became alcoholics. One of them became a millionaire. Another was the paymaster of the Youngstown Sheet and Tube Steel Mill (his wife also worked, and taught school). He knew how to invest in the stock market, was quite frugal and careful with his money, and they also did quite well financially. Even more interestingly, all seven of my brothers and sisters remembered their childhoods as quite pleasant, and none of them recalled the past with the same feelings of rejection and worthlessness and anxiety which permeated my own childhood memories. One could not argue that a supposedly dysfunctional family of origin was the primary factor in turning me into an alcoholic, or my seven brothers and sisters would have remembered the past the same way I did, and many of them would have become alcoholics too.

Alcoholism is a disease of perception, for many destructive drinkers. The major source of the problem often lies in the way children form their perceptions of what is going on, both in their families and in their surrounding society. Conditions in the family and society are processed by each individual in a unique way. My seven brothers and sisters and I experienced many of the same events, but again and again I formed a uniquely different perception of what was actually going on, and how it related to me.

But this also supplies the key to a good deal of the healing which can take place in A.A. We need to stop assigning the primary responsibility for our alcoholism to our parents and brothers and sisters, because these are secondary factors at most. The primary responsibility for a major part of our alcoholic compulsion, in the case of many alcoholics, must be assigned to the perceptions we formed of those childhood events (and all the events that followed during our drinking careers). But perceptions can be changed.

Their underlying assumptions can be challenged: Totally and absolutely worthless in all possible ways? Always rejected by everybody? Compelled always to wear ugly, worn-out clothes (or other social badges) which we think make everyone look down on us? Intrinsically incapable of accepting responsibility or exercising leadership?

The perspective from which we formed these perceptions can be changed: What were the problems the other person was dealing with? What kind of serious inner fears and anxieties were they themselves wrestling with? How did my own behavior toward those other people contribute to their reaction to me? How much of what went on was beyond the control of any single individual back then, either me or any of the other people around me? The great depression or local plant closings, union conflicts, parents of different religious and social backgrounds, second marriages, the serious illness or death of one family member, and so on? Each family member had his or her own unique set of problems to cope with, and was striving for his or her own goals. Our needs and desires fell into conflict with one another, events followed from this by the law of cause and effect, we fought or made compromises, but none of us got everything we dreamed of having.

Blame-language makes things worse instead of better. "Blame" means assigning guilt. Alcoholics are almost inevitably hag-ridden by a sense of guilt, either conscious or subconscious, which drives them back to the bottle over and over again, when the pain of the guilt becomes too great. It does no good, as we have seen, to blame the secondary causes of my problems. The real primary core of my own problems will always lie within my own head, and the way I form my perception of events. But it also accomplishes nothing (and in fact just makes things that much worse) if I then turn around and start "blaming" myself for what happened at some point back in the distant past, particularly things that happened when I was a helpless child with little knowledge of alternatives, and no power to carry most of them out. Blaming myself means heaping even more inappropriate guilt on my already guilt-ridden head.

What I can do, and must do if I ever hope to heal my life, is to recall the past and try to reassess what went on, and form new and wiser and broader perspectives of those long-ago events. I can change my perceptions. And that means that I can change what I am doing here in the present, in the now, which is the only place where I am given any kind of key for altering the story of my life. I can change how the story ends, and that is the saving power of the twelve step program.

At any rate, back then when I was a buck private at an air base in Hawaii, I myself was not much different from Spot the alcoholic dog. For both him and me, alcohol took priority over everything else in life. In the case of almost everything else I had to do, I took no joy in whatever it was I was doing, but just tried to slog my way through it until the clock said that it was time to drink.

I did play baseball, which was just about the only healthy thing I was doing during that period of my life. It may have been the only thing that was helping me retain what little sanity I still had left. I am grateful now that I had this to keep me going. Our squadron had one of the best teams at Hickam Field, and I was the pitcher. They nicknamed me the Primo Kid, in honor of the local beer brewed in Honolulu. I drank a lot of that brew. Every time I would rare back to pitch the ball, the stands would yell "Primo!" Just as in my high school days, that was my only claim to success. The weather never got cold in Hawaii, so the baseball season was almost always extended.

We did play basketball too however, in the fall and winter, and at night. It was a very different game from the one played today: I would love to have a video of that old-fashioned way of playing basketball to show some of my grandchildren. It was not necessary to be seven feet tall, and instead of the one-hand shots, we had two-handed set shots. There were no rules setting a time limit on how long a given player could have the ball before he had to shoot. If a team was skillful enough, they could play several minutes at a stretch without losing possession of the ball. Three fouls and you were out of the game. You got only one free throw for a foul, unless you were actually in the act of shooting the ball at the time the opposing team committed the foul.

I recall that, about four months prior to Pearl Harbor, I was court-martialed for hitting a fellow airman. There were already charges pending against me for spilling food on the mess hall floor: the Mess Sergeant had asked me why I spilled the food, and of course I was drunk at the time, and told him that the floor was where it belonged. That was a major insult as far as the Mess Sergeant was concerned, so he reported me to the Mess Officer. They decided to save time and money by combining the two offenses, and bringing me before a single court-martial board for both infractions simultaneously. I was charged with disorderly conduct, convicted, and sentenced to three months in the guardhouse.

Even though I was supposed to be locked up, in fact I was allowed time off to play basketball: ball games were genuinely important, and occupied a higher place in the military scale of values at that time. After the game was over, since the guards at the lockup never kept too close a tab on how long I was away, I would sneak down to the "Snake Ranch," the cheap beer joint on the base. I was supposed to return the minute the game was over, not go out drinking, so I had to be "discreet" about my presence there. I would crawl under one of the picnic tables, and a friend would feed me beers. He kept a tab of how much I owed him, and made it clear that, when I was finally released from the guardhouse, it was pay up or else.

So the first eighteen months passed there in Hawaii, and after a while, there was very little to mark one day from another. Like back in my high school days, I just existed, and drifted along aimlessly.

There were several occasions when we were placed on alert against a possible enemy attack. We would spend many boring hours at our pre-assigned duties during these alerts. Some of us for example were given 30-caliber machine guns or small arms and assigned certain target areas to guard against imagined enemies. If anyone was caught sleeping while on guard duty, the punishment was severe. Officers of the Day had to monitor those on duty, to see if they knew not only their general orders, but also the specific orders they were instructed to carry out during the alert. I myself spent many days and nights doing guard duty over in the city of Honolulu as my own assigned task. But nothing ever happened, no enemy ever stormed ashore from landing craft, and the whole thing just became a terribly boring chore that we increasingly resented whenever it came up. So I just continued to drift along through life.

In late November of 1941, Hickam Field had been alerted to the possibility of a war with Japan, so all of us men were once again put on alert, and moved into strategic battle positions in Honolulu and at other military installations on the island of Oahu. After little more than a week, however, the alert was called off and all weapons and ammunition were recalled. Once again we fell back into complacency as we assumed our normal ways of life.

It was just two days later that the fateful time arrived, the Day of Infamy. On the night of December 6th, 1941, we were allowed to draw canteen checks. That night we had a big celebration, and drank Primo beers at ten cents a bottle until everyone got very drunk. When the beer parlor closed, we had taken the precaution to hide more beer in the bushes. When we finally dragged back into the barracks, we fell into our bunks in a stupor. We had no idea what was going to happen to us just a few hours later.

CHAPTER 7

The Attack on Pearl Harbor

On the next morning, December 7, 1941, I was lying in my bed in my barracks at Hickam Field, suffering from an acute hangover while I tried to make up my mind as to what I would do to pass the time that day. It was a Sunday, so I thought I might play a little baseball or a few sets of tennis, and relax. Hawaii was not a place of hustle and bustle, just a little cluster of tropical islands out in the middle of the Pacific Ocean, where time moved slowly and people were rarely in much of a hurry. We had been called off our battle stations two days earlier, just a false alarm.

At 7:55 a.m., I was suddenly jerked into alertness as I heard the droning of aircraft overhead and then thunderous explosions as bombs exploded on the hanger line. Our barracks was immediately adjacent to the hanger area, so when I rushed to a window, I saw a large number of low flying aircraft with the round orange Rising Sun insignias standing out vividly on their wings. We could see the mass destruction occurring before our very eyes. The peace and calm of the Sabbath had been instantly transformed into a holocaust. It is always called simply the attack on Pearl Harbor in the history books, but a greater percentage of us on the ground were actually killed in the simultaneous attack which they made on Hickam Field. They wanted to knock out our Air Corps as well as our Navy.

There had been no warning. We were totally unprepared for this attack, and fear and mass hysteria spread everywhere as we realized how totally helpless we were. We had no weapons with which to shoot back, so our only resource was to run. We realized that the three thousand men in the barracks had to get out of those buildings immediately. I myself ran outside wearing only my underwear shorts and a T-shirt, stopping only to grab a pith helmet to shove on my head as I made for the door. This last totally futile impulse was symptomatic of my state of mind—a flimsy pith helmet was not going to stop a speeding bullet—but I had never had guns shot at me or bombs dropped on me before, and absolute terror was a mild description of what I was feeling.

In later years, when people would ask me if I was running that morning, I would often say back to them jokingly, "No, but I passed a lot of guys who were." What else could a person say to people who were just being idly curious? This was not the kind of delightful adventure story appropriate for casual table conversation at light-hearted dinner parties. But oh yes, I ran, we all ran. We were nothing but sitting ducks there where we were.

I and some of the other men began running for our very lives across the parade grounds, trying to get to some place that was not under immediate direct attack. I could see the tracers from the enemy's machine gun fire as their streams of bullets slammed into the ground all around me, ripping up large divots of grass and earth. The airplanes were firing with their cannon as well, and some of the bombs were dropping on the parade grounds all around us. The mechanical rat-a-tat-tat of the machine guns was mixed with continual repeated thuds and deadly booms. I could actually hear the bullets whizzing past me, along with the screaming of flying shrapnel. In the midst of this chaotic inferno, I actually saw one bomb drop out of the sky and land squarely on top of one of my friends, blowing him to bits. I saw many other men falling around me: the first American casualties of World War II.

As I ran, I glanced over my shoulder and saw huge billows of smoke already rising skyward from the hanger lane. Our only means of retaliation had been reduced to twisted, smoldering ruins in no more time than that. We could figure out nothing whatever to do to defend ourselves. The Japanese planes were flying so low, that we on the ground could make out the smirking expressions on the pilots' faces as they strafed us unarmed men below.

I could see some of the men were diving under the wooden barracks, crying, praying and swearing. I felt lost, as it was almost impossible for me to pray, never having had much experience in this practice. I began to think about my family and how I had disappointed them.

What did I do then, as wave after wave of airplanes continued to sweep down on us, firing at every American they saw? What military people have to do. I kept moving, and at each point I tried to do whatever seemed the best thing to do there at that time.

That first wave of bombing went on for about forty-five minutes, but seemed to last an eternity. When it finally ended, the men were recalled to the barracks and began to organize for the land invasion which we believed was now imminent. But first I was detailed to the hanger line to try to fight the fires there which were raging out of control. The most futile feeling I have ever had was trying to use a portable fire extinguisher against flames which were leaping fifteen hundred feet in the air. After this meager and pointless effort, we were issued 30-caliber machine guns and small arms with which to repel the Japanese soldiers whom we now expected to start streaming in from landing places along the beaches.

It turned out instead that the Japanese planes had not gone away, but had merely flown inland to regroup. Their initial assigned targets had all been thoroughly bombed, so they circled back now to strafe all the military personnel they could spot, like shooting fish in a barrel. It was impossible to fight back effectively with the weapons we had, which might have done a little good against infantry but were not designed for antiaircraft defense, so again we retreated to the nearest cover.

At one point, I flung myself against one of the palm trees which lined the main boulevard in front of the barracks, clinging to it for dear life and trying to use it as a shield against the hail of bullets and bomb fragments. A piece of flying shrapnel completely tore off the top fifteen feet of the tree. Over thirty years later, in 1972, my wife Ann and I visited Hawaii and I saw the truncated remains of that palm tree still standing: it had somehow sprouted new fronds and hung onto its life, but you could still clearly see the scars, and that it was fifteen feet shorter than the other palms which lined the street. If the piece of burning hot metal had come in a few feet lower, it would have cut me in two as well. We could also still see the marks of the bullet holes in the sides of the barracks. Everything threatened to come back to me as I gazed at these reminders of that day—all the feelings of total terror, of being moved into a different kind of reality and a different kind of time flow, of instant automatic reactions without conscious calculation, of being conscious of what was happening and yet horrifyingly helpless to stop it from happening—and I shuddered inside.

Seeing the palm tree cut in two as the hail of bombs and bullets from the second attack fell all round me convinced me of the futility of trying to use that for shelter. Six of us finally tried huddling in a corner of one of the nearby hangers for protection. Suddenly there was a horrendous explosion and I was hurled through the air and slammed against a wall. When I finished gasping desperately for breath and got my lungs refilled with air, I realized that one of the bombs had gone off only about twenty feet from where we had been crouched. As the initial shock further wore off, I saw that a buddy of mine and one of the other airmen were the only ones besides me still moving in the wreckage. The other three never knew what hit them. When we checked, one of these motionless forms seemed still to be just barely alive, so Cliff and I began carrying him to an ambulance. It was no good though, he died there in our arms as we were trying to help him.

About this time I reached the point where the will to survive was ebbing. The faith and sense of security I had always derived from being an American had taken a severe blow. Our enormous sense of pride in being from the USA, our sense of invulnerability, our belief that no one would dare take us on, had been badly shaken. We had betrayed ourselves into thinking that our impenetrable base was beyond attack. It very obviously was not. We saw unfolding before our very eyes the terrible saga of what has been called "the most dastardly act of aggression in recorded history."

This second attack did not last as long as the first. A few antiaircraft weapons had finally been manned, and some of the attacking airplanes were shot down this time around. When the Japanese came back for their third and final attack, they had to quit after only about ten minutes. Despite the demoralizing effect of the first two raids, our forces had rallied enough by this time to inflict heavy losses on the incoming aircraft.

During one of the attacks, five of our own B-17 Flying Fortress bombers came roaring overhead and loud cheers were heard. Everyone thought they had come to our salvation, but lo and behold, they had not had any ammunition loaded in the heavy guns which bristled from various mounts all over their fuselages. It was simply a routine flight of planes which had been prescheduled to be transferred from the mainland to Hickam Field, and at the time when they took off, no one had expected them to actually see action that day. Instead of landing there where we were under siege, and being destroyed along with everything else there, they simply kept on going and landed at Bellows Field instead.

Only a few of the American airplanes stationed near where we were ever got airborne that morning with ammunition in their guns, but those which did managed to knock a few Japanese aircraft out of the skies. This was only a minor comfort however compared to the massive destruction which we suffered everywhere else.

We were fortunate at Hickam Field in one respect. Japanese intelligence had earmarked our fuel storage area for bombing, but had mistakenly marked it on their maps in the middle of what was actually our baseball field. Had their intelligence been more accurate, the destruction we underwent would have risen even greater by far.

The American Pacific Fleet was severely crippled. From Hickam Field we could see many of the ships burning over in Pearl Harbor. The Navy lost 2,117 officers and men with 960 missing and 876 wounded. The Army lost 278 officers and men with 396 wounded. The Air Corps at Hickam Field lost 369 officers and men, with over 500 wounded. There were also about 70 civilians who were killed at various places on the island.

The fine American ships which were lost that day—the USS Arizona, the USS Utah, and all the other famous ships—are well known. The Air Corps was also badly hit. Most of the aircraft on the hanger line were either totally or partially destroyed by the attacks. In this case however, the damage did not have the same long term crippling effect, since the planes we lost that day were almost all totally antiquated. The Army Air Corps in Hawaii was ill-prepared for any kind of real war. The most modern bombers there were the old B-18's, and most of the fighter planes were equally outdated. The newer planes were back on the mainland.

So the aircraft destroyed were mostly ones which were going to have to be replaced anyway. It was the toll in human lives which hit the air base so hard. Proportionally speaking, the Air Force lost a greater percentage of its men than either the Army or Navy. One out of every ten men at the base met his death that day. There were around 130 men in my own squadron at that time, and 37 of these were either killed or wounded, many of whom I myself saw die.

This sudden, brutal loss of so many of my buddies all at once had a tremendous psychological impact on me and the other members of my squadron. There were five of us in particular who were especially heavy drinkers, who spent many a night at the primitive little tropical beer joint we called the Snake Ranch, lounging around the picnic tables and talking and putting down one Primo beer after another until we could barely walk. The other four were all killed. I was the only one who did not die.

Some of the airmen who had survived the raid committed suicide later. I remember one airman who came from an area close to my own home town. He called a number of his friends over to his bunk one day, and they gradually drifted over, wondering why he was calling them together like that. He then pulled out a gun and shot himself in the head, right before their eyes.

We remained in a state of shock for quite some time after the attack. Over the next few days, wild rumors continued to appear about a large Japanese invasion force which had purportedly been spotted forming just off the coast. We were kept alert by constant fear. Everyone had assigned duties, and we all expected to be thrown at any moment into hand-to-hand combat with hordes of wildly shooting invaders screaming "Banzai!" as they charged.

I had known we were at war the moment I recognized the Japanese insignia on the airplanes' wings. My sister had written to me prior to the attack, telling me I was lucky to be stationed in Hawaii instead of the Panama Canal, which was where she assumed any war would break out first. I answered her letter by telling her the real danger was to Hawaii: it seemed clear to me that the Japanese would have to knock out the American forces there first, to prevent reinforcements being sent to help defend the Philippines, which was one of the places Japan seriously wanted to take over. My sister gave a copy of my letter to the hometown newspaper, which printed it. After the Pearl Harbor attack, the Office of Special Investigations sent some of its agents to question me. They were apparently worried that I might be some kind of a secret agent, or in contact with foreign spies! I had to assure them that I was just using my natural intelligence, and drawing what I felt were some totally logical deductions from the commonly known facts.

The next year and a half in Hawaii was spent under blackout conditions. Once the sun set, there was soon total blackness outside. Each building had all the doors and windows covered so no light could escape. This added to the eerie feeling all of us had as we went about the island. Your imagination could soon run riot, thinking every little jungle noise was produced by an enemy unit secretly landed on the island, with its rifles trained on you.

Poker and blackjack games were conducted in the latrines in the barracks late at night. The smoke was thick as the airmen puffed cigarette after cigarette while they wagered their money. One night some of the smoke drifted up the stairway to the second floor where my sleeping quarters were located. I was asleep, and dreamed that the Japanese had attacked again and were dropping canisters of gas on us this time. I woke up yelling, "gas attack! gas attack!" Someone else heard me shouting, thought it was real, and within a few minutes the alert was sounded for all of Hickam Field. In fact, before it was all over, the whole territory of Hawaii was put on highest alert, in the belief that a new Japanese air attack might have begun, and that this time they were dropping poison gas. Never in my wildest imagination would I have thought that I could wield such influence over other people, even if it was in my sleep!

Based on grim memories of the First World War, the possibility of poison gas attacks was in fact taken very seriously. When we went to town, we were ordered to carry a gas mask and helmet with us at all times. I recall a sergeant who loved to drink, who got drunk one night and lost his gas mask and helmet. Someone suggested he call the Commanding General's Office to find out who had gotten his gear, and he was so drunk that he actually made the phone call. He gave his name, rank, and serial number, they heard his slurred request for information about his missing equipment over their telephone, and in short order he found himself reduced back down to a private once again.

But there was not much fun anymore. Hawaii had totally changed. The old free and easy tropical lifestyle was no more, now that the war had begun. The descendants of the original native Polynesian population changed their attitude toward us: prior to the attack, many of these islanders resented us American servicemen, but now we had become their heroes. This mattered little to me, because I myself certainly did not feel like a hero. Other people on the islands were of Japanese descent, and we regarded them with great suspicion. Rumors were spread that there were spies all about, and we were told to always be on the alert for any attempted acts of sabotage or suspicious behavior from these Japanese-Hawaiian people. Many of them resented the way they were treated by us of course, and tried to avoid any contact with us.

America had gone to war, and this would dominate all aspects of our lives for the next four years.

CHAPTER 8

Sabotaging Every Success

No matter how arrogantly we alcoholics may have sometimes acted on the surface, this was a phony front. Most of us had no feeling of real self-worth deep down at the subconscious level. The guilt that we felt over our drinking (because there is always a good deal of guilt about that in every practicing alcoholic) made this already overwhelming feeling of worthlessness even greater.

Some of us tried to deal with this by becoming frantic, driven overachievers, but no matter how much we accomplished in the eyes of the world, we still felt like failures inside. Other alcoholics did like I did instead, and just gave up trying to do anything much at all. We who were underachievers were so convinced that we would fail, that we refused even to try.

And because of our wounded sense of self-worth, we all of us—overachiever and underachiever alike—developed a talent, in one way or another, for sabotaging our own greatest successes. Three times in a row during this period of my life I was given a chance to accomplish something very significant or demonstrate that I could take on a major responsibility—I was given a sergeant's stripes, a chance to become a pilot, and a marriage—and all three times I struck out.

Because we lacked any intrinsic inner feeling of self-worth, our greatest fear was of being rejected and abandoned. We felt alone even in the midst of a crowd. We simply assumed that other people would not like us if they really knew us. We simply took for granted that we would disgrace ourselves in humiliating fashion if we were put to the test. At the subconscious level, *we assumed in advance that we would fail*. And so that was always what eventually happened, and *we brought it on ourselves*.

We became so preoccupied with our own inner feelings of misery, frustration, self-pity, vengefulness and fear, that we paid almost no attention at all to what all the other people around us were really thinking and feeling. Our perceptions of them became as skewed and distorted as our own warped perceptions of ourselves. Even when we encountered another human being who actually loved us and thought highly of us, we could not see it. We were so convinced that no one at all could see anything good in us, that our eyes were totally blinded to the fact that some people in fact did like us and saw all sorts of good things in us. When other people tried to extend genuine love to us, we were completely oblivious to them, or we turned and fled as fast as we could. I was already doing that to myself by the time I was in high school. There were good teachers there who tried to reach out to me. There were other boys, and girls too (although I could not see it), who genuinely liked me. All I could see was my failings and my flaws, and I grossly distorted reality as a result.

The world we create in our minds is governed by our own inner perceptions. If my self-perception is that I am totally worthless as a human being, then I will construe all the things which happen to me in a way which will fit into that perceptual framework. When I have to do something, I will act as "a worthless person"—because that is what I am convinced that I am—and therefore I will get a worthless person's reward. I will end up sabotaging myself every time. My misperception will become a self-fulfilling prophecy.

The Alcoholics Anonymous program has twelve steps, but the destructive alcoholic drinking itself is mentioned in only one of these steps, the first. The other eleven steps are directed toward healing these other things I have been talking about while telling my story: my resentment, blaming of others, envy, fear, guilt, and self-loathing. (The twelve steps of the Narcotics Anonymous program work the same way: the irresistible compulsion to use addictive and mind-altering drugs is only referred to in the first step.) When I came into the A.A.

program and finally began working all of the steps seriously, I was slowly taught how to quit living in the past, and living in failure, and living in resentment. I had to learn how to handle my emotions as a mature adult. I gradually learned how to start being responsible for myself and my decisions in the here and now, and in the process I was slowly led in the direction of recovering a sense of self-worth. We will have to talk about this in a whole lot more detail later on in this book, because it is the most important gift which is given to us by the twelve step program, the power *to feel good.*

But the important thing to note, in this part of my story, is that other people were only secondary causes of my misfortunes at most. Could I "blame" my parents? My seven brothers and sisters did not become alcoholics, and they were brought up in the same home that I was. One of them became a millionaire. It was my very own unique perception of my childhood that was doing the mischief—but I can learn how to change my perceptions of events. Could I genuinely "blame" other people for what was happening to me at this point in my life? I was constantly surrounded by numerous people who liked me and were trying to help me in every possible way. But I destroyed myself anyway. I did it to myself. I was my own worst enemy. My own perceptions of myself were blinding me to reality, and blocking me from taking real responsibility for myself and dealing with my emotions in a mature and adult fashion.

But I can learn how to change my perceptions. The A.A. program was going to provide a context in which I could learn how to take control once again of the reins of my own life. Unfortunately, at this point it was going to take me six more years of misery before that was going to happen. This was 1942, and the A.A. Big Book had only been published in 1939. The Jack Alexander article in the *Saturday Evening Post* had only come out in March 1941, and other than those who had read that article, most people in the United States had never even heard of Alcoholics Anonymous. Even by the end of 1941, there were only about 8,000 members across the entire United States. And even more importantly, I was going to have to suffer a lot more catastrophe in my life until I reached the point where I was willing to change. For six more years, I was going to have to make the same fundamental mistakes over and over again until even I was willing to admit that my old way of doing things did not work, and never would. Only then would I become teachable. Only then would I become willing to change. Only then would I finally become desperate enough to look at my own perceptions of the world, and see that all the blaming and excuses and resentment and self-loathing was fundamentally being manufactured inside my own head.

For six more years I was going to sabotage my every success. For six more years I was going to take every opportunity given me, and figure out some way to destroy it. And the only way I knew to deal with my heartbreak and misery was to drink even more, which simply accelerated the downhill slide all the more rapidly.

I was only a buck private at the time of the catastrophic attack on us, and yet within six months had been promoted to First Sergeant of the 362nd Materiel Squadron at Hickam Field. I was given my stripes on June 14, 1942, just two weeks before my twenty-fourth birthday. This made me the youngest First Sergeant ever in Air Force history. Now let us grant that promotions were coming quickly now that the war had actually begun, but nevertheless this was quite an accomplishment, and it showed how highly some people actually thought of me. I had enormous potential inside me which other people could see, but I could not.

It did not hurt any that the trauma of seeing all those comrades die in a single day, and particularly all five of my closest drinking buddies, had actually gotten me to stop drinking for a long period of time. It had never dawned on me how much I could accomplish in life as long as I did not drink. What even greater things could I have achieved back then if I had just stayed off the bottle, and stayed off it permanently?

My pay rose to $132 a month, more money than I had made for a long time. The First Sergeant reports directly to the Squadron Commander, and is supposed to take care of all of the day-to-day running of the squadron. The First Sergeant sets the duty roster, and decides who gets leaves. He adjudicates disputes within the enlisted ranks and among the other noncoms under him, and he decides when disciplinary measures are necessary. Most everyday decisions are made and most ordinary problems are supposed to be solved by the First Sergeant alone, without bothering the Commanding Officer. It is a position of extraordinary responsibility, and a good deal of power. But I had never had the courage to take any kind of leadership role before, nor had I ever before been put in any kind of position of authority like this one—and at a fundamental level, at this point in my life, I did not have the courage even to really try.

The youngest First Sergeant ever in Air Force history: I should have been filled with a healthy sense of pride, and thrown myself into my new duties with enthusiasm, and gratitude for being given this marvelous opportunity to show my abilities. Instead, down deep in my subconscious, I was filled with anxiety, tension, and dread. The psychological pressures inside my mind were too painful, and I had all that extra money now, so I took the only route out that I knew how to take: I went back to drinking again. The only difference now was that I drank at the Noncommissioned Officers Club. Many of the other noncoms relied on alcohol at that time to help relieve the stress of the seven-day work weeks that were part of the new wartime duty assignment. The problem was that I was an alcoholic, and could not handle drinking even a small amount of alcohol. I did not last long as a First Sergeant. I kept my stripes, but I had to be reassigned to duties that did not require the same kind of leadership qualities, and did not demand the willingness to make decisions and take large responsibilities.

This pattern of being given opportunities for enormous success and then sabotaging myself at the crucial moment, continued to be repeated over and over again in my life. One of the most devastating episodes in my life followed soon after, and was a perfect example of this.

One night while imbibing some of the local Hawaiian Primo beer at the Snake Ranch, a buddy named Ellis asked me why I had never put in for Aviation Cadet or Officers Training School. Frankly I did not think I had the potential to be an officer. This seemed far beyond my talents. But Ellis kept on working on me all night long, and he became convincing enough, that the next morning, when I arose, I made inquiries.

It turned out that one of the criteria for being accepted into Aviation Cadet school involved passing a written test over a variety of subjects. My worst fears began rising in me instantly, because I knew that if there was a math section on the exam, I was sure to fail. It was math that almost prevented me from graduating from high school. But I talked with the section which was responsible for administering the test, and they assured me that I had nothing to fear in that regard, and that I seemed to be fully qualified to do adequately on the exam. So I signed up for the test, a time was assigned for taking it, and all the wheels were set in motion.

I actually passed the exam, gained approval in all the other necessary areas, and found myself accepted into the Aviation Cadet program and assigned to go back to the states to be trained to become a pilot in the United States Army Air Corps. My mind was swirling. I envisioned the pride my family would feel when I told them. Somehow or another, neither I nor the authorities who recommended me for this schooling seemed to think about my alcoholism as any kind of potential problem.

I also had a girlfriend now, even if at long distance. After the attack on Pearl Harbor and Hickam Field on December 7, 1941, a young woman from my home town wrote a letter to me. I did not know that she had cared about me, but her letter suggested that she was deeply and personally worried about my safety. I wrote back, and soon the letters were going back and forth regularly. Our communications became more and more deeply personal. Although all our mail was read, monitored, and censored, I included some rather personal messages regarding my own feelings. I am sure some of the officers who were censoring these letters were getting a laugh out of the way I was expressing my love for my pen pal.

I had never dated her nor for that matter considered her part of my life, prior to the start of the war, but because of her show of affection toward me, I was an easy prey. Anyone who would openly express an interest in me became an instant target for my total emotional surrender, and what I uncritically thought was undying love. Alcoholics who have no real inner sense of self worth and are continually beset by deep subconscious anxieties about being rejected and abandoned, become so pathetically "needy" that they will often try to form a relationship with the first person of the opposite sex who begins paying deliberate attention to them.

The fateful day arrived when I boarded the troopship *Leonard Wood*. This was in fact the same ship I had been on when I traveled from New York via the Panama Canal to Los Angeles, when I first began my long ocean journey to Hawaii. Now I was going back home on the same vessel. It was over three years since I had seen my family. When we arrived stateside, we were sent to Camp Anzio and housed as a unit of the Cadet Corps, but were almost immediately given thirty-day furloughs to visit home before we began our actual training.

When I arrived in Niles, I was considered a celebrity, because it was a small town and one of its residents had now come home, after first being a hero at Pearl Harbor and then selected to participate in the pilot training program of the United States Army Air Corps. Needless to say, I did not respond to all this attention in a positive way. I had such a low opinion of myself, that receiving that much notice from others simply created a deep subconscious anxiety inside, a dread that simply fueled the desire for alcohol. Once I had a few drinks in me of course, my ego was well-bolstered by liquid fortitude, and I was off to the races again. I thrived on attention then, and the drunker I got, the kind of attention I ended up getting tended to become more and more negative.

As long as I could keep on drinking, it was an incredible ego experience. Everyone in town who knew me or my family wanted to meet me, have a few drinks, and discuss the war. I made myself available constantly to imbibe and provide war stories of my experiences at Hickam Field—some of them concocted of course, to make the plot more interesting. I needed so desperately to be accepted, I tried to make myself out as a great war hero, and the bait was swallowed without a challenge. Because I was one of the first people in the state of Ohio to have actually fought in World War II, expressing any doubt about my tales would have seemed unpatriotic. So even my wildest claims stood as factual.

Since I seemed to be determined to make my life more complicated, I not only immediately went to visit my pen pal with whom I had been having the long distance romance, but also on the next evening paid a visit on the old girlfriend to whom I had been engaged before the war. The old flame seemed to flicker rather brightly when I first walked in, but then she abruptly told me that her decision to break off our engagement had been permanent, and she was no longer interested in having any kind of relationship with me ever again.

The shock of this hit me so hard that I immediately went off to the closest beer joint and got loaded. The anger at being rejected by her joined with all the subconscious anger I had stored up over the years—anger over the way I had always perceived myself as being continually rejected by everybody around me—and I was ready to explode. Alcohol depresses the inhibitions, and allows us to act out all our deepest subconscious feelings and desires. Going into a bar and getting drunk in that state of mind was an instant recipe for real disaster. I deliberately picked a fight with another patron at the bar, and got pretty well beaten up. You see, I was a great imaginary fighter, but lacked the ability to demonstrate this talent in real life.

This skirmish almost ended the other romantic relationship as well. I had to cook up some cockamamie story to calm my pen pal down. But she bought it, and she became my ardent fan and sucked in all my other wild tales too. From time to time she drank a few drinks with me, but she drank the more sophisticated kind of mixed drinks which I had never in fact even tasted. I stuck with beer and whiskey shots, the old-fashioned "boilermakers" that were the common drink of working men in the Steel Country. Usually I could control my drinking as long as I was at her house. Alcoholics try to deny their problem for years because of the fact that they can sometimes control the number of drinks they put down, by iron willpower and careful counting, which creates the illusion in their minds that they are still in fundamental control of the process. So I was miserable having to control my intake while I was with her and pretending to be "a normal social drinker," but I usually could do it—and then of course, immediately after leaving her house, I would go get really bombed. My sense of still being in control was sheer illusion, nothing more.

And even then, in spite of my attempts at controlled drinking, on several occasions when I was with her I had a few too many and became obviously intoxicated. In fact, in spite of my attempts to cover up how much I really drank, on numerous occasions she expressed concerns regarding my alcohol intake. I assured her that this was a time of celebration because of returning home, that I was somewhat of a hero because of being at Pearl Harbor, and that citizens just wanted to show their appreciation for my being there, and their joy at the way I had escaped death. Smooth talker that I was, I somehow convinced her that I had no real fundamental problems with alcohol. She foolishly believed my lies and excuses, and even more dangerously, I talked myself into believing them too.

My family, who knew more about my long term history with alcohol, became very concerned about my drinking, and told me so right to my face. All this did was make me angry. When people try to confront alcoholics about their obvious drinking problem, our normal fallback positions are either to get angry, which allows us to terminate the unpleasant conversation by screaming and yelling and walking out, or to start making up excuses and telling lies.

When we recite the same excuses and lies often enough we start actually believing them ourselves, so at the conscious level, we are eventually able to do this with total sincerity. I would have been outraged if someone had told me that what I was saying was complete nonsense—that person would be implying that I was a liar, that I was not totally sincere in what I was saying—when I *knew* that I was being totally sincere and honest. I had indeed become totally sincere about believing that I had no problem with alcohol. I had had to work hard to do it, but I had convinced myself that my delusions were true, so I was looking every place except the real place—my essentially out-of-control drinking—to try to figure out why things were going so badly wrong with my life.

On this troubled note my furlough ended, and the Air Corps sent us to Fresno, California, where they stationed us for a brief period prior to beginning our real schooling. There were sixty-nine of us there, all from Hawaii, so we liked to be known as the "Fighting Sixty-Niners." Most of us liked to drink, but we had little time to do so, because we were put through what was the equivalent of a second round of basic training while we were there. We had to march in the boiling hot sun with full field equipment while a drill instructor barked orders at us. His real name actually was Sergeant Zero, which perfectly fit him. We referred to him contemptuously as Mister Nothing. He was an arrogant little upstart, who gleefully and maliciously used his position of authority to abuse everyone under him. What rankled most with me, was that I was a Technical Sergeant and he was only a Staff Sergeant, so that in any other setting I would have outranked him.

Fortunately, our next orders soon came through and we were transferred to the Aviation Cadet School itself in LaGrande, Oregon. This was a quaint little town that welcomed us with open arms. Although we were a group of wild servicemen who could be quite rowdy at times, they nevertheless accepted us and made us feel at home. They liked us and adopted us as their own, and catered to what was sometimes our rather bizarre behavior. Many of us had been on the firing line during the Japanese attack on Hawaii on December 7, 1941, and we were the ones to whom they were especially nice.

In those days a prospective pilot had to go to certain pretraining classes at a nearby college and pass some difficult courses there before being accepted for advanced pilot training. Eastern Oregon College was the place they sent us. Some of the courses we had to take were directly related to some part of our training, while others were designed to turn us into educated people who could hold serious conversations with others.

You can see how inaccurate my self-perceptions were, and how I had allowed them to pull me down. Back in high school, I was so convinced that I was a poor student that I never even tried, and refused to let myself become interested in anything I was forced to study: I deliberately took up an attitude of contempt and hostility toward everything the teachers were trying to involve me in. If I tried, I would just fail, and then they would humiliate me in front of all the other students, who would judge me, and regard me with disdain. I might as well let them know in advance how much I hated them too, and get in the first blow myself. And so I generated this entire fantasy scenario of failure in my head, and acted it out in totally self-destructive fashion.

There was in fact something even more destructive about my attitude back then. In my perception of the world, there were only two kinds of positions one could be in: "better than" or "less than." So in my mind, no matter how hard I struggled to be "better than," something always inevitably happened, sooner or later, that made me feel "less than." This happens to everyone in the world who tries to play that psychological game. This was part of why I had hated Sergeant Zero so much—oh, he was in fact an obnoxious, envious little man, pompous and arrogant about the tiny shred of authority he had been given for a short while over people who were, most of them, going on to far higher things than he would ever be able to accomplish, and he played a particularly petty version of the better-than/less-than game over trainees who were temporarily at his mercy—but it dug into me with a special kind of poisonous resentment because I was still playing that same game too much myself. I never realized that a person can obtain a deep satisfaction from simply doing an ordinary job in reasonably competent fashion, without having to try the fool's game of attempting to do absolutely everything absolutely perfectly all the time.

For some reason or other, perhaps because it seemed merely a sideline to the pilot training itself, I actually allowed myself to become tremendously interested in the things I was studying at Eastern Oregon College. Increasing my knowledge simply made me feel good. This was a surprising experience to me: studying very hard and yet enjoying doing it. Perhaps it was helped by the fact that we basically did the courses on a pass-fail basis, where we were given no official grades on our work past that point. This removed part of the underlying subconscious anxiety from my mind.

The one subject that especially interested me was American history. I had always had a profound interest in history, and this course in particular was totally intriguing. I threw myself into it with such eagerness that I ended up, on the final exam, making a higher score than anyone who had ever taken that comprehensive test before at Eastern Oregon, including the regularly enrolled students during all the previous years. We in the cadet program were given no official grades, but the professor nevertheless announced my achievement to the entire cadet corps.

My ego was blown totally out of proportion by this, and was even more inflated when I learned that I had been put in a small select group and was targeted to become the Cadet Colonel. My perception of the world was such that I based my own feeling of worth entirely on external achievement and what I believed other people thought of me. I had no inner standards of worth: no knowledge of what I had to do to be able ultimately to live with myself, and what I had to do to avoid betraying my true self. So something like this could send me into flights of grandiose fantasies. "I was the best there ever was." But underneath was always the subconscious conviction that I was going to end up rejected and humiliated. So my whole life now had to be devoted to doing everything perfectly, anything at all that came up. Failure "to measure up" in any aspect of my life would surely result in everyone looking down on me and rejecting me once again.

Initially, I had only put in for Cadet Training in order to come back to the United States, because I had gotten extremely homesick for my family. This was in spite of the fact that, when I was actually living with them, I was always resentful of the high standards they set, and my seeming inability to achieve those standards. I felt that each of my seven siblings was superior to me, and that there was no way I could ever rise to the level they set. And I felt the same sort of intrinsic inferiority to everyone else in our little community in Ohio: I just never seemed to be able to measure up to the rest of the people who lived around us. But now I had actually accomplished something praiseworthy, something I could finally point to with pride when I went home to visit. But what if I failed to be "superior" and above the others, or at least their equal, in anything at all that came up in Cadet life? There was a real torment going on inside my mind.

I only knew one way to self-medicate all these subconscious conflicts and fears and doubts, and that was to drink. So whenever we were given some time off, I would start drinking, and sometimes would end up getting myself in trouble. My accomplishments began to slip. Our behavior was supposed to be exemplary, and whenever we lost points due to some infraction, this detracted from our chances of being selected for Flight School itself. There were several of these advanced schools, at different locations in the United States. I became known as a disciplinary problem, and I became marginal because of several incidents in particular which involved my behavior while under the influence of alcohol.

The final incident that washed me out of the program was a sad one indeed. One Friday night there was a dance in the university ballroom for the Cadet Corps. Everyone else seemed to be having a fine time. I felt like the odd ball out, because I still did not know how to dance (this was like being back in high school again), and this seemed to be the only way to make the acquaintance of any of the pretty girls in attendance. I had always been an incredibly shy person when it came to the opposite sex, and was mortally fearful of being rejected.

From the beginning of my journey to maturity, I had been terminally afraid of any activity in which one could be judged as poor, good, or excellent. In other words, I wanted to start out at the beginning being excellent, and not have to go through the slow learning process that would lead up to that. That of course, was impossible. No one could start off dancing like an expert, the first time they ever tried.

My perfectionistic fantasies led me into any number of booby traps during my youthful years, and this ended up being one of the most devastating in terms of my own ego and pride. I stood around at the dance, just being a pathetic spectator and watching everyone else have fun, and was totally unable to figure out what to do. Then, from somewhere, a little dog burst into the room and ran across the dance floor. Another dog in my life! I should have remembered from high school, that dogs and I in public situations can quickly result in total humiliation.

But I was in such an advanced state of intoxication by this point, that I ran out on the dance floor and picked up the small dog and began what I thought was a waltz, much to the amusement of the entire rest of the Cadet Corps. I had to try to show off some way in order to cover my feelings of total inadequacy. Unfortunately, there was a member of the faculty present, a regular Air Force Captain, who was an extremely stiff and humorless and arrogant man, who was not amused. He immediately ordered me to put down the dog, and go to my room at once. I was drunk enough that I tried arguing with him, and would not quit, until finally some of the other cadets persuaded me to leave and go sleep it off.

The next day, there was an official meeting of the regular officers assigned to the university staff, with the cadets all present, where my final termination from the Cadet Corps was approved. The next day I was told to leave, that I had no further role there.

The requirements at Eastern Oregon College had been strict, and the expectations placed on us far higher than those put on normal college students at even quite prestigious places, but the rewards of successfully passing the program were enormous. The pride and sense of accomplishment would have been huge. And there had been an enormous bonding between all of us cadets who were involved in the program, an almost unfathomable emotional attachment between us, created by our common dedication to such a demanding program. All my hopes and dreams and sense of belonging were demolished in an instant. And what would I ever tell my family, and my soon-to-be wife? I was supposed to have been the top cadet in the Corps, the one who was targeted to become the Cadet Colonel. I was in a state of shock that almost bordered on a nervous breakdown.

The day I left the college to be sent back to a regular assignment, I can still remember every detail of walking down the sidewalk with my barracks bag over my shoulder, in a state of enormous depression, and having to walk past all the other cadets who were assembled in formation, where they could all see me slinking away in humiliating defeat. Then to my amazement, a man named Paul V. McDougal, who had been chosen to be Cadet Colonel instead of me, called the whole Cadet Corps to attention and cried out, "Hand salute!" They were saluting me with respect, in spite of what I had done! I returned the salute to the whole multitude, with tears streaming down my cheeks. It was so unbelievably strange: there in the midst of one of my greatest defeats, I received what I still regard as one of the greatest honors I have ever had bestowed on me.

Numerous people had written their farewells on a shipping tag attached to my bag, a piece of cardboard which I still treasure to this day. Some of the writing is faded so much now as to have been obliterated by time—this was sixty years ago, back in an incredibly distant past—but I can still make out many of the names and comments. There were good wishes from civilians there in the little Oregon town of LaGrande, as well as from military friends: There were the Price's, who owned the restaurant. There were Joe and Hank, Maxine Young, Myrtle Price, and Tom Parrish, who claimed I was "the best @#&% who ever crapped between a pair of Woolworth socks." There was the name of Maxine Harrison from the Top Notch, Edith Travis, Tex, Bob Kromburg, Mildred Penn, Dan, Jarrad, Joe, and Hank who said "I see the light." And others as well, faded away now so as to be no longer legible, but they liked me and they cared. If only I had realized that I did not have to "earn" other people's love by outrageous and out-of-hand behavior. All I ever really had to do was just to be me. But I still did not "see the light," and would not, until I finally fully came into the A.A. program five years later.

CHAPTER 9

First Tragic Marriage

My girlfriend had been very impressed with the idea that I was going to become an officer and a pilot in the United States Army Air Force. How could I ever tell her what had actually happened? Like many an alcoholic, I made up a creative lie. I took the time to think it through carefully. It was essential that my washing out be due to some physical condition over which I could have no control. That way I could be totally blameless. We alcoholics do an excellent job of playing helpless victim of things beyond our control, when we are trying to cover up the more unfortunate consequences of our drunkenness. I decided to say that I had been eliminated from the program because they had tested me and discovered that my depth perception was faulty. Apparently neither I nor anyone else to whom I told this fancy tale stopped to think that no one who was as good at baseball as I was, which involves tracking a rapidly moving ball and knowing exactly how far away it is and how fast it is traveling, could conceivably have flawed depth perception.

When I came back to Ohio, I trotted out my carefully prepared lie, and otherwise tried to keep conversation about this matter at a minimum. Fortunately (or so I believed at the time), she cooperated with me and did not press me for details, and gave me sympathy. Our relationship seemed to be still on. When the spouses and families of alcoholics come into Al-Anon, one of the things which they have to come to terms with before their own lives can start being healed, is that they also wanted to share the same fantasies and delusions which we alcoholics were so good at devising. Both she and I would have been so much better off in the long run if we had been willing to ask some hard questions and face some painful truths, right then and there.

———————

While the military was deciding where they wanted to give me my next regular assignment, I was temporarily assigned to the Air Force base at Amarillo, Texas, for around three months, which I did not find pleasant at all. Alcoholism is a progressive disease, and mine was still progressing rapidly: the problems you get into keep on getting worse and worse, your behavior becomes more and more confused and out of control, and (until you reach the very end) it keeps on taking more and more alcohol to get you to the state of inebriation you require.

I had already gotten in trouble because of my drinking by the time I had been in Amarillo only a week. At that time Texas law prohibited the dispensing of liquor by the drink at a bar. Night clubs only sold set-ups, and you had to bring your own liquor. The amount of alcohol I wanted by this point often exceeded the pay I was getting, and I had reached that point in the progression of the disease where the alcoholic will do and say anything, break any rules or commit any deception, in order to get his liquor.

A buddy who had once been a Mason told me several phrases I could say which would convince a Mason that I belonged to that organization too. It seems totally crazy to me now, but I went into a drinking establishment there in Amarillo and began getting friendly with a man who wore a Masonic ring, and began dropping a few of these phrases into my conversation. The man gave me several drinks, and I foolishly believed that I could continue the deception, so I kept on going. Alcohol makes your mind believe that your fantasies are real, and that you will never get caught. Well, eventually, whatever I was saying, it started to become clear to him that I was a total phony and not a real brother Mason at all, so he proceeded to beat me up badly. When I got back to base, to add to my humiliation, I was also called on the carpet and reprimanded severely for "drunk and disorderly conduct" while drinking off base.

Another time I was at a club that catered to servicemen, and I was really intoxicated and had to go to the men's room very badly. A GI was standing at the door mumbling "nobody goes in here" but I tried to shove my way past him. He struck me several times, I was told later, and knocked me out cold. I ended up in the hospital, where it took me several hours to come to, with a broken nose and two black eyes, along with a serious concussion. It turned out the GI who had done that to me had had previous encounters with the law, and several charges against him were already pending. So this time the other guy was the one who was punished: he was court-martialed and given six months in the guardhouse and a dishonorable discharge. But the point was that if my own thinking processes had not been so hopelessly muddled by alcohol, I would have instantly realized that this man was drunk out of his head, totally out of control, and very dangerous, and I would have had my guard up and not tried tangling with him all on my own. To a certain degree, I brought that on my own head, just as much as when I foolishly tried to pass myself off as a Mason.

When I was drunk, I was not a very good fighter, but I kept on getting into places and situations anyway in which I got into fights and then got beaten up badly. It was almost like a death wish. Many alcoholics are like that.

After three months of living like that, I was told that my orders had come through, and I was going to be sent off to New Guinea. Supposedly those who had already served in the Pacific Theater of Operations were not to be returned to that area, but the military was simply not following their own stated guidelines, and not for the first time by any means.

I was given a thirty-day furlough prior to shipment, so I returned home to Ohio. My girlfriend and I had decided that we were going to get married before I went back to the Pacific. My mission on the train trip home was to have a really major fling at John Barleycorn. What was my reasoning? Celebration? Anxiety over marriage? By that point in the progression of the disease, alcoholics respond to every external situation—anger, disappointment, joy, success, too much excitement, too much calm, or simply boredom—by turning to the bottle. For a change, I had won some money in a poker game just before leaving, so I kept on getting off the train at every station where we stopped, to replenish my liquor supply with yet another bottle or two. I was in such bad shape by the time we arrived at my home town, that they had to hold me up and half carry me off the train. My family, and my girlfriend in particular, were totally stunned at the sight of me dead drunk and rubber-legged, being dragged down the little metal steps where you got off the railway coach.

I decided that I would "prove" to them I was not an alcoholic by using all my will power for the next thirty days to practice controlled drinking. I do not think I got seriously intoxicated a single time, and I managed to convince people that my drinking was only casual social drinking. I would go to the local bars in Niles, Ohio, where I was treated as a hero, and everyone offered to buy drinks for me. I had several military ribbons on my uniform and no one knew what they were really for, so I let them think they were for extraordinary acts of bravery under fire. The ribbons were just for being there, not for heroism. I certainly did not tell them how I had run away as fast as my legs would carry me when the warplanes began shooting on Pearl Harbor day.

Somehow or other I managed to count my drinks, and hold myself back from getting visibly drunk. The warning I had received when I was poured off the train from Amarillo worked for that entire month. A lot of alcoholics can do that for relatively short periods of time. It does not in fact prove that you are not an alcoholic, because it is too much of a strain and too exhausting psychologically to keep up very long. I have actually seen alcoholics carry that off for up to a year even, by just sheer white-knuckled will power, acutely miserable all the while, but the collapse back into drunkenness and totally out-of-control drinking always eventually occurs. Attempts at controlled drinking, even total abstinence, by will power alone provide no long-term solution to alcoholism.

My girlfriend insisted on a formal wedding. I felt like a duck out of water, surrounded by all the fancy dresses and suits. But I even managed to restrain myself from getting drunk at the reception afterwards, by sheer dogged will power, even though drinks were being served.

Then we were off on a train for a short honeymoon in Cleveland, all of sixty miles away. These were the days of the old steam engines, and I can still smell the sharp sulfurous stench of the coal smoke drifting back from the smokestack, and hear the steam hissing out in white jets from the engine when you walked past its mammoth black greasy bulk there at the head of the train. When the train was in motion, the cars lurched and swayed unpredictably from side to side, and you could hear the constant clicking of the wheels passing the rail joints over the various other rumbling sounds and metallic creaks and groans. The total effect could actually be quite hypnotic, like being rocked to sleep in your mother's arms while she hummed a lullaby. And unfortunately, that was exactly what happened. I was so psychologically worn out from the strain of trying to control my drinking and cope with the stress of the formal wedding, and from the pressure of all my subconscious anxieties, that I actually fell sound asleep from sheer exhaustion there in my seat as we huffed and puffed through the Ohio countryside. I certainly did not come off looking like the great romantic lover or the totally smitten suitor. It is a wonder my new wife did not dump me right on the spot.

Instead of sending me straight off to New Guinea, the Air Force then sent me the opposite direction, to Seymour-Johnson Air Force Base in Goldsboro, North Carolina. Although we were told that our dependents could not accompany us, my new wife in fact came east and got a small apartment in town. During that short time she got pregnant, something I did not learn about until I was already back in the Pacific. By the time I got back to the states again, I would have not only a wife but a lovely baby girl.

———————————

Then the military shipped me back west again, to California, and I boarded a troopship and sailed off to New Guinea. The jungles seemed astonishingly beautiful at first, at least when they were flying us into the interior, and could look down on them from on high. A place called Nadzab was our destination. We could see all sorts of brightly colored birds fluttering through the lush, green, leafy treetops. But I soon came to regard it as the most God-forsaken place in the entire world. Once you were down on the ground, life was harsh in those jungles. The heat was overwhelming and thousands of insects buzzed and hummed and darted, and filled the air around you with their swarms. I ended up in a four-man tent in the middle of all this. My very first night a monsoon hit us, and the water rapidly rose to almost the bottom of our cots. The rain drummed on the canvas relentlessly all night long, and I tossed and flailed about, trying unsuccessfully to escape the hordes of mosquitoes which attacked ceaselessly, worse even than the ones along the stagnant creek where we had gone fishing when I was a child. Sleep was impossible. I was worried about a whole lot more than just the ferociously itching bites that started appearing everywhere I had exposed skin: some of the mosquitoes in this jungle, I knew, carried the tropical disease malaria. Once you had been infected, you were beset over and over again by totally disabling cycles of chills, fever, and prodigious sweating. And in fact I did eventually contract that disease before I got out of the Pacific islands.

The fear of Japanese air attacks which could come at any moment, drove us almost insane. Fresh meat, eggs, and other things Americans would normally eat were considered luxuries, and we were not provided with luxury items. What was handed out to us at meals was barely fit for human consumption at all. The local natives wore bones through their noses and dyed their bushy hair in bright colors that simply looked totally bizarre, if you were a small town boy from 1940's Ohio, who was not used to that sort of thing. Of course, now that I have lived in modern California all these years, with teenagers wearing rings piercing their eyebrows and tongues and belly buttons, and hair dyed every color of the rainbow, I might not even notice it at all!

I was assigned to work in the Technical Supply section of Aircraft Maintenance, which at first meant simply processing and filing technical orders pertaining to airplane parts, an incredibly boring job. I soon figured out a way to start working on aircraft, because I could not stand the endless paperwork.

The biggest problem of all at this point, for an alcoholic like me, was finding something to drink out there in the jungle. The Air Force supplied each of us with a six-pack of beer as our alcohol ration every three days. Note that this perfectly matched the average consumption of a true normal social drinker, which is two drinks a day at most. To me, this ration would have been absurdly small—impossibly too little—even if we could have actually drunk all the beer in that six-pack. But with no refrigeration in the sweltering jungle heat, the best you could do was stick your mouth right over the can of hot beer the second it was opened. Even then half the contents would gush out in a frothy geyser all over the ground and your uniform. GI's are brilliantly inventive though, and there were many unsung scientific geniuses among our ranks. We learned to put the beer in a sack wet down with carbon tetrachloride when we were lucky enough to find some, and twirl the bag around in the air. As the cleaning solution evaporated it would cool the beer down some.

Legitimate whiskey from Australia cost sixty dollars for a fifth. There was no way I could afford that. Sometimes I could purloin some lemon or vanilla extract, which came in small bottles but had a lot of alcohol in it. My Commanding Officer called me into his office once right after I had tossed down some of the lemon flavoring, and the minute I reported in, he took a big breath and exclaimed, "Sergeant, what in the hell have you been drinking? You smell like a fruitcake!" And then there was fermented coconut milk, an ungodly homemade intoxicating beverage. You drilled a hole in the coconut, poured some sugar into the hole, and then plugged it with a cork and left it to ferment. The wait was excruciatingly long, and the taste was cloyingly sweet even after it had fermented, but it was alcoholic. It also gave you agonizing attacks of diarrhea. Those of us who drank this regularly had soon wasted down to skin and bones.

One evening after a particularly heavy drinking bout, I decided to go out and win the war single-handed by searching out Japanese in the jungle. Drunk out of my mind, I got several guns, as much ammunition as I could carry, and plunged out into the pitch black night, into the endless, humid, swelteringly hot expanses of densely interwoven trees and vines. All I accomplished was to become hopelessly lost. It took hours of wandering around, still half drunk, before I could find the base again. I was so sick by the time I staggered in from the jungle that they had to put me in the hospital. I was eventually diagnosed as having contracted dengue fever, which was spread in tropical climates by infected mosquitoes. You suffered from fever, a rash, and worst of all, extremely severe pains in the joints: one of the old traditional folk names for it was breakbone fever.

When I finally got out of the hospital, they sent me to Biak, a Pacific island right on the equator, which was even hotter than New Guinea, and then to Mindora in the Philippine Islands. I was miserable and just wanted to get out.

Since the United States was so obviously winning the war now, a point system was set up allowing some of the troops in the Pacific to return to the states. A GI got points for length of time overseas, marital status, and having children. I clearly qualified for the first shipment home, but was denied the right to be put on that list because my position had been declared "essential to the mission." I protested so strongly, that I was finally granted permission to go to Manila and plead my case at headquarters there.

When I got to Manila, I went in and demanded permission to speak to the Commanding General himself. His Executive Officer brusquely told me to leave. I was so outraged, I became rather vocal, and the discussion became more and more heated. Eventually General White himself, who was the Commander of Far Eastern Air Forces, heard the ruckus and came out of his office, and asked calmly, "What is the problem?" Seeing the stars on his shoulder, in a suddenly very subdued tone of voice, I nervously told him that my assignment was not essential to anyone at all, and that I had earlier been denied a furlough when my wife became critically ill with uremia while giving birth to our daughter.

In fact, General White immediately ordered that my name be put on the shipping list. For a third time, oddly enough, I went on board exactly the same troopship, the Leonard Wood, and sailed back to the United States. We docked in Los Angeles, and then were sent by train to Camp Atterbury in Indiana prior to discharge. This apparently friendly Hoosier setting turned out, strangely enough, to be one of the most dangerous places I was in during the whole war! To begin with, while on the train riding there, I fell out of the upper bunk and dislocated my left shoulder. I had to be taken off the train, and sent to a doctor who put my arm in a sling and wrapped it close to my body, before I could continue my train trip.

The very day after arriving at Camp Atterbury, the Red Cross notified me that my stepmother had died. I was granted an emergency leave, and took the first train to Niles, Ohio. Getting off the coach with my arm in a sling, everyone assumed I was a battle casualty. War heroes got bought lots of free drinks, so I soon began taking advantage of this cheerfully. My wife met me at the train with our baby daughter in her arms. This was the first time I had ever seen her, but it was love at first sight. My little girl was the joy of my life. She was so beautiful and seemed to respond to my attention with pleasure and delight.

My biggest problem with everyone else was my appearance. My weight had dropped to only a hundred and five pounds, and my skin was green from taking Atabrine for the malaria I had also contracted in the jungles. All the adults looked at me with horror, as though I had become some kind of freak.

It was all so strange after almost two years in the jungle: hot water to bathe in, fresh food, comfortable beds for sleeping, and the incredible luxury of ice water to drink. It was a shock. I did not know how to react to all this, or to ordinary Midwestern people living ordinary civilian lives. I felt like a total stranger with my wife and her family. Everyone seemed to be holding back, and there was something strangely tentative in the air at all times. I could not relax at all and feel comfortable in their presence.

My stepmother's funeral came three days later, and this was the first time I had ever thought to consider the sacrifices she had made when she took on raising us children. She had worked very hard to make our lives a little more tolerable, and I at least had never appreciated it. I felt very guilty about this, which added to my incredible inner stress.

Over and over I longed for a drink, but was afraid to, because I was so in dread of being cast out if I were seen drunk again. I snuck out to the bars when the compulsion got too bad, to nervously put down a few every now and then. It was pretty horrible. Everyone who knew me wanted to buy me drinks, and I could have easily had the kind of drunk I really wanted, but I held myself under rigid control, and crept back home after just a few rounds. If this kind of white-knuckled control game were what Alcoholics Anonymous offered, no alcoholic in the world would ever join that organization or sing its praises. But in fact, this is not at all what A.A. is about, and this is not at all what life in A.A. is like after you have been in for a while. If you, the reader, are putting off coming to A.A. because you think that this is what is in store for you, please cast that idea totally out of your mind. A.A. will teach you how to live a way of life so satisfying that, down in some deep place inside your being, you will literally *not even want the drink*. It gives people the most priceless gift in the world: genuine freedom from their unbearable torments.

I had to go back to Camp Atterbury then for a brief while longer. I was on pass in Columbus, Indiana, on August 14, 1945, when everyone started going wild as the word spread that the Japanese had surrendered. I was determined that a big celebration was in order, and ran down into the street to get to a liquor store before they closed. The next thing I remembered was waking up in a hospital bed the next day. I never got my celebratory drunken spree, in fact had never even managed to put a bottle or a glass to my lips. It turned out that while running down the street toward the liquor store, someone had thrown an object out of a second story window, which had hit me on the head and knocked me out cold for some hours afterwards. I had somehow survived the first day of the Second World War in spite of being shot at and bombed by waves of hostile Japanese airplanes, and almost ended up being killed by my own countrymen in the peaceful town of Columbus on the last day of the war.

Some fifty-seven years later, I met the co-author of this book for the first time and we began hatching out our plans for writing it, in that very same town. I had been asked to speak at the Indiana State A.A. Convention which was being held in Columbus that year, and could not resist telling the tale of my last visit to their town. My co-author assured me that Hoosiers had gotten a lot more civilized over the past half century, and that he could almost positively guarantee me that no one would drop a flower pot or other heavy object on my head this time around, and in fact I had a marvelous time and got out of town totally unscathed on this occasion!

But to go back to August 1945: three days after being released from the hospital, I was discharged from the military, and headed back to Ohio, extremely nervous and apprehensive. I had learned no trade in the Air Force that could be converted to civilian use. What would I do to support my wife and new baby girl?

My father-in-law, who worked for General Electric, got me a job in the lamp division there, but it did not last long because my alcoholism was too advanced by that point. In typical alcoholic fashion I worked very hard to impress the people at General Electric with my sincerity and my desire to do a good job. We alcoholics *are* sincere when we tell people how we have seen the light, and have learned our lesson, and are going to do things differently now, and how totally dedicated we are to doing things right from now on. We can look people in the eye when we say those things, because in one part of our conscious minds we genuinely believe it. It is just that the power of the unconscious conflicts, and the power of the physiological addiction itself, will still always win in the long run—no matter how many promises we make, or how many mighty oaths we swear. Believing that a fantasy is true, no matter how sincerely it is believed, does not help people deal with real-world situations in which they are in fact totally at the power of forces they cannot control—including not only the forces down inside the unconscious level of their own minds, but also the kind of physiologically addictive compulsion which we saw in Spot, that poor drunken barroom dog who begged for dishes of beer at the Snake Ranch in Hawaii. I was by now hopelessly physically addicted to alcohol too. Spot the alcoholic dog could not have stayed away from beer just by exercising will power, and at the primitive purely physiological level I was no different from poor Spot.

So in spite of my promises, and all my good intentions, on several occasions I reported for work at General Electric under the influence of alcohol. They finally fired me, and then my drinking turned into a daily affair. My wife became so disgusted that one night she refused to even let me in the house when I tried to stagger in the door. The next day, my clothes were all put out on the front porch, and I was soon notified that she had filed for divorce.

I moved back into my dad's home, but refused to follow anyone's advice. I kept on drinking, and was not eating properly, so my already poor health kept on getting worse and worse. I pleaded with the judge when I was called into the divorce court. I pledged that I would never drink again, and with all my heart I believed what I was telling him. He did not know enough about alcoholics to realize how ultimately empty and meaningless these kinds of promises were in reality. He also took into account the traumas experienced during my military career, and the short time I had had to adjust to civilian life, and decided to put the divorce case on hold.

I developed a deep resentment and self-pity because no one from my own family had come to court with me to defend me. Resentment is the number one killer of alcoholics, and as this resentment and self-pity smoldered inside my mind, I ignored my pledge and went right back to drinking again. I drank out of anger, even though the alcohol only fed the flames of helpless rage, and plunged me into an even deeper agony of despair. My malaria began acting up again, and I was shaking and having fevers and chills, and so miserable I wanted to die—the disease attacks in periodic cycles, once you have the infection lodged in your system—and I had to be admitted to the hospital. But the judge found out that the hospitalization was necessary, not only for the malaria, but also for the excessive drinking to which I had once again returned. So he immediately granted the divorce, and that was the end of my marriage. My beloved baby girl I was not to see again for forty years.

CHAPTER 10

My First Encounter with A.A.

While I was lying there in the hospital, a friend attempted to get me into a Veterans Administration establishment for longer-term care. But this was the year 1945, and even though I was obviously in very bad shape from the malaria I had contracted in the jungles of the Pacific, I had also been identified as an alcoholic, and the V.A. hospital simply refused to accept me as a patient. The assumption was that alcoholics would be obstreperous and uncooperative, and sometimes even violent, and that their inability to stop drinking would mean that they would ultimately destroy their bodies and brains and drink themselves to death, regardless of anything medical personnel attempted to do to help them. There was no help for alcoholics in the military while they were still on active duty, and there was likewise no help for them after their discharge, no matter how honorably they had served their country. We were the abandoned ones. Our disease made us too ugly and unlovable, and too hopeless.

It took a long time for changes to occur. The first organized military alcoholism treatment programs were not going to appear until I myself set up the first two, at Mitchel Air Force Base from 1948 to 1951 and at Lackland Air Force Base (with Dr. Louis Jolyon West) from 1953 to 1957. These programs shed a few bright rays of hope into the otherwise rather dark and gloomy situation at that time.[5] But by the end of the 1950's, the military authorities had once again abandoned any serious attempt to help alcoholics in the armed forces.

Large numbers of military alcoholism treatment programs did not start to be created until a decade later, during the latter half of the 1960's, and it was not until 1971 that Senator Harold Hughes was able to put through an amendment to the Military Selective Service Act which finally legally required the Secretary of Defense to set up procedures and provide all necessary facilities to treat and rehabilitate members of the Armed Forces who were dependent on drugs or alcohol. It was called the Hughes Amendment, and created Title V of Public Law 92-129, which began to produce dramatic changes whenever its legal requirements were actually enforced. And it took just as long for veterans to begin to receive help after they had been discharged from the service: in fact, it was not until 1967 that an official V.A. policy statement directed that hospitalization for the treatment of alcoholism should be processed in the same way as a request for treatment of any other health issue "susceptible to cure or decided improvement."[6]

But there where I was, lying in that hospital bed in 1945, it was going to be twenty years at least before major positive changes began to be made. I was still a young man, only twenty-seven years old, but I was sick and desperate, and there did not seem to me that there was any place where I could turn for help. I seemed to be simply condemned to drink myself to death.

Shortly before my hospitalization, I had been fortunate to obtain a job at a General Motors plant. It was a good paying job, and interesting to me. Pay was based on your production output, so I worked very hard to prove my worth. The plant went on strike immediately prior to my entry into the hospital, so I was not regarded as having missed any work.

The only thing I knew to do after I left the hospital was simply to report back for work at General Motors. But my alcoholism was still untreated, and brief periods spent "drying out" in a hospital or de-tox ward do no long-term good in halting the inexorable progression of the disease as long as nothing is being done about the underlying alcoholic compulsion and distorted perceptions of the world. Also, although I still had a job, my work situation there immediately began to become more trying.

When I returned to the job, the management called on all its employees to increase their production to make up for the losses sustained during the strike. The strong union members among the employees were very hostile to this request. I, on the other hand, with my military training, believed that I had an obligation to the people who signed my paycheck, and worked as hard as I could to increase my output. The union people told me to slow down and stop doing that, and I bluntly refused. Hostility toward me seethed, and there were fellow workers all around me just watching for me to make some mistake which they could use as grounds for having me fired.

So my job turned into a hellish situation, and I was continually depressed over the loss of my baby daughter. My ex-wife told me she would remarry me if I remained abstinent for a year. The problem was that I had gotten to the point all alcoholics eventually get to, where no matter how much I wanted *not* to drink, I could not stay away from the bottle.

It was during this period that I had my first contact with Alcoholics Anonymous. It was not going to work for me this first time around. I did manage to get almost three months of desperate, white-knuckled sobriety by going to A.A. meetings every week, but then went back to drinking once again. As I reflected later on however, one of the reasons it did not work for me was because the little A.A. group I went to was well-intentioned, but taught and practiced only a small portion of the real program. As I began to analyze what had been left out, and what had to be taught in order for the greatest amount of real healing to occur, I was able to set up a program at Mitchel Air Force Base two years later which had a far higher success rate, extremely impressive in fact. I had to learn that I must do some things in working with newcomers which they did not do at all, and I had to learn that I must *not* do some of the things which they had done, which simply made people feel worse about themselves and ultimately drove them off.

In 1945 most people in the United States had not yet heard of A.A., but I was living in Niles, Ohio, only forty-five miles east of Akron, which was where the movement had first begun ten years earlier. So unlike most parts of the country at that time, there were people scattered all over northeastern Ohio who had in fact heard about A.A., and who were aware that, for the first time in history, a method had been worked out for getting drunks sober and keeping them sober which had an enormous success rate, far surpassing any other techniques that had been tried up to that point. My father-in-law even had heard about A.A., and was trying to get me to go to their meetings before my first wife and I were separated. I ignored his advice; alcoholics tend to brush aside things which are said to them by non-alcoholics. But then while I was out drinking, I met a man whom I had known most of my life, who was considered one of the town drunks there in Niles. He also told me that I ought to get into Alcoholics Anonymous, in spite of the ironic fact that his own contact with the program, whatever that had been, had certainly not been sufficient to stop him from continuing to drink himself to death.

I can partially remember deciding at one point to call the A.A. phone number and ask for help. I stumbled into a telephone booth in a drunken stupor, at a point when I was also starting to come down with another bout of malaria, and then promptly passed out and fell out of the booth before I could dial the number. I actually do not remember falling out of it, but some of my friends told me the next day that this was what happened.

———————————

When I was finally hospitalized though, a person I had known for most of my life came to visit with me. He was an active member of A.A. now, and talked to me for a long time about his own drinking career. I listened, but could not truly identify with his drinking history. I did however agree to go to a meeting with him, and went to my first A.A. meeting on January 19, 1946. This group met in Warren, Ohio, only four miles from my home. There were still not very many A.A. meetings around, even in my part of the country, and the next closest one was in Youngstown, Ohio, ten miles away in the opposite direction.

The people at this A.A. meeting talked about the severity of their drinking and their long history of alcohol consumption. I was at least twenty years younger than the next youngest member. I cannot accurately recall, but I do not think there were any women at the meeting. As far as most people at that time were concerned, women who drank uncontrollably were not alcoholics, but simply moral degenerates.

In fact, as I looked around the room, I kept on telling myself that I could not possibly be an alcoholic, because my experiences were so different from theirs: I was part of a different world, I did not believe that I had drunk the way they did, and above all I was only twenty-seven years old. I guess I felt as though there was some magic number, like forty-five or fifty, where no one could conceivably be an alcoholic until the person was at least that old. Later on, Dr. Jellinek at the Yale School of Alcohol Studies, along with other alcohol researchers, established that alcoholism is a progressive disease or illness whose early stages can be diagnosed in people who are quite young. When I finally got sober, I was going to be privileged to study with this man, who was one of the most brilliant and insightful people I have ever known. We can use these early indicators now (employing the Jellinek Curve and other diagnostic devices) to identify people, at a very young age, as having already started the alcoholic progression. So the idea that I was "too young" to be an alcoholic was nonsense, but I was trying as hard as I could to avoid looking at the truth about myself, and grasping at any straw to maintain all my excuses and denial.

Some of the people at that A.A. meeting talked about having been skid row bums, and having begged or stolen to get alcohol, and other behavioral traits like that. Again I said to myself inside my own mind, that I had never done any of these things, so I must not be "one of them." A.A. was for alcoholics, and since I clearly wasn't one of those, whatever it was that was actually wrong with me, their program was not going to help cure it. Now this too was nonsense. Like most alcoholics attending their first A.A. meetings, my mind was still involved in selective memory loss. These memories were pushed down into my subconscious, out of sight, because of all the guilt I felt about them.

When I began to go to more meetings later on, and my mind began to clear, these buried memories began to resurface one by one over a period of time. If you the reader have read the earlier chapters of this book, then you already know that I had in fact begged for money, and had lied and connived and tried to work scams and cons continuously. I had "walked off with" bottles containing alcohol on many occasions, but argued to myself that this was not "stealing" because of one excuse or another. I would say something like "the Army Air Corps will never miss a few bottles of lemon and vanilla extract," and so on. I had wandered penniless, far away from home, on more than one occasion, and had survived by doing things like eating apples from a tree in a farmer's field, and mooching meals from people who picked me up hitchhiking, and I had once nearly been arrested for vagrancy until I talked the policeman out of it.

But at this point, I was blocking off all these memories, and keeping them buried down in my subconscious out of guilt and shame and humiliation, so at the conscious level I felt that I simply could not identify with what these A.A. people were talking about. And unfortunately, some of the older men actually told me that I was not old enough to be an alcoholic, and they would scoff at me and tell me that they had spilt more liquor than I had ever drunk. I felt like "the odd man out." It is sad and tragic, but I have heard of a few older A.A. members rebuffing younger people in this fashion even down into the 1970's and sometimes even 1980's, and making them feel excluded from the group. This is a very bad thing to do. The sooner alcoholics can turn their lives around, the better off they will be. There is no reason to ruin over half of your useful adult life, where you end up having to be faced later on with all those regrets for what you "could have done" with your middle years if you had just come into A.A. sooner.

The "God talk" at that A.A. meeting in January 1946 also really turned me off. I would start thinking of the strident, hysterical tones of the radio evangelists my parents had made me listen to as a child, and the excessive moralisms and demands for blind faith in what seemed to be total nonsense, and what seemed to me to be the mindlessness of that kind of hyper-religious cant, and this was the only way I could think of to interpret what these A.A. people were saying. And I knew I did not want that, and would never be able to stomach anything like that. One of the things the little A.A. group in Warren failed to teach newcomers was the marvelous spirit of tolerance in A.A., and the way in which the members are allowed to work out their own understanding of spiritual issues and real eternal values and the things which give true meaning to life.

I should also say however, that hating God and being totally hostile to any kind of spiritual concepts at all, is one of the standard symptoms of untreated alcoholism in my understanding of the disease, along with rebelliousness, broken relationships with family and neighbors, antisocial behavior of various sorts, being excluded from all decent society and turned into an outcast, failure to achieve even basic job and educational requirements, and so on. These things all have to be dealt with in order to heal someone's life in the A.A. program.

But I have been sober now, and a continuously active A.A. member, for almost fifty-five years at this point, and I have never ever talked about the spiritual aspects of the program to other people in any kind of preachy religious language. It is not necessary to sound like a radio or television evangelist. And I have not only stayed sober myself, but have helped bring literally thousands of people into the program by talking about it my way, so that is the way I will write about it in this book.

It is important to remember though, that the most important reason why I do not speak all that much about the spiritual side of the A.A. program is because I know that I lack the words and the eloquence to do it adequately. At this point in my life, I rather regret that I never had the training or experience or religious education that would enable me to express these things better. When I meet people in the program who do have the background to talk about spirituality with depth and profundity—those men and women who are "the real thing" and are speaking from the heart and from real personal awareness of the spiritual dimension of life, not those who just mechanically parrot religious-sounding phrases—I both appreciate and greatly admire them. If you still cannot stand it when you hear other people in the program talking about their higher power, and faith and grace and other spiritual concepts like that, you still have some psychological healing to do.

But back in January of 1946, all I could think was that I wanted no part of what these A.A. people seemed to me to be saying. And because of the mystery surrounding the recovery process, and the general rejection of alcoholics by most of society at that point in history, I was convinced that if I kept going to A.A. meetings and began admitting that I was an alcoholic, I would simply condemn myself to being totally humiliated and looked down on and despised by my family, and by all my friends (and enemies) there in my community. Because of the public stigma attached to alcoholism, I was willing to go to any lengths to deny that I was one. I was more willing to destroy my life and die drunk, than I was to face the public contempt which I was sure I would receive if I admitted that I was an alcoholic.

The disease concept of alcoholism, which Mrs. Marty Mann was going to help introduce to the American public, had not truly developed yet. As Marty liked to put it, there were three basic points that had to be stressed over and over again to change the general public perception of alcohol abuse: "(1) Alcoholism is a disease and the alcoholic a sick person. (2) The alcoholic can be helped and is worth helping. (3) This is a public health problem and therefore a public responsibility."[7]

Marty backed me to the hilt when she learned of the program which I set up at Mitchel Air Force Base in 1948, and was the one who got me into the Yale School of Alcohol Studies for further training in 1949. My own philosophy of alcoholism treatment which I was developing was based on a perspective very similar to hers, which was what enabled us to work together so smoothly.

I want to talk about the modern disease concept of alcoholism in this book, because even today, almost sixty years later, when I am talking to people in the military about setting up treatment programs, or trying to convince soldiers and sailors and Marines and Air Force personnel to come into one of these programs and get their alcoholism treated, I can sometimes feel like we were still living back in 1946. I encounter non-alcoholics who still want to take a purely punitive approach, and alcoholics who feel that they will be totally stigmatized if they admit that they are suffering from an illness.

———————————

At any rate, I had gone to my first A.A. meeting on January 19, 1946. Wib, my first A.A. sponsor, was a persistent person who knew my wife and her whole family. He was desperately trying to save our marriage. I went to meetings with him for the next three months. There were both open meetings (which any person could attend) and closed meetings (for alcoholics only). Most of the meetings were speaker meetings, with a leader and two or three speakers.

The disease concept of alcoholism had not truly percolated into that part of small town Ohio, so the common mode of therapy was simply to deliver "drunk-o-logues," where those with more time in the program went into long, lurid detail about all the troubles they had gotten into with their drinking, and encouraged the newcomers to start speaking up and doing the same. Members thought of themselves as drunks, sots, dipsomaniacs (a word I have not heard now in many years), or simply as no good down-and-outers, dwelling morbidly on all the guilt and shame which they felt. Alcoholics have to face the bitter reality of what they were actually doing to themselves with their drinking, and the shambles this made of their lives, but if you go no further than that, very little real healing can occur. There was not much in the way of real therapy in the little Warren A.A. meeting.

Newcomers who came in seeking help had it dished out on a contemptuous, rather arrogant take-it-or-leave-it basis. There was also the prevalent feeling that you were a clandestine member of some ultrasecret society, holding little covert meetings while you looked over your shoulder continuously for fear that someone might find out what you were doing. That also is not conducive in the long run to real mental health.

The philosophy expressed at these meetings in Warren, Ohio, did not coincide with my problems. In particular, I do not know of anything that can elicit as much suffering as a divorce. I had had a beautiful wife and child whom I loved, and then, in terms of the way it felt to me, I had simply been tossed aside like used clothing. It was an almost unbearable tragedy, and I thought my mind was going to crack at times from the pain that would fill all my thoughts. On top of that, I had so many other problems in my life that I was rendered almost totally nonfunctional most of the time. There was not only the terrible hurt from the divorce, but also the feeling of having been totally rejected and abandoned by my own family. Although desperate to remain sober, these other gnawing problems kept pushing me over the edge. It seemed a complete mystery

William E. Swegan   137

to me how anyone could remain sober on the basis of what was actually talked about at these meetings.

Frankly, that was not a one hundred percent healthy group of people in the little A.A. group in Warren, Ohio, in 1946. But there were also some good and positive things going on. To begin with, they got the starting point right: they were not drinking. That has to be the primary rule in any workable recovery program, because until alcoholics stop drinking totally and completely for a reasonably extended period of time, there is not even a remote possibility of solving any of their other problems. There were good moral standards set, and this too is vitally important, and sometimes forgotten in present-day A.A. groups. Alcoholics need to have their superegos (their internalized sense of right and wrong) bolstered up in order to truly mend their lives effectively. And the use of vulgar language was taboo in A.A. meetings in those days.

Continual use of vulgar and obscene language is not a sign of good mental health, but instead a symptom pointing to a good deal of unresolved anger and hostility and mindless generalized rebelliousness against the whole world still buried down in the subconscious. Rules against the use of vulgar language began to be ignored in A.A. meetings during the 1960's, largely I believe because of the new influx during that period of people who had also been deeply involved with drugs, which meant that they were much more antisocial in their behavior, at a much deeper psychological level. I do not believe it has been healthy for the A.A. movement.

But the basic problem I was encountering in that context, was that I could not come up with any idea, from listening to the members of the little Warren group, about how A.A. could actually work. It was a two-step group. They dealt with the first step (powerlessness over alcohol) in their continual drunk-o-logues, and they tried to practice the twelfth step (carrying the message to others), but the other ten steps in the twelve-step program got almost no mention at all. There was very little said for example on the fourth step, that is, identifying and then learning to deal with our crippling resentments and fears, which I badly needed at that time, or on the steps used to heal our sense of guilt, which was almost totally overwhelming me at that time, even if I had great difficulty consciously admitting it.

And above all, I could not make myself identify with them. When I saw similarities between their drinking and mine, I simply dismissed these parallels. Whenever I could point to someone else's story and say, "but this never happened to me," I used that as a basis for denying that I myself had a problem. I continued to believe that alcoholism was "a problem of other people." When I am talking to newcomers nowadays, I try to continually stress that the psychological and physiological and genetic problems for each alcoholic will always be a unique mix of different factors. I emphasize to them that you may not in fact have drunk the way I did, and you may not have had the same particular subconscious conflicts that I was struggling with, but that you are strongly advised not to believe, simply because of this, that you do not have a major problem with alcohol. What you have to ask yourself is what alcohol has actually done to you in your own life.

Your psychological makeup will almost certainly be different from mine. Your genetic and family and social background may be strikingly different from mine. With some people, it is mostly a physical addiction, with no truly major internal psychological conflicts and problems, and no genetic history of alcoholism in their families. On the other hand, in the long run alcohol does not ultimately differentiate between its victims. It will always eventually shatter the lives of all those who become addicted to its compulsive and destructive nature.

I wish somebody had told me that back in 1946. As it was, however, I did the best that I knew how to do, and in fact managed to achieve almost three months of sobriety while going to the A.A. meeting in Warren. My ex-wife had told me she would remarry me if I remained abstinent for a year, and this was one of the driving motivations which kept me going to that meeting, and kept me away from the bottle. Unfortunately, no one ever gets permanently sober for the long term in A.A. if it is being done to win the approval of some other human being, no matter who that human being is—a spouse, a parent, a commanding officer or boss, a good friend, or whoever. If we try that, we simply put our lives back under the control of external forces which we will never be able to totally control. I had to learn that the hard way.

One day I ran into my ex-wife by accident on a bus, and she told me that she had now changed her mind about that promise she had made. Even if I stayed sober, she had decided that she never ever wanted to be in a marriage with me again. My greatest subconscious fear, that of being totally rejected and abandoned by those I loved, had not only come to pass, but I could no longer deny or avoid knowing that the rupture was permanent and irredeemable. I felt like I was at a total emotional bottom.

I quit my job, and eventually found myself hitchhiking to Cleveland, Ohio. On an impulse there in Cleveland, I decided to reenlist in the Air Force. I took the physical and passed, but then had to wait until my orders were cut.

I hitchhiked on to Toledo, Ohio, and ended up on skid row. It was there that the grim realities of life as an alcoholic hit me. I was cold, hungry, destitute, and sleeping wherever I could find a place to curl up. And it was the way I felt inside that was the worst of all. In some ways each alcoholic is unique, but at a more fundamental level all alcoholics are the same: genuine chronic alcoholism always progresses, and our external lives always keep on getting worse and worse over the long run, and our inner psychological misery always keeps on building up inexorably higher and higher. The bitterness, resentment, self-pity, anxiety, guilt, regret, and feeling of anguished futility finally tumbles around in your tortured mind non-stop and gives you no rest by day or by night. And it has to be labeled "alcoholism" because the crucial factor in driving us onward to our final doom is drinking *alcohol*. Until the drinking stops, no one ever gets better.

Life on skid row is the ultimate in total depression. It is a symbolic total capitulation to the disease. It is giving up in terminal despair. It can be a dirty, run-down section of a big city, where derelicts with greasy hair and grimy clothes sleep on newspapers in alleys and drink cheap fortified wine out of bottles in paper bags. But skid row is above all a place in the mind. If you the reader think you may have a problem with alcohol, remember that above all: your body can be living in a mansion in the most expensive part of town, while your mind is living on skid row. I can see it in newcomers in their eyes. Their clothes do not matter, their worldly positions and rank in society do not matter. When you see the numb despair in their eyes, the pain and hatred and hopelessness, you know that down deep inside they are living on skid row.

I physically escaped the alleys and the cold and hunger at that point when my orders finally came through. I was assigned to the Reserve Training Base at Romulus, Michigan, and had a warm bed to sleep in again and food to eat. Romulus is part of the greater Detroit metropolitan area, about halfway between downtown Detroit and Ann Arbor over to the west. In spite of my drinking, I had never in fact been reduced in rank during my Air Force career. I had been made a First Sergeant back in June of 1942, which in those days was a rank between Staff Sergeant and Technical Sergeant. The Air Force ranking system had been changed by that point, so that someone who functioned as the first sergeant of a unit was now usually given the rank of Master Sergeant. So when I first reenlisted, I was automatically and unthinkingly assigned the rank of Master Sergeant, the top-ranking sergeant's position. I got to parade around with these stripes and rockers on my sleeve for three weeks before someone realized the error and I was dropped down to Technical Sergeant. My hour of glory was extremely short-lived. I was not going to make the Master Sergeant rank honestly until much later on, after I had started taking A.A. seriously and actually stopped my drinking for good.

Since Romulus was a reserve base, nearly all of the flying was on weekends. There was not that much to do the rest of the week. I was put in charge of the flight records of the reserve officers, which was monotonous and required no real skills. After that short, frightening stretch living on skid row in Toledo, Ohio, my life seemed to have once more settled into its old pattern of monotony and boredom and too much drinking. Physically I was no longer on skid row—I had a job, clean clothes to wear, a warm bed to sleep in, and good food to eat—but deep down inside my mind I had never left that place. I started to drift again, simply existing, without meaning or purpose. Mainly I just felt numb inside, and no longer cared about anything really. It was either that, or be overcome with self-pity, bitterness, guilt, self-loathing, and despair.

It was going to be another two years before I finally began to understand more about how the A.A. program had to be worked, and became willing to make the total inner commitment—just for myself and not in the attempt to win anyone else's love or approval—that is required in order to genuinely work the twelve steps.

CHAPTER 11

The Blonde in the Merry Circle

So I was back in the Air Force again, stationed at the Reserve Training Base at Romulus, Michigan, about twenty miles west of Detroit. It was the last day in April in 1946. That night I went into a bar called the Merry Circle. I was alone, and ordered a drink. A beautiful blonde lady was waiting tables and came over to serve me. We began chatting, and it was a strange case of instant attraction. Somehow or other, we just seemed to fit.

I drank too much, as usual, and left without my hat. Losing your hat in the military was a no-no. I had drunk myself into enough of a blackout, that I could not remember the name of the night club, even though the indelible picture of the lady who had waited on me was still stuck in my mind. Her I could not forget. So I went searching the next day, and by a stroke of luck found the Merry Circle and retrieved my hat. But that was the least important part of this mission. I asked the people working there about my waitress and found out that this was her day off, but I also found out when she would be back on duty.

The following Monday, three days after our first meeting, I walked into the Merry Circle once again, and found her right there at the front door, checking identifications. We talked and talked all that night, continuing on long after her shift was over. Ann was the widow of the first trumpet player with the famous Xavier Cugat band, which was the best-known Latin music group in the country at that time: rumbas and sambas, and conga drums, and music that Americans all over, Hispanic or not, loved to listen to. Her deceased husband's friends in the night club business had gotten her this job so she could support herself and her two little boys. She showed me their pictures, and I told her how special children were to me. And we kept on talking, about things that were more and more personal.

Finally, out of a clear sky, I asked Ann to marry me, and she agreed! I had no transportation, so we took her car and headed off for Bowling Green, Ohio, to get married. This was May 2, 1946. We were married for over fifty-three years, until her death just three and a half years ago.

In those days an enlisted man had to get permission from the Commanding Officer to marry. The official position was often along the lines of "If the Air Force wanted you to have a spouse, we would have issued you one." But I called my CO from Bowling Green to ask his permission. His response was a little different from what I had expected, and rather amusing: "You are going to get married anyway, so go ahead." Upon returning to the base, he asked me what prompted me to get married. I quickly replied, "Love."

In fact—and I hate to spoil the fairy tale atmosphere of this story—Ann had been left widowed with two small children, and was frightened to death about trying to raise them on her own. She was needy and insecure, and would have said "yes" at that point to the first man who showed any interest in her at all. And in my own way, I was no different. I would have clung desperately to any woman who showed me any attention at all. Two insecure and needy people, who are both deeply afraid of any kind of rejection and abandonment, and petrified at the thought of having to make it through life on their own, do not make good marriage partners. This is part of the dilemma of the alcoholic marriage: both the alcoholic and the non-alcoholic partner will have their own personal problems, equally deep and equally difficult to handle. Ideally, both partners will become involved in their own recovery programs, and will begin learning how to deal more positively with their own internal issues, but even at best, each partner is apt to have times when he or she will have to struggle to deal with what is happening at that period in his or her life.

Nevertheless, Ann and I did stay married through thick and thin for over fifty-three years, all the way to the end of her life, even though it was sometimes not quite like the stories in the fairy tales. She died on January 10, 2000, of pneumonia resulting from a cerebrovascular accident (what is commonly called a stroke). The last few years of her life, when her mind began to slip progressively, were especially troubled ones for her, and I grieved for the inner torments she was suffering, and sometimes had to use every single tool and device the A.A. program had taught me to keep going myself. But I loved my wife very much and still miss her terribly. I only wish that she could have been reading this book as we were writing it.

But to return to the story, Ann and I had gotten married, but our situation was a difficult one. We had little money to live on and my drinking was a constant problem. Our military operations were transferred from Romulus, Michigan, to Selfridge Field, which required me to travel almost forty miles to work every day. We could not afford to move from where we were, because my wife had been living in a housing area in Wayne (only five miles from Romulus) where the rent was very reasonable. It took almost six months before I received the extra military allowance for quarters that came with my newly married status. The first payment did not in fact arrive until the day after Christmas, so that the two kids had to learn the meaning of Santa Claus one day late. I joined a car pool so I only had to drive one day a week. The rest of the poor people in the car pool never knew whether I would be drunk or sober the next time it was my turn to get behind the driver's wheel.

On the other hand, despite my drinking, the two kids and I got along very well. They seemed to like me from the start, and there was never any bickering over them. That was one of the nicest parts of my life.

During the Thanksgiving season, I obtained a furlough and worked part time in a factory near Dearborn, Michigan, in an attempt to cover some of our expenses. The day before Thanksgiving, the company gave everyone a turkey and half a day off. Of course this was also payday, which meant to me that I should go out and celebrate. After a few drinks in a friendly bar, I then went on home, but a big argument got started the minute I walked in.

I got mad, tucked the turkey under one arm, walked out in a huff, and proceeded to the nearest bar to really tie one on. I plopped the plucked dead turkey down on the counter of the bar and ordered a drink. After several refills my wife, who knew exactly where I had gone, walked into the bar, and demanded the turkey. The bartender suggested that she take both of us home, and Ann told him with disgust, "No, all I want is the turkey. You can have him."

Ann was a very good cook, but had had no experience with turkey before. On the advice of a neighbor, she wrapped the bird in a greased towel before baking it. It stayed in the oven for what we calculated was the proper length of time, and she took it out and we began slicing it. We could neither one of us figure out what had gone wrong, but it was the most "foul fowl" we had ever tasted. I myself suggested that we might be better off just throwing the turkey out, and eating the baked towel for Thanksgiving dinner.

To add to our problems at this time, my drinking had finally reached the point where I was neglecting my basic job responsibilities in especially serious ways. It was a Reserve Base to which I was assigned, which meant that the most important part of our responsibilities came on the weekends. The Reserve Officers came in from their civilian jobs, and spent the weekend flying to obtain their necessary regular flight hours. One weekend when I was scheduled for duty, I went on a drinking spree and failed to put together the necessary forms so the reserve officers could do their flying that week. Some had driven many miles to get in their required flight time, including some colonels, who were very angry.

The Commanding Officer had a long conversation with me, which included the threat of reducing me back to a private. In fact, if he had not basically liked me, my punishment would have been much more severe. He told me I was restricted to base for two weeks, which meant that I had to stay there at Selfridge Field and could not return home to my family. After four days, I told him that my family needed me, that this was creating serious difficulties for my wife and two small boys, and pleaded to have the restriction lifted. He felt pity for me and lifted the restriction. Terrified by this close call, I did in fact manage to stay out of trouble for the next few months.

The problem was, that it is in the very nature of the disease called alcoholism, that none of those who suffer from it can control or manage their drinking for much longer than that, simply because someone else is threatening the alcoholic with punishment or some other dire consequence. If you the reader are in a military command position, and are not an alcoholic yourself, this is important to remember. If you have personnel under your command who repeatedly get into drunken incidents, you can call them on the carpet and threaten them with severe punishments, and perhaps get a few months of improved behavior, *but it will not last very long.* You can easily fall into the illusion that if you simply made the scoldings or the threats or the actual punishments more severe, you could stop the person from drinking permanently. But in fact there is only one real solution: alcoholics can recover if and only if they are sent to a proper treatment program (and are sufficiently motivated to take advantage of that opportunity). Otherwise, as the alcoholic's commander, your illusions about the nature of alcoholism are in fact just as unrealistic as his or hers are.

Christmas of 1946 was not much fun. The kids begged for a Christmas tree, but they cost fifty cents, and I literally did not have fifty cents to pay for one. I went to a lot where trees were being sold, waited until the attendant who was selling them had his back turned, shoved one of the evergreens into the trunk of my car, and drove off rapidly. The kids were pleased and excited when I got home with my stolen property, but inside I was being overcome with guilt. I did not like the fact that I had now turned into a thief. Also, though we now had the tree, we had no trimmings to decorate it with.

Later that afternoon I borrowed some money and went to town and got drunk. You see what my scale of values had become: I could not get a Christmas tree for my own children by any honest means, but I would do whatever was necessary to get money for alcohol. I did not come home until many hours later, in the wee hours of the morning. I had somehow obtained a huge bag of popcorn from a movie theater. I suppose I initially thought we could get a needle and thread, and make popcorn strings to hang on the tree, but I was too drunk by then to handle anything that complicated. I simply got up on a chair and turned the bag of popcorn upside down over the top of the little evergreen. Some of it got hung in the needles of the tree, but most of it landed on the floor. My wife Ann was very upset over this episode!

The next day however, December 26, my first housing allotment check arrived in the mail. We felt like we were rich people. We went hog wild on our late Christmas celebration, and the kids had a ball. Even if Santa Claus had to come a day late, I am grateful to this day that my first Christmas with my two oldest boys ended up with them being able to enjoy it before the holiday season was all over.

We also discovered that our little family was going to become larger. Ann found out that she was pregnant, with the baby due in May. With two boys, our initial wish was that our third child be a girl. It did not matter at all, really, and we felt ourselves richly blessed when the third son was born. But this one was a difficult pregnancy for Ann: she had to go into the hospital several times because of false labor pains, and we both underwent a good deal of anxiety.

Due to threats from my Commanding Officer, I had stayed out of trouble for a while, but then, as we alcoholics always do, I got myself in serious difficulties with the military once again because of my excessive drinking. I decided to try going to a few A.A. meetings once more, this time in Detroit, Michigan. About eight years earlier, a man named Archie T. had started the first A.A. group in the Detroit area after spending six months living with Dr. Bob and Anne Smith in Akron and getting sober himself. Those were the real early days, and A.A. was still a brand-new phenomenon at that time.

For a few months, abstinence was the name of the game. But it was unfortunately much like my previous experience with A.A. I was physically present at the meetings, but I could not feel a part of the program. I felt set apart from the rest, in part because I was a G.I., since military people were often considered second class citizens in those days. I had suffered from feelings of rejection all my life, and I could not shake this feeling in A.A. meetings either. Eventually I had a relapse, and these then became more frequent. A.A. was not going to work for me this second time either.

But those were good meetings; I have no criticisms to make about what the people in the Detroit area were doing in 1947. Compared to A.A. meetings today, there seemed to be more compassion shown the new member. People flocked to me, to talk to me about my problems, and to give me support in my efforts to maintain sobriety. The problem this time clearly lay with me: I was so suspicious about everyone, that I could not really believe that they were sincere; and when they tried their best to be genuinely friendly, I simply shied away and held them at arm's length.

It still seemed a total mystery to me, how these people were staying sober. That of course was because, although I was physically present at the meetings, I never attempted to actually start practicing the twelve steps, nor did I take any kind of personal moral inventory. And in bizarre fashion, it was I who was always questioning whether these sober people were honest themselves. I would ask myself, "Are these people actually sincere in wanting to lead a sober, more productive life?" And my answer to that question was that I remained dubious about them, and about their own honesty, and their real motives.

In all the years since then, working with newcomers, I have found that this is a somewhat normal reaction for people who have ambiguous or clouded motives for attending the meetings. If I, as a newcomer, am refusing to commit myself absolutely to working the full program, and if I refuse to tell anyone else in the group the real truth about who I really am and what I am actually feeling, I will tend to assume that everyone else in the meeting room must be just as phony as I am. "If you are like me, then no sensible person in this whole world would totally trust you, or anything you say about yourself."

So since I insisted on continuing to play my old phony roles, and could not be truly honest with myself or anyone else, and was refusing to actually start working the twelve steps in my own life on an everyday basis, my second contact with A.A. did not work either. I was eventually drinking just as much as I ever had.

Then, fairly early on into 1947, I was transferred to Offutt Air Force Base at Omaha, Nebraska. I left my family in Wayne, and reported to my new assignment, intending to get the lay of the land before bringing them out. Omaha in those days was not one of my favorite towns. The stock yards were quite extensive, and the odor filled the air for miles. I had been given no advance information about what might be available in the way of housing for my family, but was hoping for the best. When I arrived however, I discovered that there was not only an acute shortage of housing there, but also frequently great animosity among the civilians toward military personnel. It was the first community I had encountered since my days in the San Francisco area prior to World War II, where the local people were so deeply anti-military. My wife was clamoring for me to find some housing so she and the children could come out to Omaha too, but I continued to have no luck in finding anything we could afford, and my drinking was again becoming a serious problem.

A truly nightmarish episode happened at that point. I was in a bar drinking one night. I was going in and out of blackouts, so I can only remember portions of what actually took place. Someone at the bar told me that my wife and children were in an automobile accident and that she had been killed. I reacted without doing any investigating, and called my Commanding Officer in the middle of the night and told him that I had to have an emergency leave. When the alcohol finally wore off enough for me to begin to think a little bit rationally and stop going into those intermittent blackouts, I was already on the road, driving to Detroit. After searching through my pockets, I found orders stating that I had been granted the emergency furlough. That at least was a relief: I had not gone absent without leave from my base.

But then I picked up a hitchhiker who was standing by the road, and once he was in the car with me he pulled a gun on me, and barked out the order, "Take me to Detroit." Well this was no problem, I assured him. That was where I was going too, and he was welcome to come with me. To my surprise, he did not give any indication that he meant to harm me in any way, but apparently was just very desperate to get to

Detroit himself. When we arrived there, he got out of the car, actually thanked me for taking him, and then took off. It is nevertheless difficult to exaggerate the relief you feel once you are no longer alone in a car with a gun-wielding man, who is so mentally unbalanced that you have no way of truly predicting what he might do next.

You especially cannot imagine the additional relief I felt when I discovered my wife and children were actually safe and sound, and completely unharmed. But we also decided that she and the boys were not going to stay one minute longer in Michigan. We packed what little belongings we possessed and called the moving van to pick them up.

When we began driving back, the closer I got to Omaha, the more nervous I became. I realized that the furlough had been granted under false pretenses, but also recognized that going in to my Commanding Officer and saying, "But a man at a bar where I was drunk out of my mind said that this was what had happened," was not going to be an acceptable justification. And in fact, my Commanding Officer was furious and told me that I was a disgrace to the human race, and that if there were any other problems from me, I would be a private on the spot.

And the worst was yet to come. At first we could find no housing anywhere, and all of us had to sleep in the car for the first week there. Then I found us a place to live in what was actually a converted roller skating rink, which had been cut up into tiny apartments. There were few conveniences in these primitive living quarters, and the family was uncomfortable and miserable.

The building had never been designed for anyone to actually live in on a full time basis, so the heat was unbearable until the cold weather came, and then we almost froze. There was no insulation of any sort to provide protection from the freezing winds. The weather in Omaha is brutal in the winter: on some days it is quite possible to freeze to death fairly quickly if you are caught outside for too long, even with normal winter hat and coat and scarf on. This is out in the Great Plains, where the shaggy-haired buffalo used to roam across the trackless prairies, pursued through the endless snows by packs of savage wolves. In fact, a crack at the bottom of our front door frequently provided us with our own personal snow drift, heaped up inside our living room, as the wind howled outside. And we had the new baby, our third child.

The landlord would not buy coal for the furnace, so one night while intoxicated, I went into the basement and took a lot of the furniture he had stored there, and broke it up and tossed it in and burnt that to keep us from freezing. The next morning, when he found out what I had done, he was furious, but we reported him to the Health Department, and he finally got the message and ordered some coal for us to use.

One time my wife was sick in the middle of the night and a doctor had to be contacted. Reluctantly he made a house call. His price for that was five dollars, he explained. After he had treated my wife, I asked him if he would like a beer. He readily accepted my offer, and one drink led to another. When he finally left, he and I were both thoroughly drunk, but he did not charge me anything for the house call!

It was a great relief when, after only about a year in Omaha, I was selected for a new position at Mitchel Air Force Base on Long Island, just outside New York city. The engine on our car went out just before our departure, but the Red Cross, an organization which I have always held in high esteem, provided us a loan to get the engine overhauled and make the trip. Even then, we had to just limp across the country, all five of us and our belongings packed into that rundown old car—one of us still a baby in diapers—plagued by continuous mechanical problems.

That was such a long time ago, and we were all so terribly young then. The little baby in that car is fifty-six years old now. When I did my fourth step in A.A. later on, I had to come to terms with all the things I had been doing wrong in my life during those years, but looking back on it now, I also realize that, in so many other ways, we were all just doing the best we knew how.

We stopped off in Ohio to visit my family, but there was a lot of tension. I was still made to feel like an outcast, and we decided to cut this visit short. I left them, once again feeling totally rejected by the people I loved most. We stopped off next in western Pennsylvania, where my wife's family lived. They stayed there while I went on to New York to find living quarters for us, which took several months. Military people everywhere were plagued by that problem: the salaries we were paid were too low to afford most civilian housing.

I was having more and more problems with the physical difficulties which are associated with alcoholism. I suffered from constant hangovers, and began to develop the shakes if I had no alcohol in my system. My wife was eventually driven to contacting my Commanding Officer, and complaining about my drinking and how it was affecting her and the family. He in turn threatened to have me reduced in rank if I did not quit my errant behavior.

In fact I knew that my drinking had gotten totally out of hand. Down at the subconscious level at least, I was suffering from massive guilt over this, and I began to experience periods of total hopelessness. I loved the Air Force and I did not want to become a casualty because of my inability to stay sober. But I did not think I could actually get sober and stay sober, and I certainly did not intend to change my basic lifestyle in any way.

I decided to start going to A.A. meetings again. This was the third time I had tried the program. Again I initially found it totally mystifying. I thought that somehow or other I could go to meetings and that in some magical fashion I would learn how to stop drinking, without changing anything else I was doing in my life.

What the A.A. people in fact kept on telling me was that I had to change everything about the way I was living my life at that point, including my most basic attitudes and my everyday behaviors, with numerous suggestions and examples of the kinds of things I needed to do. I quite literally did not hear a thing they said about that kind of issue: it just went in one ear and out the other, without leaving any conscious memory behind at all. If you asked me what the people talked about at any particular A.A. meeting, even five minutes afterwards—even if the entire meeting had been spent talking about one of the ways we could change the way we lived our lives—I could not have told you a word they said. I would remember at most a few fragments of conversation, mostly totally irrelevant, or completely off the point, or remembered only in garbled or distorted fashion. Or if I did remember something they said about us having to change the way we were living our lives, I would "explain it away" as something that did not apply to me.

Alcoholism is in part a disease of perception. In fact, most human psychological problems arise from issues of perception. Relationship problems are also created by this same factor: two human beings perceive the same events differently, and then come into conflict with one another as a result.

Psychologically I was forced to totally block out most of what was said at the A.A. meetings, because consciously hearing what they were saying would require me to look at myself and the way I was actually living now. I would be forced to radically reevaluate my own perceptions. And I could not stand to do that. My subconscious mind believed that the guilt would be too painful to stand. So my psychological defense mechanisms would click into place, and I would avoid actually hearing a single word.

This is part of the mystery of human perception: we can normally only see and hear and consciously feel things that fit into our preexisting mental frameworks, even if that framework is seriously distorted by subconscious guilt. Something that does not fit into that already established framework will usually be as though it literally did not exist at all. Therefore to make it in the A.A. program, everyone must first reach a decisive point which is called by various names: hitting bottom, surrendering, making a real commitment, undergoing a total inner psychic change, or whatever. When I am writing for Employee Assistance Program publications, I call it "becoming motivated." To accomplish this, there must be a fundamental shift in the basic foundations of all our perceptions of the universe. Sometimes this happens when we finally encounter something so big, so grand, or so marvelous that we cannot ignore it, even though it does not fit anywhere at all into our previous belief system. At other times, the preexistent framework of our beliefs may have to be demolished quite brutally. We may have to have the ground jerked out from under us. But some sort of fundamental ground shift has to occur before our perceptions are altered, and we can begin looking at ourselves and the world around us through new eyes.

―――――――――――

The A.A. group I was attending met in Valley Stream, a town in the western part of Long Island. In fact, it is only about sixteen miles as the crow flies from the heart of New York city. One of the members of the group, Warren T., agreed to become my sponsor, and became a constant mentor. He was there when I needed him, and was a constant source of assistance.

I was not very cooperative however. So when my wife and I came to have particularly acute financial difficulties, I went off the deep end and started drinking again. She called Warren, and he came over to our house. I was not thrilled to see him there, because I had been drinking all morning, and was now scheduled to travel over to New Jersey to play baseball at MacGuire Air Force Base. I exchanged a few words with him, and then took off, leaving him there to deal with my wife, who was obviously in a total state by that point. He in turn was obviously very upset with me, and no one could have blamed him.

Warren was a good man though, and did not give up on me. I went with him to more of their weekly meetings. The intelligent thing to do, of course, is to make it the first time around. Why would an intelligent person make himself go through what I had to go through for those two years? Nobody in A.A. regards people who keep on going back out and drinking again as heroes. Nevertheless, I am living proof of one old A.A. piece of advice: if you do not make it the first time in A.A., go back to meetings again. If you do not make it the second time, go back to meetings again. No matter what happens, keep on going back to meetings, even if you have to drag yourself back, crawling on your hands and knees.

CHAPTER 12

Getting Sober:
July 5, 1948

I felt trapped in a situation from which there seemed to be no exit. All I knew how to do was to keep on drinking more and more, in a world where everyone seemed to be against me. I struggled this way and that way, but could never seem to break through the walls which surrounded me on every side. Everything I tried to do ended up in bitter failure, and there seemed no way out. I seemed doomed to drive away everyone I had ever loved, and then to drink myself to death in despair over my fate.

But my sponsor Warren continued to stick with me, and I kept on dragging myself back to meetings. And the people in the little A.A. group in Valley Stream, Long Island, never turned me away when I kept on walking back through their door having failed yet again. They were certainly not happy with me, but they did not cast me out and never made me feel as though they wanted me to just go away and never come back again. And even I had to admit eventually that they clearly cared what happened to me.

For people whose minds are as full of emotional conflicts as most alcoholics, we will find that we cannot change our perceptions of the world (and of ourselves) until there has been some enormous shifting of the foundations upon which our perceptions are based. In fact, almost every recovered alcoholic whom I have ever talked to can pinpoint, almost to the moment, when that decisive ground shift occurred for him or her. But since every alcoholic is to some degree unique, this shifting of perspective can take very different forms.

For some alcoholics it can seem in some ways like an old-fashioned traditional religious conversion experience. Mrs. Marty Mann, who was to be my mentor later on when I was setting up my first military alcoholism treatment programs, had been confined in 1938 as a hopeless alcoholic herself in Blythewood, a psychiatric center in Greenwich, Connecticut, for over five months, and her case seemed untreatable. But at the beginning of January in the winter of 1939, her psychiatrist, Dr. Harry Tiebout, obtained a multilithed typewritten copy of a pre-publication draft of the A.A. Big Book, and suggested that she start reading it. At first, reading the book had no more effect on her than going to A.A. meetings had had on me, until one day she became so angry at the business manager of the psychiatric center that she stormed up to her room, literally seeing red. She had decided to go out and get two bottles of whiskey, get thoroughly drunk, and then come back and kill the business manager with her bare hands and wreck the place. (I know that those who knew that extraordinarily elegant and impressive lady may find those lines unbelievable, but that is what alcohol does to even the best of us.)

Suddenly her eyes fell on that copy of the Big Book lying open on her bed, and in the middle of the page she saw one line which seemed to be carved out in big, raised, black letters standing out above the rest of the page: WE CANNOT LIVE WITH ANGER. The next thing she knew, she was down on her knees, weeping into the bedspread until it became soaking wet, and praying. She felt a presence in the room which filled the whole room with a sense of life and light streaming in, the presence of something which she later came to call God. She was an active member of the A.A. fellowship from that point all the way to the end of her life in 1980. I will always be grateful to her for the backing and support she gave to me when I was setting up military alcoholism treatment programs at Mitchel and Lackland Air Force Bases.[8]

But most alcoholics do not experience anything like the extremely vivid phenomena which she did. If we look at the two original founders of A.A., Bill Wilson had a spiritual experience as extraordinary as hers at the time of the decisive crisis in his life, but Dr. Bob did not. Dr. Bob, A.A. Number Two, went out on one last drunken binge at the annual convention of the American Medical Association, then came to his senses and realized what he was doing to himself. In fact, Bill insisted that Bob down one last bottle of beer to steady his hands so he could go in and perform the rectal surgery which he had scheduled at St. Thomas Hospital on June 10, 1935. That is the official date of A.A.'s birth as a movement, because Dr. Bob never drank again after that. That morning, he had said to Bill, "I am going through with this." Bill, puzzled, asked if he meant the scheduled surgery, and Bob told him that too, but more importantly, "I'm going to do what it takes to get sober and stay that way." So that is the way Dr. Bob described the fundamental shifting of the foundations, the moment of crisis and decision in which he changed the whole basis of his perception of the world, and as a consequence, the whole subsequent course of his life: "I am going through with this." It was an act of real commitment, a fundamental reorganization of his priorities. Everything else he wanted or thought he needed was now made subordinate to that one overriding concern.[9]

Each alcoholic is unique, so there are many other ways that the shifting of the foundations can take place. Even then though, most recovered alcoholics can tell you, almost to the exact moment, when the crucial shift occurred. Some found themselves given up for dead, by both the medical doctors and everyone else around them, and then made the simple but elemental decision, "I want to live." And with every last bit of their failing will, and against all the odds which seemed to be implacably stacked against them, with the aid of some incomprehensible healing force which they called their Higher Power, they fought and lived.

Others, greatly blessed, walked through the door of their first A.A. meeting and heard the easy laughter and saw the joy on the faces of the people in the A.A. meeting, or felt the enormous love there—for that is something you can feel—or they felt "the spirit of the tables," which is the presence of that extraordinary superhuman healing power which is somehow part of the atmosphere of a good A.A. meeting. And these people made the instant decision, "I will do whatever it is they say they do." Because they wanted what they saw or felt at that meeting, literally more than anything else in the entire world. And that transformed and reshaped all their other perceptions of themselves and the world from that point on, and they could put the bottle away, and no longer found themselves compelled to drink. And they can usually tell you the day, the hour, and almost the exact minute when this shifting of all their mental foundations occurred.

In my case, I can tell you exactly when it happened, and the way it happened for me. It was July 5, 1948. I was standing in front of a mirror, and I looked at myself, and actually said aloud these simple words, "I am unacceptable to myself." It was an incredibly simple, but utterly gut-level realization. I was suddenly totally appalled by who and what I had actually become. The whole framework of my life, my attitudes, and my thoughts collapsed within me when I suddenly saw clearly what all my old beliefs had led me to. I became willing for the first time to actually *work* the twelve steps and throw myself wholeheartedly into the A.A. program. And I have never felt it necessary to take a drink since that day, almost fifty-five years ago.

If you the reader are an alcoholic who is still drinking, neither I nor anyone else can tell you—with your own totally unique set of problems and life experiences, and your own particular mix of psychosocial, genetic, and physiological contributing causes, and your own individual pattern of self-destructive drinking—exactly how you can reach this point, or exactly what form that basic shifting of the foundations is going to have to take with you. But I can tell you that you are going to have to let some sort of light, or realization, or insight, or overwhelming spiritual reality, break in on you from without. You will not be able to produce it from within yourself by clever thinking, or long reading of weighty books on psychology or theology, or "being more careful about your drinking," or practicing greater control over your consumption.

A.A. seemed a complete mystery to me until that day when I stood before the mirror, and *actually looked at myself.* If you the reader are an alcoholic who is still drinking, this may be the only thing I can say that might be useful to you. You will need to quit looking all the time at other people and how they behave. It does not really matter whether they are good people or evil people, whether they are intelligent people or impossibly wrong-headed and misguided. It does not matter whether they accept you with open arms, or totally reject you and abandon you. It will do you no good to be filled with envy over the good things they have, or to say or do things to get even with them for the wrongs you think they have done to you, or "show them" what you really think of them. One way or another, you are going to have to do the equivalent of standing in front of a mirror and looking at yourself, and yourself alone, bracketing out and ignoring everything else in the world.

When I finally was willing to do that on July 5, 1948, the real truth of my own existence hit me with that bitter realization: "I am unacceptable to myself." In order to set up totally new foundations for my life, the old foundations had to be completely destroyed. That was the day I fundamentally died to my old way of life and was born to a new way of life, even though I did not realize the latter at the time. There on that day, it seemed only a totally negative thing, leaving me psychologically naked and with nothing left at all in my possession. Stunned and rather numb, the only thing I could figure out to do was to keep on going to A.A. meetings.

This of course was exactly what I was supposed to do. The difference now was that I actually listened to what they said and heard their very simple suggestions and began actually acting on them in my everyday life. That was all it really took—it is a very simple program—and I never was compelled to take a drink of alcohol again. It is now almost fifty-five years later. The story of the first thirty years of my life was the tragic story of a young man set on a course of complete self-destruction. The story of the years which followed reads like a totally different book with a totally different central character. Of all the gifts which the A.A. program gives us, this is perhaps the greatest gift of all: the power to completely change the story of our lives, the power to rewrite the script, the power to change the way the story ends, the power to completely reinvent, not only ourselves, but the very way we perceive everything in the world around us.

I threw myself into the A.A. meetings now. Our lives in New York took on a new meaning. I began to enjoy the freedom that is associated with sobriety. Despite our financial hardships, and the many emotional frustrations still remaining, through the help of many dear civilian friends there on Long Island my life took a dramatic turn for the better.

I am sure the basis for many of us staying sober was the close relationship we had in that little A.A. group. There were dances, picnics, and other social gatherings that kept us a close knit organization. I could air my problems with almost anyone else in the group, and I would get support and a feeling that they genuinely cared about my family's future. That was part of the essential spirit of the Valley Stream group: a sincere desire on the part of most of the members to be of assistance to the new people, as well as anyone who might be having difficulties. The closeness of the members made us look forward to the meetings.

It changed many other things in my world. GI's were used to being regarded as second class citizens by most of the civilians in the areas surrounding their bases. They had no voice in local government, and rarely could they purchase anything on credit. So we GI's tended to be rather reserved in our dealings with them.

Having civilians in the area around our base offer us real, openhanded, generous help was a totally new experience for us military personnel. As I began spreading the message among other alcoholics there at Mitchel Air Force Base, and taking them to A.A. meetings at Valley Stream and Hempstead and other towns in the vicinity of our base, all of us found a friendly, welcoming atmosphere. The civilian A.A. members were outgoing, and extended us the kind of support which made us feel like we truly belonged. It removed our feelings of rejection and isolation, and helped turn our lives around.

The meetings in those days were somewhat different from the present ones. There were both open meetings, and closed meetings for alcoholics only, just as there are nowadays. But the format was different. There was no reading of the preamble at the beginning, for example. On the east coast, in and around New York city, we introduced ourselves by saying, "My name is _____ ; my sobriety date is _____ ." In those days, I think that introducing yourself by saying, "My name is _____ ; I am an alcoholic" was more Midwestern, and may have come out of Akron, but I am not sure. When I went out to California later on, in 1965, and would introduce myself in meetings by giving my name and sobriety date, people just thought I was doing that because I was bragging, so I switched over to the other style.

I do not really think that things like this are very important though. When people in A.A. begin worrying too much about this sort of thing, it becomes like the kind of traditional dogmatic religion where the members are terrified that they will be condemned if they use the wrong word in some ritual phrase. A.A. is concerned with spirituality, and was not intended to be some new, rule-bound, legalistic set of doctrines and dogmas and complex rituals. No one ever resolved crippling subconscious conflicts, nor do people ever heal the resentments, fears and guilt which are destroying their happiness and their lives, by repeating a handful of mechanical words and phrases over and over. You remember that I had learned how to "say words" in A.A. meetings back in Warren, Ohio, in 1946, but I still kept on feeling bad about myself, and after less than three months, went back to drinking again.

One thing I do miss about those days, is that almost without exception, there was a prohibitive attitude toward the use of foul language in the meetings.

Although the members were overwhelmingly male, there were already a few women members. Mrs. Marty Mann's example was starting to be followed by a few other female alcoholics, although nothing yet like the present day. There was a strong ethic present in those early groups: women who came into the program were absolutely not to be talked down to or treated in any kind of patronizing manner. Above all, it was a point of honor that the male members not come on to them sexually or try to make passes at them. When the women's liberation movement began to become a major force in the United States in the 1970's, I discovered that I had already been thoroughly sensitized to these vital issues by my participation in early A.A. during the late 40's and 50's. I sometimes come across as a modern-day "women's libber" myself, with my insistence on the use of inclusive language, and sensitivity to the feelings and issues of women alcoholics, but these were attitudes which I was taught (and learned for myself) back in the old days in early A.A., long before the modern women's liberation movement really began achieving any widespread public notice in this country.

An atmosphere of secrecy prevailed at all times. People would sneak into the meeting places, rather than walking in with total unconcern about who might see them. Anonymity was a major issue, because alcoholism was not considered a disease or illness in those days. It was people like my mentor Marty Mann, the founder of the National Council on Alcoholism, who had to lead the crusade to change the American public perception of alcoholism in that regard. People who were gainfully employed had to protect their jobs, and knew that if the word spread that they were going to meetings for "alcoholics" that they could easily lose their employment. There were no Employee Assistance Programs operating in the workplace, and the unions had not yet geared up to deal with this problem. As a result, each employee was left totally to his or her own devices in seeking help.

I truly believe that there was much more empathy toward the person seeking help in those days than there is at present. A new member was given undivided attention. One person might be chosen as the individual's official sponsor, but many of the members who had some time in the program could be counted on for a friendly ear and useful advice. There were very few A.A. groups back in 1948, and the number of members was greatly limited: we were still very much a small, struggling movement scattered in little pockets here and there around the country. Those who had already been sober for a while went to great efforts to provide the new members with a sense of belonging. In terms of the feeling of acceptance which was extended to newcomers, and the effort undergone to make them feel like they belonged, early A.A. was much more intense than the present-day program.

Current A.A., by comparison, has a tendency to ignore new members. There is usually not the same drive to include them and take them under the group's wing. I think this is because, in recent years, we have had too many people coming to their first A.A. meetings from treatment programs, or being forced by so-called court referrals.

The court referred people are in fact given no real choice about attending A.A. meetings. They will have been found guilty in court, one too many times, of drinking and driving, under rules which have in recent years become far more stringent about what constitutes impairment and can be prosecuted. A judge will give them the alternative of either getting slips of paper signed showing that they have attended so many meetings, or doing a long period of jail time. As a result they come into the meetings totally against their will and their own wishes. They tend as a result to be either withdrawn or disruptive in the group. They are not usually very receptive of assistance. In fact, more often than not, there is little desire to admit that any difficulty exists in their drinking behavior. A court referred person tends all too frequently to regard himself or herself as the victim of circumstances, instead of being the one who has the problem. Sometimes several subsequent incidents must occur before they finally become convinced in their own minds that they are indeed in the right place.

In the case of the people who start coming to A.A. meetings after first being in a treatment program somewhere, there is a tendency to assume that they already received everything they needed to know about getting sober there. And so we are apt to draw the false conclusion that it is unnecessary for us in the A.A. group to take these newcomers under our direct, personal care and show them by personal example how the program of Alcoholics Anonymous is actually lived on a daily basis.

Strangely enough, this assumption was even being made in the late 1980's and early 1990's when there was an over-proliferation of insurance-funded treatment programs which were often achieving no more than a 2% to 4% success rate. These tended to be over-psychologized operations, with too few people on their staff who were themselves recovered alcoholics, so in fact many of the patients who came out of these treatment centers knew very little about the A.A. program, and tended to believe that they could stay sober with psychological gimmicks alone. And insurance funds were so easy to obtain during that period, that all too many of the people who came out of those treatment programs had simply gone into treatment for a sort of temporary respite from their drinking. They were not really serious about wanting to stay sober on a permanent basis, so when they came to A.A. meetings, they could sometimes be almost as uncooperative and frivolous and fundamentally unmotivated as some of the court referred attendees.

As an additional problem, too many A.A. groups seem to still be assuming that the majority of new members will be coming in via treatment programs, and that they do not need to make old-fashioned twelfth-step calls to reach out to alcoholics who are still suffering, in spite of the fact that most of the new treatment centers which were established in the late 1980's and early 1990's have now gone out of business and are closed.

So why and how did people come into the A.A. program back in the early days? Most frequently, they themselves recognized that they had a problem, or their families pressured them to seek assistance. When they contacted us, we made a twelfth-step call on them to explain how our program worked and to invite them to join us.

There were also people whose employers sent them to Alcoholics Anonymous for help. There were no Employee Assistance Programs of the modern sort in 1948, but some supervisors here and there were aware of the A.A. program, and these more enlightened bosses would sometimes send employees to us, when the employees' drinking became a source of major difficulty on the job, and all the supervisors' other efforts had failed. There is more knowledge about alcoholism and its treatment in the workplace nowadays, but even then we had a few people in the business world who, though not alcoholics themselves, had a certain amount of very limited knowledge about the program of Alcoholics Anonymous and what it could accomplish. We were very grateful for them.

But in most cases, as far as their place of employment was concerned, we felt a primary need to protect alcoholics who came to A.A. from being identified in public as alcoholics. It could easily cost them their jobs.

Back in those days, when A.A. began, those of us who came into the program were hard core drinkers, who were already at least semi-convinced that we ourselves had a very big problem. We all realized at some level that we had reached the end of the line, and that this was our last, best hope. That made us more teachable, and more willing to commit ourselves totally. There was an intensity, a spirit, an atmosphere of mutual supportiveness and belonging, an incredibly positive attitude and pride in ourselves in the good sense, and an enthusiastic willingness to take on whatever challenges came along. We threw ourselves into the program and we had the time of our lives. Those were in fact good old days, and I am still so very grateful that I was there, and can treasure those memories.

The use of drugs was almost never mentioned back in early A.A. I do have to talk about that, in explaining what was different between then and now. Drug addiction had not yet become a major problem in this country, and I do not believe that there were very many dually addicted A.A. members at all in those days. That did not begin to affect A.A. in a major way until the 1960's and the Vietnam war era. I do in fact believe that people in our society who become involved with severely addictive drugs like heroin and crack cocaine are of necessity more antisocial than alcoholics. Alcohol use is legal, but drug addicts have to employ illegal means to procure their drugs, which is necessarily linked to profound differences in their attitude towards the world. As a result, the two groups—alcoholics and users of severely addictive drugs—have dissimilar behavioral problems.

At the surface level, one obvious change began to occur when increasingly greater numbers of dually addicted people (and people who were in fact basically drug addicts, even if they also used alcohol) began coming into Alcoholics Anonymous: cursing and offensive behavior was not permitted in early A.A. at all, but the standards began to be lowered more and more drastically as more and more drug addicts began attending meetings. Not just individual behavior but group behavior underwent a distinct change. My negative reaction to this is not just "old-fashioned prudishness" on my part. At a very profound psychological level, this relaxing of group standards meant the A.A. groups were no longer able to be so effective in strengthening the newcomers' ego defenses.

In those days, we understood far better that we were attending A.A. to improve our character. We knew that one of our basic tasks was to teach alcoholics how to fit in more smoothly with the standards of the society they lived in, so they could start to feel good about themselves. We knew that learning how to do this better would in turn remove a good deal of the psychosocial pressure which was a contributing factor in driving many of us to drink.

As someone who never was involved with drugs myself, I do not truly know the thinking nor the compulsive nature of the drug-oriented people from the inside. I find it personally more difficult to relate to, or counsel, a person who is either dually addicted or purely drug addicted. Nevertheless, by the end of my career in directing military alcoholism treatment programs (I retired from Alameda Naval Air Station in California in 1983), I was treating people with drug problems as well. They too needed help, and desperately. And I saw repeatedly that drug addicts who truly commit themselves to working all of the twelve steps unflinchingly and unreservedly can recover from the irresistible craving into which they used to fall. All that is necessary is to take the phrase in the first step that reads "we admitted we were powerless over alcohol" and replace the word alcohol with the words "our addiction."

But to return to Long Island and 1948: we held our meetings upstairs over the firehouse in Valley Stream. Then as now, you could not hold an A.A. meeting without an ample supply of coffee, so we took turns making the coffee for the group. One week it was my turn, and everything was going well. We were already halfway through the meeting when suddenly the sirens in the firehouse starting screaming at full blast, and the next thing we knew the firefighters came rushing up the stairs, burst into our meeting, and ran through the middle of our group and into the kitchen. It turned out that the coffee pot had boiled over and set their fire alarm off. So I became known as the one who created the fire alarm in the firehouse.

Warren T., as I have told you, was my first sponsor. The way he continued to stick by me was what got me sober at the beginning. I do not know whether I would have made it without him, and his patient persistence in working with me.

When he moved from the area, a veterinarian named Phil D. became not only my sponsor but a very close friend. He had a very successful practice. He and his wife Bea were generous, warm-hearted people who made it their project to help me and my family in every way they could. They would often come over and collect one or two of our boys, and take them back to their house to play with their son Jimmy. Without exception, our boys would come back home with new toys and clothes. It was against the normal rules for A.A. members to accept assistance like that from other A.A. members, but Phil and Bea would not take no for an answer, and to be honest, even a sergeant in the Air Force made so little in those days that we were very grateful for what this meant to the boys.

Phil and Bea and Ann and I became very close friends. We visited each others' homes and went on picnics together. While I was away at the Yale School of Alcohol Studies later on, they made it a point to drop by our home frequently to make sure my family was doing all right, which helped to relieve my apprehensions about being away from them for so long. And Phil and I went all over that part of Long Island—Hempstead and many other places in the area—speaking at A.A. meetings together. It was a very warm bond which we had.

It therefore caused me great sadness when I began to see signs that Phil and Bea were starting to slip in their allegiance to the program which was saving our lives. In fact, I had always had a certain suspicion that their real dedication was to their friendship with us, and that their commitment to the A.A. program was somewhat superficial. Phil was often rather quick to express doubts about the true benefits of belonging to the program, and would challenge other members on their beliefs. What made this so heartrending to me was that I liked both of them so much, and I did not want to see them slide back into their old, destructive way of life. When Phil and I were traveling around and speaking to other groups, he had talked enough about what it was like before he came into A.A. that I knew that returning to that would be catastrophic, for Bea as well as him.

After I was reassigned to Kent State in Ohio in 1951, and had to leave Mitchel Air Force Base, we continued to keep in contact for a while. We corresponded and exchanged phone calls quite often at first. But once we were separated by all those miles, the relationship began to weaken, and eventually we totally lost contact with them.

I did not find out what happened to them until many years later, when I was attending an alcoholism seminar in San Francisco, on the other side of the continent. There was a young man who was a member of the Air Force and was attending the same program, and I recognized at first glance that I somehow knew him, but was puzzled because I could not for the life of me remember when or where. But then when I heard him say there at the meeting that his name was Jimmy and that he came from New York, I instantly knew that he was Phil and Bea's son. When I went up to him afterwards, and asked him if he was Jimmy D. from Freeport, and then explained who I was, he almost fainted.

Sadly enough, it turned out that his father Phil had returned to drinking and then lost his veterinary practice as a result. His mother Bea had committed suicide. Phil ended up living in a Salvation Army treatment center, and eventually died there. They were such good people that this was a sad disclosure indeed.

Alcoholism is a killer disease, and the end can be nightmarishly dreadful. Alcoholics Anonymous, since its inception in 1935, has been the only method of treating this disease which has had very much success, and that only works well if people are motivated, and willing to commit themselves wholeheartedly, and continue to live in the program and practice its principles. But this does not mean that those who do not make it are bad people, or morally flawed and despicable. Phil and Bea were good people. I treasured our years of friendship, and I wept for the needlessly tragic way their lives ended.

There was an old A.A. slogan, frequently posted on the wall in meeting rooms: "There but for the grace of God go I." Somehow or other, my life was spared, and Phil's and Bea's were not. All I can do now is try to pass it on—what my life was like, what happened, and what it is like now—in the hope that alcoholics who still suffer can learn something from me that will spare them that kind of doom. It is a matter of life or death itself.

CHAPTER 13

The Road to Maturity

The ability to feel and act mature is a goal which we deeply desire. Small children try to imitate the adults around them. Little girls like to play dress-up with their mother's clothes. Children play at being cowboys, soldiers, doctors and nurses. They feel pleased and proud when they get to do things like drive a car for the first time. They want to feel "grown up." But truly acting like an adult is more than just clothes and games and activities. The degree of maturity which people genuinely possess is not necessarily determined by their calendar ages at all; it has more to do with what they have actually learned from their life experiences.

We do not begin life as mature adults, but as tiny infants. Sigmund Freud coined the phrase "His Majesty the Baby." Infants want things their way, and they want them right now. If they do not get what they want instantly, they scream and cry. If someone tells them "no," they grow red in the face and pound their fists. In July 1948, when I first started taking the A.A. program seriously, I was thirty years old according to the calendar, but at all too many places along the road to maturity, I had gotten stalled. Like His Majesty the Baby, I often wanted to be king and master of all I surveyed. If all my personal demands were not met on the spot, I all too often reacted by simply lashing out at whoever I felt was responsible for not complying with my selfish dictates. My behavior was basically childish and infantile.

What we human beings really want is to feel good. Feeling like an adult is an important part of feeling good, and learning how to actually act like a grown-up is one of the major ways we can achieve that goal of feeling good about ourselves. In my own case, I lacked the insight to feel good about myself. I was so immature emotionally, that I had no tools for living in the kind of way which is necessary for feeling the way I wanted to feel. So part of the time, I simply lashed out at the people who were not doing as I wanted them to do, and the rest of the time I collapsed back into a kind of numb and despondent attitude where my only real goal in life was simply to exist.

Part of my problem was that I was an alcoholic. My alcoholism and my immaturity were all tangled together. The effect of excessive alcohol intake on the brain keeps the mind from functioning in ways which will allow the normal maturation process to take place. And on the other side, the emotional conflicts created by my childish thought-processes put me in so much pain that I drank even more alcohol to try to escape.

———————————

In 1967, the physicians of the United States put themselves on record as supporting the disease concept of alcoholism: "Resolved, That the American Medical Association identifies alcoholism as a complex disease and as such recognizes that the medical components are medicine's responsibility." But the complexity of the disease meant that the physicians, with their pills and other medications, could in most cases treat only part of the problem.

In 1990, the National Council on Alcoholism and the American Society of Addiction Medicine adopted a joint definition of alcoholism which spelled out the nature of the problem in greater detail:

> Alcoholism is a primary, chronic disease with genetic, psychosocial, and environmental factors influencing its development and manifestations. The disease is often progressive and fatal. It is characterized by continuous or periodic: impaired control over drinking, preoccupation with . . . alcohol, use of alcohol despite adverse consequences, and distortions in thinking, most notably denial.

I can agree fairly closely with that definition. It was put together by those two organizations (the NCA and the ASAM) on the basis of what people like me had discovered from setting up alcoholism treatment programs over the preceding fifty years.

As the statement says, one of the components can be genetic. In my own case, that was almost certainly true. Although there was no abuse of alcohol in my immediate family while I was growing up, my grandfather had been a serious alcoholic. But since the genetic component in alcoholism is very strong, more likely than not this hereditary tendency simply skipped a generation before manifesting itself again in me.

The genes which are involved make you statistically far more likely to become an alcoholic, but do not guarantee that you will become one. Some individuals who are brought up in families where they are regularly exposed to severe alcoholism, and where genetic factors are almost certainly involved, nevertheless do not become alcoholics themselves. Some of these in fact react in the totally opposite direction. They develop a strong aversion to alcohol as a response, and not only do not drink alcohol at all themselves, but are strongly critical and antagonistic toward anyone who does imbibe. My father was like that, and it increased the tension between him and me when I began to abuse alcohol after my graduation from high school. When he saw me drunk and out of control, it triggered some of his own most traumatic childhood memories, of seeing his own father staggering into the house hopelessly drunk. Because of his own overpowering inner fears, he could not react to me properly, and I in turn read his response as just one more bitter parental rejection.

In my case, genes which I had inherited from my grandfather probably played a role in my vulnerability to the disease. But genetics alone could not provide the whole answer to my alcoholism. My seven brothers and sisters shared combinations of the same basic parental genes from which my own genetic makeup had been derived, which meant that by the law of averages some of them at least must have inherited the genes which created the tendency, and yet none of them became alcoholics. Only I did. So other causes—what the NCA and ASAM statement called "psychosocial and environmental factors"—had to have also been involved. There have to have been factors in the internal psychological dynamics of my childhood family, along with pressures arising from my interactions with the surrounding society, which also helped push me toward out-of-control drinking as a response.

And since each of us is a unique personality, there also will be a component which is totally individual. If you have worked with as many alcoholics as I have over the years, it becomes clear that identifying "good" vs. "bad" families (dysfunctional families we call them today) cannot come even close to providing full answers. In some instances, we find people who were in fact brought up within a fairly positive environment, but were unable to recognize its positive aspects, so that the opposite of the normal results were obtained. At the other extreme, we can also see some individuals who encountered many highly negative experiences during their childhoods, but were able to mature and enjoy a productive life in spite of this.

Now insofar as we are talking about me and my own alcoholism, it is extremely important to make one thing absolutely clear. My own background and circumstances influenced who I was, but I am responsible for who I became. I developed the habit of waiving my own responsibility, and insisted on blaming others for all my problems. If I go back to doing that now, I will quickly become once more what I was then.

I have had to ask myself what might have been going on in my family during my early childhood which might have contributed toward my ultimately becoming an alcoholic. But I also have to acknowledge that some crucial factor involved there has to have come from me, and me alone. Even though my seven brothers and sisters were brought up in the same home where I was, none of these factors had any negative effect on them. For some reason I alone developed both conscious and subconscious negative responses, not only toward our parents but also toward my siblings, and in some way I alone lacked the ability to appreciate the positive aspects of our home life. I would regard an event from a totally negative perspective, while some other member of my family would turn it into a positive learning experience. I did not seem to have the proper tools to implement a positive life style.

Again, it is vitally important to make it clear that I am not trying to evade my own personal accountability here, because it was in fact my own responsibility, then and now, to work out how to live a trouble-free life. I am merely trying to understand a little better what the issues were which I failed to learn how to handle properly back then. That is the only way I will ever be able to stay away from alcohol permanently. I have to learn how to identify it better when similar issues occur in my life today, so that I will not fall back once again into trying to deal with them the way I did back then.

All problems have an origin. I entitled this chapter "The Road to Maturity," because in the case of alcoholics, so many of our problems can be caused by conditions which arise at various points during the maturation process. An important part of healing our lives is therefore learning how to grow up, and how to start functioning as an adult.

The forces which will eventually lead people into becoming alcoholics can sometimes start affecting their lives from the very beginning. Personality clearly starts being formed from the moment of birth. In fact, some contend that this process begins *in utero*, before birth itself even occurs, so that external events which take place while the mother is still carrying her child can have an effect on the child's later behavior and response to the world. And what happens during the first two or three years of a person's life can also be very crucial.

I do not recall any of my own experiences from very early childhood which could have been responsible for some of the peculiarities of my later personality and ways of acting, nor have I been able to reconstruct any events from that very early period, by questioning by older brothers and sisters, which would account for the way I was. Nevertheless, the often radical differences between my responses to the external environment and those of my brothers and sisters, indicate that there must have been some decisive factors affecting me which did not affect them, or did not impinge on them in the same way.

The majority of people want to be loved and accepted, and I was no exception. If problems prevail which cause conflicts, a feeling of rejection may become a factor, a condition I was well aware of. Some children are in fact rejected from the beginning in certain ways by both their parents and the other members of the family. Their birth may have created some untenable circumstances, and the family in reaction spurns all their attempts to become a positive component of the family structure.

Although my siblings always contended that this was not the case in our family, I felt it was. When small children start competing for family love, and the more successful ones begin receiving far more than routine acceptance, this can create a serious division in the family. As a child I was constantly driven to seek extra praise and extra recognition as a means of feeling a part of the family circle.

One's family cannot in fact always be there to respond to one's wishes and demands. Sometimes it is simply not physically possible, in any realistic fashion, for the rest of the family to be there for support or help in certain kinds of situations. But each time something like this happened, from my own childish perspective, I interpreted it as a rejection of me personally.

My inability to control my temper created situations which caused disruption in the whole family from time to time. My anger invariably stemmed from my inability to control people, places, and things. When some negative circumstance arose, I became furious and turned this anger onto the rest of my family, which created enormous disharmony in my relations to my parents and brothers and sisters.

There were times, even back during my earliest years, when those outside the family circle provided me with the love and acceptance which was necessary to guide me back to something closer to a normal behavior pattern. I would have been in even worse shape than I was, by far, had it not been for one neighbor couple whom I mentioned when I wrote about my childhood. The wife would fix me doughnuts or pie or other special treats, and her husband would take me fishing with him. Between the two of them, I got fed and fussed over almost daily.

This is an area where becoming an active member of a warm, close A.A. group can become such an enormous help in the healing of an alcoholic's personality problems. Friends like this outside the family can often be effective in restoring us to a more harmonious relationship even with those within our families, which will ultimately heal many of those painful wounds which had originally been inflicted by our families.

It is not just the earliest childhood years which can create problems. In fact, during the process of maturation, some people may have lives that are almost problem-free during their earliest years. But then a sudden shift in family circumstances may alter the whole tenor of these children's lives, and change their whole attitude toward the world and begin eliciting negative behavioral responses.

Some of the most serious problems which arise during the maturation process can also be produced by factors totally outside the immediate family. In my work with alcoholics over the years, I have seen this repeatedly. Even people who are free of inner emotional conflict during the earlier parts of their childhood can encounter pressures from the society around them which can create personal problems later on.

In my own case, I think that external social pressures on my life played an important role for several years at a crucial point in my growing up, and that this was a major contributing factor in the development of my own problems. Because my family had so little money, I could not dress in the right clothes or point to the right kind of family car to feel good about myself within the sometimes rather vicious social ranking system of my high school. In addition, during that same period, my stepbrother not only caused enormous problems within the family itself, his actions also (at least in my perception at the time) caused us to be looked down on by everyone around us.

And there was another issue at one point, which I neglected to mention back in those chapters I wrote about my early years. When Adolf Hitler and his Nazi movement took over Germany, and he then began spreading his control over other parts of Europe as well, the United States tried to stay completely out of it at first. Nevertheless, during this period, people discussed and debated the issue continually. My stepmother was of German background, and publicly defended Hitler. She was certainly not the only person in the United States who refused to totally condemn him. Younger people nowadays tend to be surprised by this, but there were some respectable American figures, like Charles Lindbergh for example, and Frank Buchman, the founder and leader of the Oxford Group, who to a certain degree defended Hitler for a while. (This was one of the reasons why A.A. began separating itself as much as possible from the Oxford Group very early on. There were several other key reasons, but this was certainly one of the factors.)

Nevertheless, my stepmother's statements in support of Hitler and the Nazis did not go down well with most of the people in our small Ohio town. The whole family, including myself, found many people who treated us with aversion and contempt. I hated her for what she had brought down on the rest of us, and I felt desperately alone in trying to deal with the pervasive social animosity with which we all began to be targeted on many occasions. She was too German in her own attitudes and ways of dealing with people, and the rest of our family were pretty much typical Americans. What she was doing did not make any sense to the rest of us in the family. The problem for me though was there were too many other people in our small community who would not allow me to disassociate myself from her position.

Alcoholics who come from families which were excluded, rejected, feared, or looked down on by some of their neighbors for any kind of racial, ethnic, religious, or socioeconomic reasons, need to look at that as one possible factor in their feeling of rejection and alienation: being black, Jewish, Hispanic, or Native American; or being poor or speaking English with a foreign accent, can take its toll on children while they are growing up in many American towns and neighborhoods. Living as a child in a big Polish Catholic neighborhood, where you are the only Hungarian Catholic or you are the only Protestant of Scotch-Irish background, can cause the same kind of problem. Anything that makes a child feel "different" and not part of the group can produce feelings of alienation and rejection. If your parents came from very different backgrounds, that can introduce this destructive kind of mutually suspicious hostility and conflict into the family circle itself, and you yourself are apt to still bear some of those emotional scars.

Even positive attributes can cast a child into a minority status. Children who are motivated academically and do well in school, can be the target of a good deal of hostility on the part of their less able classmates. Some of the lesser ranking students, feeling like failures, may go to great lengths to viciously deride and make fun of the brightest children, in an attempt to tear them down and make them feel like inadequate failures too. An extremely beautiful young woman may be targeted by some of the other schoolgirls, who spread malicious false rumors and other derogatory remarks across the whole school. These things hurt, and they leave scars in later life too. Enormously successful adults who nevertheless feel like hopeless failures inside find their way into the ranks of Alcoholics Anonymous with surprising frequency.

But to return to my own story: I got stalled and stuck at many places during the normal process of maturation. In all too many areas of my life, I had failed to grow up and learn how to be an adult. The contributing factors were multiple. My immaturity needed to be addressed, but during my childhood and youth, there was actually no one at all I could have turned to, who would have been able to help me to deal effectively with my psychological and social problems. My internal conflicts were too great, and it would have needed someone with considerable professional skills, or the equivalent, to be of any real help to me at the basic underlying level. And the fact was that I did not recognize this at the time as *my* problem. I thought the problem lay totally in the area of other people's actions towards me, and that the only solution would lie in having everyone else around me change. I was very angry inside, because I felt like such a total victim.

This was one of the most important things that happened on July 5, 1948, when I looked in the mirror and saw myself honestly for the first time. I finally realized that the real crux of the problem lay in me. But crushing as that blow seemed at the time, it implied something enormously positive and potentially productive. It meant that I was not at all a completely helpless victim. My whole attitude and perspective changed to the core. If the real problem was me, then I could start trying to figure out some way to change me. I wasn't really totally helpless, and I was not at all condemned to be the perpetual victim of other people. The most important gift the A.A. program has to give us, is the gift of freedom. At the subconscious level anyway, I knew in that moment of deep insight that a path to freedom lay open to me for the first time in my life.

Truly sweeping changes began to take place in my life and my way of dealing with other people during the weeks and months that followed that decisive insight. My co-author at one point noted to me with amazement, that by September of 1948, as he put it: "You seemed to be a totally different person. I wouldn't even have been able to recognize that this was the Bill of the first thirty years of your life." And it was indeed true that I became a different person. I had made that crucial break-through that every suffering alcoholic has to make, in one way or another, in order to start the healing process. And although it is not always the case, with some alcoholics the major transformations then begin to occur with incredible rapidity. That was what happened with me: the dam broke and the mighty waters of change and healing, which had been held back for so long, swept through that break in an onrushing torrent.

At some point during my years of working with other alcoholics, I worked out a list of fifteen simple characteristics of a stable and mature person. I do not remember actually where I first got that list. I may have taken something I read somewhere, and then modified it on the basis of my own knowledge and experience. But at any rate, I have used this list for many years, both in talks to groups and in my one-on-one counseling work, to emphasize the need for a more positive approach to life, and to show alcoholics how they can escape from the devastating effects on their lives produced by their abuse of alcohol and other drugs. I think of it at this point as "my list."

The items in this list may appear excessively simpleminded to many when they first read them. They may seem trite and sometimes unbelievably corny. But in fact, most of an alcoholic's worst problems are surprisingly simple at heart, when you really try to describe the issues in ordinary language. In reality, even the most sophisticated and highly trained mental health professionals find that a good deal of their time working with patients in counseling sessions is spent trying to teach them how to better deal with these extremely simple basic human problems. Getting over-involved with exploring a patient's deep Freudian subconscious, or the appearance of Jungian archetypes in that person's mental imagery, or other sorts of complicated and subtle things like that, is not necessarily all that productive much of the time. You have a patient who in reality does not know the simplest things about how to act like a real adult in ordinary human life, and you have to figure out simple ways to lead him or her back into the maturation process, where the patient can learn how to get un-stuck from places where he or she got badly stalled back at some point in the growing-up process.

Tools for Personal Freedom
Fifteen Guidelines to Mature Behavior

1. Accept constructive criticism gratefully, and see it as a means for self-improvement.
2. Do not indulge in self-pity.
3. Control your temper.
4. Do not wear your feelings on your sleeve.
5. Meet emergencies with poise.
6. Accept responsibility for your actions.
7. Outgrow the all-or-nothing stage of life.
8. Accept reasonable delays without becoming emotionally frustrated.
9. Do not indulge in senseless worry.
10. Avoid being boastful in socially unacceptable ways.
11. Do not be envious of other people's successes.
12. Be open-minded toward other people's opinions, and do not feel you have to always be right.
13. Do not be a chronic fault-finder.
14. Plan things in advance, and avoid spur of the moment responses.
15. Vigorously defend your principles.

Learning how to use these fifteen simple guidelines effectively will produce a much happier and more trouble-free individual, and provide for positive interpersonal relationships. Help in learning how to use these "tools for personal freedom" is available in many of our present treatment programs, or through individual counseling. A good and wise A.A. sponsor can often be helpful here too.

It is vitally important for alcoholics to take all of these fifteen guidelines seriously as part of their recovery. Because of their inability to recognize that they too have human frailties, or because of a sense of false pride, some people continue to proceed along the road to self-destruction, unmindful of the fact that methods exist which can enable them to solve their dilemma. Help is available—if they are willing to swallow their pride and their fear of failure, and become willing to seek assistance for their problems.

A person also has to stop drinking, completely and totally, in order to work successfully on these issues. Alcohol is a depressant, and in my case I had difficulty in exhibiting an acceptable behavior pattern while under its influence. My subconscious defenses which controlled my behavior were removed and I became desirous of being the master of all I surveyed. I revolted against any response which differed from my philosophy of life. The results were often disastrous. People who go to A.A. meetings but continue to drink get nowhere really until they stop that behavior. I myself had to put the bottle away, and keep it put away, before I could make any progress. But on the positive side, a commitment to actually doing this will begin to exhibit positive fruits so quickly, that we will find it progressively easier and easier to stay away from alcohol.

How did these fifteen guidelines to mature living relate to my own specific problems? Since each alcoholic is a unique individual, you the reader, even if you are an alcoholic, may find that some of your problems were different from some of my problems. Nevertheless, the clearest way to explain many things is to give concrete examples. So I am going to give specific examples of some of the things I myself had to learn how to do, in the hope that this will enable you to see more clearly the nature of the issues involved. To make it easier to follow what I am doing, I will put numbers at the beginning of each section, showing how those particular problems in my own life related to some of the items on that list of fifteen basic guidelines.

No. 3

Anger was perhaps one of the most destructive of my behavior manifestations. I was unable to control my temper when I was growing up as a child, I argued with my wife, I got in disputes with my fellow airmen over trivial things, and I got into arguments in bars which sometimes ended up in pushing, hitting, or wild fist fights. While under the influence of alcohol, I always felt at the time that my anger was totally justified. But the fact was that I was cruel and physically abusive toward others, and I had no right to treat other people that way, even if it were true that I was right and they were wrong.

I could not control people, places and things—this was the basic underlying problem. But this would make me feel so frustrated that my anger would finally simply explode in totally destructive fashion. The only way to cure this is to realize that none of us can really control people, places and things. The only thing I can one hundred percent control is my own reaction to these external situations.

The majority of people want to be loved and accepted, and I was no exception. But I cannot make another person love me, I must be someone who can be loved. Generally, alcoholics have difficulty in this area because of the negative impact they have on their family and friends. Some alcoholics are readily accepted when sober but turn others off when they are under the influence of alcohol. Personal charm can be destroyed almost immediately when alcohol is ingested, and I was a victim of this process. I should have recognized this immediately the first time I drank alcohol and got drunk at that Christmas party when I was eighteen: everyone at the party was regarding me as hopelessly obnoxious by the time it was over. Instead, I kept on getting drunk, and offending people and making them uncomfortable, and disgusting them over and over through the years that followed.

No. 1

It was not as though no one ever told me that some of my behavior was very objectionable or inappropriate. Constructive criticism was often offered when my behavior became unacceptable. Although this was an opportunity to improve my interpersonal relationships, I usually became offensive or non-responsive. That is a big problem all we alcoholics have: we claim we do not know why other people do not like us, but the truth is that we do not listen when they tell us exactly why! And these are frequently things that we could change, very simple things, at little cost to ourselves.

Sometimes I exploded in anger at them, but fear of being rejected often made me shut my ears to them instead: it caused me to inhibit my reactions to many kinds of events or circumstances. Down in my subconscious I wanted to be angry but was afraid they would totally reject me if I expressed it; I felt they were attacking me unfairly but simultaneously felt a painful guilt at the thought that they just might be right. The inability to resolve this inner conflict led to much anxiety on my part. Anxiety can become very painful, and this caused me to reach for the bottle as a means of resolving it. The solution was negative, and it only created additional problems.

No. 2

Instead of using constructive criticism as a way to grow and improve my behavior, I refused to change, and instead went off and just felt sorry for myself. Self-pity is generally caused by low self-esteem. I took their criticism, not as a statement that "we do not like the way you are treating us in this particular situation," but as a total condemnation of me as a person. I used this technique of feeling totally rejected and unloved as a technique to justify my response to many problems: "If they regard me as a totally worthless person anyway, I'll show them how much I despise them too." This gravely affected my ability to be liked and accepted.

Self-pity has a way of eating into the very fiber of one's soul. I become desperate and begin looking for some way to medicate this overwhelming pain. Alcohol is used as a common remedy for this emotional deficiency, and I used it often. But sitting and drinking and brooding in fact just makes us feel even sorrier for ourselves, so it makes the chronic self-pity sink even deeper into our minds.

Nos. 6, 8, 11, 12, and 13

All these childish traits which I had never outgrown, made me tend to be a poor loser. I could not stand it when you did better than me at anything. I was always envious toward those who experienced success or good fortune. I wanted to achieve success too, but without devoting much effort toward becoming successful. I wanted a free ride. It sometimes takes a long time and a good deal of hard work to become what one wants to be—a capable dancer, a good student, or any of the other things I had always longed to be but never took the time to work at.

The biggest problem here was that I could not bear to recognize that I myself was the one who was responsible for what I did or did not achieve. This was what made it so painful to compare my success or failure with the achievements of others. So in order to compensate for this condition, I became a faultfinder, and constantly went around condemning the efforts of others. Continually being hypercritical of others and trying to put them down all the time, without devoting any real time to my own self-improvement, simply prolongs and delays achieving any positive goals of my own.

No. 12

The need to "be right" dominated my interactions with other people, a practice which alienated my friends and made my foes hate me even more. In any difference of opinion, even with things that were ultimately not all that important, I was convinced that somebody had to be "right" and the other person had to be "wrong." Naturally, I felt that the one who had it right was clearly me, and that I had to force you to admit that. I played this right vs. wrong game as though it were a contest for the World Series championship.

It is sometimes hard, even when one is totally sober and clear-headed, to determine where to draw the line between being nice (and not hurting people's feelings) vs. standing up for principles one believes in (No. 15 in my list). This difficult issue, unfortunately, was seldom a matter of concern to me after my having a few drinks of alcohol. In this I was no different from many other alcoholics, and I had a tendency to express my opinion and disagree with the thoughts and actions of others very loudly and aggressively while intoxicated. On some occasions I defended my opinion by turning to physical violence.

A return to sobriety sometimes disclosed the fact that I had lost a good friend permanently due to my unacceptable behavior while under the influence of alcohol. One often does not realize the difficulty involved in the establishment of a real friendship until after it has been lost forever, and it is too late to undo your drunken words and actions.

It was the way I was playing the right vs. wrong game back then which was doing the damage. That is a very dangerous psychological game. Different perspectives necessarily mean different perceptions. If two people see the same automobile accident, their accounts of what happened will not be the same. Two people can look at the same set of circumstances and have entirely opposite interpretations.

Each human being is unique: that is why they are referred to as "individuals." Our individualism is constituted by our own particular life experiences, by the way we process and interpret those events, and by the philosophy of life we develop on the basis of those interpretations. When I begin playing right vs. wrong as a destructive psychological game, what I am attempting to do is to sustain some semblance of emotional stability for myself, but at enormous cost. If I can convince myself that I am right and you are wrong, then my own perception of the world (or so I try to tell myself) must be grounded in something objective and permanent that I can understand and control. But in order to do that, I have to deny you your individuality. I can only affirm myself by denying you. Unfortunately, I played that game to the hilt from the time I was a small child. Put some liquor in me, and it became even worse.

Nos. 1, 4, and 6

As individuals mature, if they have done so with a conflict-free personality, they are usually able to accept responsibility for their own actions. If they have needlessly or inadvertently upset other people, they apologize and change their behavior. But there are others who "wear their feelings on their sleeves," as the old saying goes, and are incapable of processing the criticism of others without an angry response. I was one of this type of personality, and it manifested itself in an anger which usually produced a severed relationship between myself and the other person when it finally erupted. Admitting to being wrong was very difficult for me, so I shifted the blame instead to my family, employment, community, or spouse.

No. 7

When two people are in conflict, sometimes the best solution is for each person to give a little. But compromise is a difficult procedure for people who are immature. They develop an "all or nothing" response to external factors. They do not understand that getting 50% of what I desire is not necessarily all that bad, getting 75% of what I would like to have is actually doing quite well indeed, and getting 90% of what I really want is phenomenal success. People who refuse to acknowledge this fact of life will never be able to live in reasonable peace with anybody else over the long run.

No. 13

I spent years going around finding fault with other people. I held them up to a standard of absolute perfection, and they always came up lacking. Being this kind of perfectionist was very destructive. It allowed me to downplay other people's performance, but all I was really doing was trying to compensate for my own feeling of inadequacy. When I was criticizing someone else for something trivial, it gave a temporary boost to my own fragile sense of self-worth. But as long as I held up absolute perfection as the only worthwhile standard, what did that do to me? I became so fearful of failure, any failure at all, that the need to succeed was totally inhibited. This became a very painful part of my personality. I was afraid to try anything, because if I did not do it perfectly the first time, you would be able to criticize me as viciously as I had been criticizing you.

Furthermore, the standards that I used back then for evaluating other people and criticizing them and putting them down, were often absurd. I was continually preoccupied with rank and titles and wealth and the material things other people had. Little did I realize that personal achievements, money, and credentials do not make one a decent human being. The only evaluation I do now, is to recognize that I prefer to spend time when I can with other people who are simply decent human beings—they are more fun to be with, and it is much more enjoyable and relaxing—but you can have compassion and empathy for the others, and you can care what happens to them.

Allowing others to do their thing without being critical is a mark of a mature individual. Diplomacy and being tactful are essential to a lasting friendship.

Nos. 9 and 10

Day dreaming and conjuring up grandiose ideas which are often unachievable, is a trademark of the alcoholic. I spent many hours devoted to daydreaming about impossible accomplishments. I would eventually start talking arrogantly to other people and treating them contemptuously, as though I had actually achieved these things and was the very cock of the walk. Having a good deal of alcohol in me made it easier to go off into this fantasy world. This never got me anywhere, but provided a change of pace from the other kinds of thoughts that otherwise seemed to occupy my mind.

So for example, it distracted my mind from one of my other favorite things to think about. I loved to worry a great deal about all the things that *might* go wrong. This sort of excessive preoccupation with what were also only imaginary scenarios was likewise a waste of valuable time. I would begin fantasizing about all the possible events which might occur—disasters which would alter my life catastrophically if they did happen—and fall deeper and deeper into negativity until this would finally provide me with yet another excuse to start drinking again.

Of course the problem with alcohol as a temporary solution to the problem of excessive worrying, was that my drinking usually landed me in situations which actually did do me great harm, and cast me into even greater worries than I had had before.

Our job in A.A. and in alcoholism treatment programs is to produce healing. But no healing can occur until the person is willing to look at the real problem which needs to be fixed. It is painful to acknowledge blame for a condition which one has never been willing even to recognize, or whose existence one's sense of pride finds totally unacceptable. Emotional contributions to alcoholism are seldom recognized by alcoholics until they are in some type of treatment and are prepared to change their lifestyles.

It is not just the internal sense of feeling good about oneself which is at stake. When we violate these fifteen guidelines, we invariably eventually end up alienating all the other people with whom we come into contact. The friction between ourselves and other people caused by alcoholism can destroy family harmony and constitute the basis for separation between family members. But contrariwise, when we begin to heal, our relationships with other people also begin to improve.

When I hit bottom on July 5, 1948, I had alienated my family back in Ohio, my wife, and most of the key people at Mitchel Air Force Base where I was stationed. When we interacted, arguments, quarrels, blaming, or threats of punishment erupted. I was at strife with the entire world around me most of the time. But as I began my recovery, this continual friction and arguing began to fade away. There is an enormous healing power in the A.A. program: I can heal not only my own soul, but my relationships with the other people around me, in almost miraculous fashion.

In my own case, the abuse of alcohol was both cause and effect of my overriding problems. Nevertheless, it is not my intent to "preach" against alcohol, nor to employ fear tactics in addressing the problem of alcoholism in our society. It is a very serious problem, and does not need proof of its destructiveness. The proof is listed in the police reports, vital statistics, and in our court systems. It is hoped that the material contained in this book will assist someone who has a problem with alcohol to seek a solution to it, so that this person will become able to lead a more rewarding and carefree life.

My list of fifteen principles is extensive. Not all of them may apply to you, although most of them did in fact apply to me, some much more than others. Through the application of the principles which were relevant to me, my own life has in fact become more successful and rewarding, without me having to use alcohol or any other mind-altering substances.

I have heard people say in A.A. groups that simply attending A.A. meetings will, all by itself, automatically provide the individual with the will to get sober and stay sober from that point on. At the first A.A. meetings I went to, back in northeastern Ohio, there were too many people who talked and acted that way, and it certainly did not get me sober. This is two-stepping: trying to work the A.A. program on just the first and twelfth steps alone.

Inherent in this attitude is a refusal to recognize the enormous therapeutic and healing power of the program, and to take advantage of this power. In fact, this is very dangerous. I could not get sober at all in meetings run like that, and I have noted through the years since, that even when a few people do get sober for a while that way, of all the factors which lead to relapse later on, reluctance to address emotional problems is the major reason why alcoholics and addicts return to using alcohol and drugs.

Even nowadays, I sometimes hear some A.A. members denounce the practice of talking about personality and character disorders. They try to set up a false either-or dichotomy: spirituality or "psychologizing." They claim that you must only speak of God as the sole source of recovery (but often, amusingly enough, use profane language to express their spiritual beliefs, which has always seemed particularly grotesque to me). In fact, they seem to be afraid of discussing character defects, principally because they usually will not accept the fact that they themselves have some of them too. This is three-stepping: trying to work the program on just the first, second, and third steps alone.

It is not a two-step or a three-step program, but a program with twelve steps. In particular, until people have done a fourth step, no deep healing and no real therapeutic benefits can start happening. The fourth step is the place where we do a real self-inventory, and see how we actually do think and behave in terms of issues like the ones laid out in those fifteen guidelines. You can pick some other list or set of guidelines to measure yourself by, where slightly different words are used, but you will still have to look at that basic kind of issue in your life. You should then note that, as it says in the Big Book on page 71, it is only after "you have swallowed and digested some big chunks of truth about yourself" by doing this kind of fourth step, that you will have finally "made a good beginning" in working through the program. People who try to two-step and three-step, do not even get to the beginning of the real program.

In the fourth step self-inventory, I have to discover who I really am. This means having to go back and recover a lot of memories that I have pushed out of sight. This is because, as part of the process by which the personality develops from birth to adulthood, the most negative and painful experiences are inhibited and shoved down into the subconscious. With the passing of time, one loses the ability to easily recall these painful memories back up to the conscious level, but they are still there in the mind, lodged down in the subconscious. They are not only still there, they interfere with the ability to lead any kind of normal life: they are manifested on the conscious level as resentments, intolerance, self-pity, over-dependence, hate, anger, and many other negative feelings and behaviors.

Now once the personality develops, at the basic level it cannot be changed. If during the period between birth and adulthood, we have built up negative responses to life's problems which were simply inhibited and never resolved, then various kinds of character disorders will also usually be produced. These will create further barriers blocking us from any kind of fully productive life.

In real healing, we are not trying to change the basic personality, which will always be there as the core of our personal identity. But we learn how to employ positive measures which will enable us to start behaving in a much less destructive way. Recovery from emotional problems of this sort requires that we build defenses against acting out in the areas of our painful emotional conflicts. In other words, we must "build character" as part of developing stronger ego defenses against our personality defects.

So we have to pull old painful memories out of our subconscious minds, and think about them at the conscious level in order to identify the real problem areas. But we also have to consciously and deliberately create defenses against acting out those emotional conflicts in the way we used to. We not only have to work hard at identifying why something going on right now is getting us so upset, we also have to work and work at training ourselves to carry out a different set of responses to those painful emotions.

This is why just attending meetings is not the answer all by itself. There must be some changes in our conscious behavior before long lasting recovery is to be found. We must build character, replacing our old negative responses with a new set of deeply ingrained positive responses which we will eventually learn to employ almost automatically. That is what the sixth step in the A.A. program is talking about, engaging in character formation to replace our old character defects (as they are referred to in that step) with a higher and finer kind of character. But the Big Book never claims that we can change people's basic personalities. Why would we ever want to, in a program which promises a return to real freedom as its principal goal? I am not trying to force you to have the same personality as me, or vice versa. We are not trying to brainwash people into becoming pale, bloodless, identical clones of one another.

Furthermore, we must always remember the warning in the A.A. Big Book, close to the beginning of the chapter on How It Works: "We are not saints . . . . We claim spiritual progress rather than spiritual perfection." Personality itself cannot be changed. However our personalities developed during our childhood and youth, that is the underlying personality we will always have to live with, with all of its basic defects still remaining down underneath. We can build character to set up ego defenses against acting out these defects in the terribly destructive ways we did in the past. But if we are sensitive to our own emotions and ongoing stream of consciousness, no matter how long we have been in the program, we will still regularly become aware of twinges here and there, where some urge arises in our minds to do things the old way.

I saw a beautiful blonde young woman at an A.A. meeting last night, and a little voice in my head said "Wow!" and I felt a little urge there. But all the work I have done over the years in building my character came into play, and I felt another wiser voice saying gently but firmly, "Now Bill, think about something else and don't act on that!" As long as I remember to listen to that second thought, the voice of reason, my life goes very smoothly. The program works, it really works, and my life over the past fifty plus years has been richly blessed as a result.

I would like to conclude by telling a story I once heard about a young person who went to his dad and proclaimed he could not control his temper. It had progressed to the point where the anxiety associated with the problem rendered him almost nonfunctional.

His dad had a knowledge of many of the psychological factors which led to addiction. So he gave his son a handful of nails and told him each time he lost his temper, to come back to the house and pound a nail in the fence close to the house. In bewilderment, the boy took the nails and did what he was told to do.

After driving thirty-nine nails in the fence, he went to his dad and said that it had worked, he was able to control his temper now. So his father told him that each time he successfully controlled his temper, he should come back and pull one of the nails out of the fence. This was building character. After a few days, he proclaimed to his dad that he had now learned how to control his temper so well that he had finally pulled all thirty-nine nails out of the fence, and there were no nails remaining.

His dad took him by the hand and led him out to the fence. There were no nails in it, but there were thirty-nine nail holes scarring the surface of the fence. The father explained that the fence had lost its original identity, and it could never be returned to its original state any longer, regardless of the measures taken.

This is one of the most important points in the story: the fence could never genuinely be returned to its original identity, no matter how hard the boy worked to try to repair it. This is an unpleasant but fundamental finding of modern psychology and psychiatry. Just go for a few sessions with a really good psychiatrist if you do not believe me, and learn a few more things about what urges and traumatic fears and memories still lie buried down in your own subconscious! In fact, most people who have been in the program for long enough to gain some genuine humility, learn to listen to the inner workings of their own minds sensitively enough to recognize this fundamental truth. If we do things to ourselves in growing up which create personality problems, the scars of these old personal issues and painful memories will remain all the rest of our lives. But we can build character, and learn how to pull the nails out of the fence, and even more importantly, we can learn how to live our lives in such a way that we will not need to pound any more holes in them.

When we violate the fifteen guidelines I laid out here, we pound more nails into our lives, the nails of anger, temper, envy, fault-finding, and so on. When we start working daily at following these new guidelines and begin building character, we become able to pull the nails back out again. But the holes and scars will always be there. Our original identities—what we would have been if we had had perfect childhoods in a perfect society, and responded perfectly to those perfect surroundings—can never be recovered.

At one level we can sometimes make amends out there in the external world, and partially make up to other people for the harm we did them in the past. Sometimes we cannot truly undo even that. When I lost my beautiful baby daughter, the child of my first marriage, I never even saw her again until forty years later, and then it was just for a brief visit. She had no desire to have any deeper, continuing relationship with me. She must remain forever in my memory as my Lost Child.

And no matter what we do in the way of external amends, we will find that deep down inside our own minds we are left with some holes in our lives, and sometimes they are more than just little nail-holes; sometimes they are great, gaping chasms. The most important thing we can do, though, is to learn how not to keep pounding additional new holes. We are not saints, but we can learn how to quit tearing through the world like a raging tornado of destruction and negativism, and we can learn how to do a little good for other people for a change. If you have been where we alcoholics were lost for so many years, this is reward enough in itself.

CHAPTER 14

Beginning the First Military Alcoholism Treatment Program

When I initially began working with a few of my fellow alcoholics at Mitchel Air Force Base—people whom I knew could profit from the A.A. program as much as I had—I certainly had no conscious intention of setting up the first organized military alcoholism treatment program in the country. It was just that my little efforts, once started, seemed to keep growing on their own. And as I went along, in a rather uncanny way, people kept appearing in my life and offering almost unbelievable opportunities to expand and improve on what I was doing. By the end of my stay at Mitchel Air Force Base, I had been trained at the Yale School of Alcohol Studies, and officially appointed by the Air Force to work full time with alcoholics on the base. I had in fact achieved enough successes in that little pilot program to convince the Air Force to let me try it again in a full-scale treatment project at Lackland Air Force Base later on. We were able to obtain a fifty-percent success rate there, which was phenomenally good in working with alcoholics in that kind of context.

But at the beginning all I was doing was trying to work my own A.A. program, and in particular the twelfth step, where it talks about the way we need to try to carry this message to other alcoholics who are still suffering. We carry the message in the simplest possible way: we stand up and tell what it was like, what happened, and what it is like now. But in doing that, we deliver the vital message that the disease is treatable, and that we ourselves are living proof that people can recover from alcoholism and live free of drink. Not only that, we display by our emotions and our actions—in ways far stronger than words—that we have found a new freedom and a new happiness, and that we have started developing things like courage, self-confidence, compassion and caring, which we sadly lacked in our lives before.

In September of 1948, I approached my Squadron Commander with the idea of giving a talk on alcoholism to the members of our Squadron. At first he looked at me as though my sanity had left me. I told him of the success I had had over the past two months or so in working privately with several of the other hard drinkers on the base, and he finally consented.

In fact I had no idea how to present the program to this sort of audience, so when the day arrived and I had to stand up and address the other 159 members of my Squadron I was filled with great apprehension. I began by saying, "I am an alcoholic and have found a way to live a useful life without having to drink alcoholic beverages." The whole room broke out in uproarious laughter on the spot. They knew all about how much I used to drink. My old character defects started to click into place automatically, and my first reaction was to go sit back down and quit this foolish idea on the spot. In fact, I really wanted to just crawl through the floor and disappear. But something different happened than had ever happened to me before in this kind of situation. I squared my shoulders, and kept on talking.

As my talk progressed, I noticed to my surprise that there appeared to be an interest in what I was saying. A different kind of good feeling began to steal over me. After my speech was over, two people came up to me and quietly asked for my help. In the days that followed, two rapidly became four, and four became six, and six became eight. Something big was off and running, and I had no idea what was going to happen next, but knew that my part of the job was to go where I was being led. This was the beginning of an awesome responsibility in helping others to seek a better way of life.

My co-author asked me how in the world I managed to handle that experience of being laughed at in public in that fashion. What enabled me to keep on going, and not only complete my talk, but finish it with a feeling of confidence and satisfaction deep inside? This was not the old Bill of the earlier chapters in this book. The person who was going into action now looked like a totally different man, he said. What enabled me to follow through on what I had started, and keep on doggedly transporting people to A.A. meetings, and working with them privately, through all the months that followed? The old Bill fled as fast as he could from anything that required real leadership and responsibility and consistency and following through on things. When the old Bill was given any kind of major opportunity to actually achieve something worthwhile, he seemed to perversely figure out some way to sabotage himself and destroy everything on the very eve of success. What was different now? How could such an enormous sea change have occurred in such a short period of time?

I had to think about that question after he asked. What happened was difficult to put into words. At some level I had always wanted to help other people, I believe. I recognized that it made you feel very good to do something that genuinely made another person's life better. But this desire was buried deep down inside, and very rarely allowed to surface. It had gotten covered over with that enormous towering structure of selfishness, resentment, envy, aggression, self-pity, fear, isolationism, and guilt which had been erected in my mind. When I looked in the mirror and all that edifice of negativism came toppling down on July 5, 1948, at first I felt totally empty. If you took all the destructive things out of my life, there did not seem to be anything left at all.

But in fact there was that simple little desire to lead my life in such a way that I could actually be of help to some of the other people around me. It was still sitting there intact, where it had always been. Only now, when it was no longer covered over with so many other irrelevant, unnecessary things, I could see it clearly for the first time. Somehow I knew that there would be authentic meaning and value to life if it were led according to that kind of principle. If I lived my life that way, I could look in the mirror at myself without ever having to feel that kind of total horror and repugnance again. Instead of merely existing, I could live a life which, in its own small way, would actually be worth something. It would all matter. Life would be worthwhile.

Alcoholics Anonymous is a spiritual program, not a religious one. Religious groups have doctrines and dogmas, elaborate rituals and special prayers, and all sorts of special rules about how their members are supposed to talk about the sacred. A.A. has none of that really. A person can talk about the spiritual dimension of life, and even more importantly live at a deeply spiritual level, without using any kind of traditional religious language at all. When I have a desire to genuinely help other people in some concrete way, I am dedicating myself to what is a spiritual value. I am embracing a higher meaning for my life, and recognizing some of the eternal truths of the universe. It is the complete opposite of a life built on selfish striving for material things and praise from foolish people who have no more values than I do.

Or we could put it another way. If somebody like me could get sober, I had something of value which I could give to other people. And I discovered that I wanted, more than anything else in the world, to give this marvelous gift which I had been given, to all the people around me who were destroying their lives just as I had done, and living in a world without value and without hope.

There was a man named Yev Gardner who also went to the A.A. meeting which I attended every week on Long Island.[10] He was short and carried his head to the side. When he talked, he would look over to the side or out the window. He was neither imposing nor a charismatic public speaker. But he was a beautiful man. What was important for Yev was to do the program instead of speak the program. There was some family money, so that although he did some work in real estate there on Long Island, he could live modestly but comfortably without having to spend much time on business affairs. He was able to devote the rest of his time to trying to help other people, and that was what was really important to him.

I did not realize it, but Yev had become the right-hand man of one of the greatest American social reformers of the past hundred and fifty years, Mrs. Marty Mann. She was the first woman to obtain long-term continuous sobriety in A.A., was on the faculty of the Yale School of Alcohol Studies, and had founded the Yale-linked NCEA (National

Committee for Education on Alcoholism) in 1944. At the end of 1949, the last strings connecting that organization to the Yale School were cut, and it became the extremely influential NCA (National Committee on Alcoholism, later changed to National Council on Alcoholism in 1957). Marty had come from an extremely wealthy background, and had a wide range of powerful and famous friends. She socialized with a large number of the best artists and authors of that time, both in New York and London. She was especially close to one of the people who ran *Vogue* magazine, and also knew the editors, publishers, and art directors at many other major national publications, as well as large numbers of prominent national politicians and generals and admirals.[11]

But she could talk to anybody in any situation, and the power of her caring and honesty and ability with words would win even the hardest heart. I later got to know her well, and she was just such a warm and decent person that I treasured every opportunity to see her and talk with her. Marty, God bless her, she was something.

She and Yev made a great team. Yev was Deputy Director of the NCA. He kept things organized and made sure the bills were paid, but also used his tact and diplomacy to soothe the troubled waters when tensions arose. It seemed to me, that without Yev as a liason between them, Marty and Bill W. (the founder of A.A., and a man who did have a considerable ego) would have found it difficult to work together as smoothly as they did.

But I knew Yev and Marty simply as two very good and decent people. Let me give you an example. After my public presentation before my Squadron, I was soon transporting a whole car load of GI's to A.A. meetings outside the base every week. But then my old car finally broke down for good, and it became clear it was past all repair. I had no one on the base to whom I could turn for assistance. In those days enlisted men could not get credit on their own to purchase anything from merchants off of their bases, and the civilians who ran businesses in western Long Island were no different from anywhere else in the country. I had started holding A.A. meetings on the base, but had already realized that alcoholics in the military did much better if they went to meetings where the majority of the group were civilians. It was too hard to escape military rank distinctions in an all-military meeting held on a base. A lower-ranking person was extremely hesitant to disagree too forcibly with someone who was his or her military superior, for fear of reprisals if the other person became too angry.

Yev Gardner became aware of my plight, and came to me one day and asked me to go to town with him. I had no idea what his purpose was, but climbed in his car, and we drove off. He took me to a car dealer and told me that if I picked out an automobile I could afford, he would co-sign for me on the loan. I was flabbergasted. Yev did not know me that well yet. It was just that he saw that these GI's I was taking to meetings needed help, and this was one way he could help them, so he would do it.

I picked out a black Studebaker. This was the period when they had come out with a streamlined design, sloping down both at the front and rear, long before any of the other automobile makers started imitating that kind of design. People joked that the hood and the trunk were so similar in appearance, that "you could not tell if a Studebaker was coming or going." But I loved it, and I bought it. My little unofficial military alcoholism treatment program was back in business again. Yev's great act of kindness permanently sealed my allegiance forever to him and to the A.A. program.

Just as a side note, when I drove it home, it turned out that my wife Ann hated black cars, and particularly Studebakers. Nothing in this life ever works absolutely perfectly! That is an important program lesson we all have to learn.

Yev Gardner came to me another time, and asked me, "Would you like to work with military alcoholics full time?" It turned out that Marty had used her connections to obtain for me, if I wanted it, an assignment to the Chaplain's Office there at Mitchel Air Force Base as a Chaplain's Assistant, with the understanding that what I would actually be doing is working with alcoholics. This was a truly strange place for someone like me to be assigned, but the problem was that there was no slot in the Air Force's list of possible assignments for a full-time alcoholism counselor. In fact, the military services refused to admit at that time that they even had alcoholics. Being labeled an alcoholic on any written document meant severe disciplinary punishment, up to and including instant dismissal from the service with a less than honorable discharge. Calling me a Chaplain's Assistant on the official records and then quietly assigning me to work specifically with personnel on the base who drank too much was a surreptitious way of acknowledging that they did in fact have quite a few alcoholics in the Air Force. But doing it that way meant nothing had to appear on the official records about how many drunks there were in the service.

It was the only way Marty and Yev and their friends in the high command could figure out to give me a full-time assignment setting up an alcoholism treatment program, but it was certainly not an easy role for me to assume. For all practical purposes I had no religious background. I had had no religious training as a child, and attended church only rarely. I was required to attend a school for Chaplain's Assistants, where I felt like a totally displaced person. Nevertheless, the Chaplains who ran the school were surprisingly interested in what I was doing, and even asked me to present several lectures on the subject to the other students. I had barely got through high school, and here I was a teacher, actually being listened to with respect. After that look in the mirror on July 5, 1948, a completely new Sergeant Bill was emerging, whose life was now built on an entirely new basis, that of simply trying within my own considerable limitations to help other people instead of fighting them and scorning them. But the strength and abilities of the new Sergeant Bill still amazed me as much as it did other people, in fact probably even more so.

The Chaplain's Office was in fact an extremely poor place for putting an alcohol education and treatment center on a military base. It was not until after I had gotten to Lackland Air Force Base that I was able to get out from under this unfortunate label. Many alcoholics could not identify at all at first with the spiritual concept of recovery. Others had little or no religious background (just like myself), or even worse, believed in God but thought that they had been deserted by him. All too many members of the American military in those days put God at the absolute bottom of their list of priorities. This meant that when I attempted to contact a person with a severe drinking problem, to offer to help, the fact that I was operating out of the Chaplain's Office often meant that anything I said at all would simply fall on deaf ears.

Bill W., the co-founder of Alcoholics Anonymous, wanted to create a world where alcoholics who admitted their problem would not be punished. In Chapter 10 of the A.A. Big Book, "To Employers," he asked bosses to give their employees a real chance to get sober in A.A. first, before they fired them for drunkenness. Mrs. Marty Mann, as head of the NCA, fought for this idea even more vigorously. When people are finally willing to admit that they are alcoholics, we should not punish them for admitting the true nature of their problem, but give them a real opportunity for effective treatment. Marty was already speaking all over the United States at that time, explaining the new disease concept of alcoholism, and telling her audiences about the successes of the new A.A.-related treatment methods, but above all calling on the non-alcoholics in the United States to begin taking more responsibility in a positive way for dealing with one of America's top three public health problems. Quit scolding and lecturing and punishing—and above all quit falling into denial and pretending the problem is really not that bad—and start putting workable treatment programs in place, just as you would for tuberculosis, diabetes, or cancer.

But this was only 1948 when I started my little alcoholism treatment program at Mitchel Air Force Base. The A.A. Big Book had only been published nine years earlier, and A.A. was still not all that well known. Marty Mann had only started her National Committee for Education on Alcoholism (as it was originally called) four years earlier, in 1944.

So in the United States in general, and in the military in particular, most people at that time still regarded alcoholism not as a disease but as a moral failing. The non-alcoholics would say, "When I have had enough to drink, I use some simple willpower and stop. Why don't you?" We expect people to use their willpower to restrain themselves from robbing banks, shooting other people with pistols, and cashing forged checks. We punish them if they do this, as a deterrence. If I walk into a police station and admit that I robbed such-and-such a bank on such-and-such a day, I will be locked up on the spot. The assumption was that alcoholism could and should be controlled the same way. Very few people realized that alcoholism was a disease, and that alcoholics literally could not stop themselves from drinking alcohol, unless they received proper treatment.

The Air Force policy at that time was to deny pay to those who sought assistance for their alcoholism, if they either had to be hospitalized or were otherwise unavailable to perform their prescribed duties. This put severe limits on what could be done in the way of providing treatment. You could not give people a three to five day period for detoxing, as long as that was what you called it. If they went into d.t.'s when they stopped their continuous drinking, at a time when they were supposed to be at a duty station, they could get in truly serious trouble. You could not have a recovering alcoholic in a treatment class if that person's military superior had assigned that man or woman some other duty at that same time. As a result, many people who wanted to recover were afraid to seek help simply due to the administrative restrictions placed on anyone seeking assistance. No one in the military made enough money to afford to have his or her pay docked.

If you were an alcoholic, you also took an even bigger chance if you agreed to seek treatment. You were then marked. If your response to treatment was not favorable, you would then automatically be given an undesirable discharge. Many suffering men and women chose to try to hide their drinking rather than take that extreme risk.

The public policies of the 1940's were insane. They produced exactly the opposite of what they were supposed to produce, especially in the armed services. Instead of reducing the number of alcoholics in the military, and restoring the maximum number of people to useful and productive lives, they forced sufferers into hiding and kept those who were sick people (not evil people) from ever getting well. As a result, there was an unnecessarily large number of what one might call "functioning alcoholics" in the military: alcohol abusers who hid and covered up their drinking, and somehow managed to keep from being discharged, while barely being able to function at their assigned jobs. In spite of my own out-of-control drinking, I had managed to go for years without even being reduced in rank. But I certainly remember what a poor job I did during those years.

In 1948, with the new philosophy of alcoholism treatment which I supported, I was a man far ahead of his time, at least in a military context. So I hit a good deal of resistance from some of the Commanders and senior enlisted personnel at Mitchel Air Force Base. They did not want me working with problem drinkers. As far as they were concerned, punishment, not "coddling," was the way to control over-indulgence in alcohol.

I was considered a freak by some and a crusader by others. Despite this, my head was held high and I proceeded with the mission of helping those who needed my counsel. The numbers of those I had helped to become free of alcohol continued to grow for quite some time. But the underlying problem still remained: until general military policies toward alcoholism were changed, it was going to be a continuous uphill battle for anyone like me trying to set up an alcoholism treatment program on any military base in the United States. And changes in basic policies were not even going to begin to take place until the latter 1960's, and especially the 1970's, when Senator Harold Hughes began putting more enlightened alcohol legislation through the U.S. Congress. In fact, the battle is not over yet, even now in the year 2003.

How did I keep going then, at the end of the 1940's, when I was often subject to such hostility in my attempts to treat alcoholics and restore them to productive lives? It was due to the support of a very small handful of people, to whom I shall be forever grateful. The most important of these of course was Marty Mann, who acutely realized the importance of changing the negative attitude toward alcoholism in the military. This was one of our major public institutions, upon which we counted, in times of national emergency, to save our lives. Having her as a staunch defender of my work at Mitchel was a major part of the motivation I needed to continue, despite the resistance of those who opposed the presence of my mission on the base.

It is hard for me to express the enormous gratitude I feel for the kind of life which a higher power has granted me, and the people whom I was privileged to know over the course of the past fifty-five years. As I look back over my life now, I realize that not many people are fortunate enough to be blessed as I have been.

Marty was on the faculty of the Yale School of Alcohol Studies, and she and Yev Gardner got in contact with the Command Chaplain at Mitchel Air Force Base, and eventually got his wholehearted support for an amazing opportunity which I was going to be given. As a result, in early 1949 I received a call from Marty's office asking if I would be interested in attending the Yale School as a student. She had obtained a scholarship for me, so I would not have to pay tuition. All I had to come up with was travel and living expenses.

I could hardly believe what I heard over the phone. I had barely gotten through high school. Surely I could not have been chosen for a program of that caliber, and with a scholarship too. But it was true. I was ecstatic.

Then came the real-world problems. First, it was against Air Force policy to give enlisted personnel permission to attend a prestigious Ivy League school like Yale. Second, I was going to have to obtain an official leave of absence from my assigned duties in order to go there, and this was no easy thing to obtain. Third, I still had no money at all for my other expenses, even if the scholarship covered the tuition itself.

But at that point, Chaplain Thomas Adams, the Command Chaplain for Continental Air Command, pitched in his support for me, and spent many hours justifying my attendance at the Yale School and convincing the higher command authorities to authorize my going for schooling there. He finally got the Air Force to approve my enrollment in the program, but could not talk anyone into supplying the additional financial support that I would need.

It was then that another good man, my Base Commander, Colonel Musgrave, came to the rescue. Roosevelt Raceways, the harness racing track near Mitchel Air Force Base, had established a special fund to be used for recreational purposes for the enlisted personnel at the air base. Colonel Musgrave, a creative man, talked them into bending the rules enough to give me a grant to cover my expenses while I was attending the school.

But I still had to get there. The Yale School of Alcohol Studies was conducting its program that summer at Texas Christian University in Fort Worth, Texas. The money from the race track was not going to be enough to cover my transportation costs there, and classes were at that point ready to begin. Literally at the last moment, I managed to locate an Air Force flight going to Carswell Air Force Base in Fort Worth, and was allowed to ride along with the crew. I arrived the afternoon before the first class session began. I had made it.

I was the first military person to attend the Yale School of Alcohol Studies. They were fascinated with the fact that I had managed to set up the first officially sanctioned military alcoholism treatment program in the country, and that I had been appointed full time to run that program by the Air Force. They wanted to know what I was doing in the program I had set up, and how I was doing it, and what was working effectively, and where I thought the central problems lay.

On my side, the knowledge I gained during my attendance at the school was simply overwhelming. You need to remember that the instructors were some of the most learned and famous people in alcoholism studies at that time. I still use to this day innumerable things that I learned from them. Dr. E. M. Jellinek was there, the biologist and neuroendocrinologist who worked out the famous "Jellinek curve" which still bears his name, a chart based on his careful statistical studies of A.A. members, which demonstrated the progressive nature of the illness which we call alcoholism and its various stages in order of their progression. He knew so much about so many fields of study, often ranging far outside his own area of formal training. He was fluent in at least three languages that I knew of, and had worked all over the world. He had actually been trained originally as a biometrician, using statistics to study biological phenomena, then had developed enough professional competence in neuroendocrinology to be put on the Yale University faculty, where he then became interested in the effect of alcohol on the human body and nervous system. But I actually learned an incredible amount about the fundamentals of psychiatry from him,[12] an area in which he had never been formally schooled at all. He had that sort of sweeping range of knowledge.

Selden Bacon was also there, another quite famous researcher on alcoholism, and Leon Greenberg, and of course Marty Mann herself. Adapting to that world of incredible intellects was one of the most challenging things I have ever taken on, but it was one of the most exciting periods of my whole life. You cannot imagine what it was like to see minds like that tossing ideas back and forth, back when modern alcoholism studies was first beginning, and the thinkers debating all these issues at the school I was attending were the most formative people in this whole new field of studies.

It was Roosevelt Raceway, you will remember, which made a grant to me for my expenses there at the Yale School. In earlier years, this harness racing track had been an air field, called Roosevelt Field, named after Quentin Roosevelt, President Theodore Roosevelt's son. This was the very place from which Charles Lindbergh had taken off on May 20, 1927, when he flew the *Spirit of St. Louis* nonstop to Paris. Lindbergh's incredible flight had taken the world into a new era of history. Airplanes were soon crossing the Atlantic on a regular basis, and eventually the Pacific as well, until the whole world was bound together in a way it never was before.

If July 5, 1948, was my own spiritual "Pearl Harbor," then going to the Yale School of Alcohol Studies in the summer of 1949 was my own psychological "Lindbergh flight." The knowledge I gained, but above all the inspiration and motivation I absorbed from those incredible teachers, expanded my horizons and raised my life up to an entirely new level. I now saw that all the people who were dying of alcoholism, and hurting and destroying all the people around them in the process, did not have to die and did not have to harm and injure. We knew how to do things about that now, things that worked. I saw now that my job was to spread the message that a new world had appeared. The alcoholics among us no longer needed to be cast out of society and abandoned to their miserable doom. It was time for the preachers to stop lecturing them and condemning them as moral degenerates, and it was time for the courts, both military and civilian, to stop locking up alcoholics on principle as nothing but criminals. Alcoholics no longer had to die. It was time to heal the sick and raise the dead.

And there is another extremely important point here, which I hope the reader has not missed. *I did not sabotage myself this time.* I not only completed the course of study, I returned to Mitchel Air Force Base with my "ammunition belt" loaded with ideas and concepts to put into practice. I arrived back home with my flag held high, and ready to really fight now.

I was already deeply committed to salvaging Air Force personnel who were alcoholic before I went to the Yale School, but I was ten times as committed now. I knew that someone had to combat the pervasive attitude of strong negativism present in so many parts of the base, so I preached to these often hostile military commanders over and over: (1) alcoholism was a disease, (2) the alcoholic was salvageable, and (3) the alcoholic was worth saving. The number of those who were willing to come into my treatment program continued to grow for a year or so, and a more positive attitude toward the problem of alcoholism began to evolve on the base.

I still have some mixed feelings about the depth to which I sometimes became involved in working with alcoholics during that period. My family had now grown to five boys, and my wife had her hands full. In retrospect, I realize how little help I was to her at many times. Many a night I would get up out of my warm bed to go the aid of an alcoholic, which I did feel was my duty. But I was needed at home too. I simply do not know whether I acted wisely and well on some occasions. Was I being selfish, or was I doing something that a good man had to do? Real moral decisions are not always clear, and presented in simple black and white.

My treatment program, as I said, continued to grow and to be successful for a year or so after my return from the Yale School. But then, as we moved into late 1950 and early 1951, the number of people being referred to me for treatment began to drop. The figures finally dropped so low, that I could no longer justify being given a full time assignment by the Air Force, where all I was doing was working with alcoholics. My Commanders however had become impressed with my ability to teach people and speak in front of groups—my work with alcoholics had required that—and I had also attended the Yale School, which gave me some credentials, so the decision was made to reassign me to teaching ROTC classes at Kent State University in Ohio. I will talk about that in a later chapter, because that is where I got to know Sister Ignatia, the nun who worked with Dr. Bob at St. Thomas

Hospital in Akron, where the two of them had set up the most famous A.A. treatment center of them all.

But the question has to be asked now, about why the numbers of people coming in for treatment began to drop at this point in time. Part of it was probably that Mitchel was a very small Air Force base. There were only so many alcoholics there to begin with, and you cannot get alcoholics into treatment successfully until they reach the appropriate point in their drinking careers. Someone who is still getting away with it will never take the program seriously. The next opportunity I had to set up a treatment program, which was two years later in 1953, I was given a choice of several bases, and deliberately chose Lackland partly because it was so huge.

The other workable strategy was to set up a treatment program on what could even be a small base, but bring in people who needed help from other surrounding bases to this central treatment unit. This required cooperation and coordination at a higher command level, and the Air Force was possibly not ready for that yet. Nevertheless, I chose Lackland two years later partly for that reason as well. If I could obtain sufficient cooperation, there were a large number of other air bases in that immediately surrounding area, and it would be easy to send men and women for brief temporary postings to Lackland while they went through treatment.

At Mitchel, another problem arose because I had no psychiatrists to help me, and no way of hospitalizing incoming patients for detoxing. Alcoholism is a complex disease. Many people need help from psychiatrists and psychotherapists in order to get stabilized in sobriety. For many alcoholics, going off of alcohol is also physically very difficult. What are called "the d.t.'s" are bad enough, but some especially heavy drinkers actually go into convulsions and die after the alcohol is removed from their systems. A one-person operation, with no hospitalization or medical help to turn to, was very difficult to run successfully. Again, at Lackland I was going to solve that. The psychiatrist Dr. Louis Jolyon West and I set up a team effort which was extremely successful. As an M.D., he could also prescribe appropriate medication during withdrawal from alcohol, or even afterwards if psychiatrically mandated.

When I first started the treatment program at Mitchel, there were still many people on base who remembered how much I drank and how much I got into trouble over my drinking, so they did not really take my title of Chaplain's Assistant seriously. By 1951 unfortunately, too many people were seeing me as part of the Chaplain's Office, and that was the kiss of death as far as alcoholics coming in for help. They assumed that I would simply preach at them, and scold them, and threaten them with hellfire. After I got to Lackland, I was finally able to get out from under the Chaplain's Assistant title, and it made my job enormously much easier. The new title I eventually got there was Psychiatric Social Worker. It is an interesting commentary on the alcoholic mind, that practicing alcoholics would far rather be regarded as insane than religious.

But the biggest problem at Mitchel came from the fact that, in spite of my informal efforts at persuasion, Commanders and Senior Noncoms were not referring people to me, even when some of those under their command were obviously in serious trouble from their drinking. It usually takes outside pressure from some source—a military superior, a boss at a civilian job, or a spouse—to actually push an alcoholic into a treatment program. At Lackland two years later, I dealt with this in part by devoting a substantial part of my time to conducting mandatory training in formal classroom sessions for noncommissioned officers and other people in command positions. I talked about how the disease of alcoholism affected people, and taught them to recognize some of the symptoms, but even more importantly stressed to them that a proper treatment program could turn these drinkers' lives around, so that they could be returned to their units as fully productive individuals. I also tried to make it clear that genuine alcoholics were not going to change if all that was done was to lecture them and threaten them and punish them more and more severely. Our purpose in the alcoholism treatment program was to take the problem off their hands and solve it for them, so dealing with the drunks who were under their command would no longer eat into their time.

In other words, to set up a fully successful treatment program on a base, one had to spend as much time working with the non-alcoholics on base as one did with the alcoholics. I had not fully recognized that at Mitchel.

And there was also the fact that Commanders and Senior Noncoms were deeply afraid that they themselves would be given black marks on their records if they admitted that they had out-of-control alcoholics in their units. The whole attitude toward alcoholism in those days was so punitive and condemnatory, that they in fact may have been right. One of their superiors might well have said, "This person has lost control of his unit. Look at all these personnel who have had to be sent off to alcoholism treatment! We need to send in someone who is tough and can take charge and bring some discipline in there."

It required people like Marty Mann and Senator Harold Hughes, working at the national level, to start changing these attitudes. It was not in fact until the 1960's and 70's that general public opinion began to change, and it took even longer for any of these changed attitudes to begin percolating into the Air Force and the Army. When I went back into military alcoholism treatment as a civilian in the 1970's and 80's, the Navy was the only branch of the military which had a fully supportive and deeply committed approach to alcoholism treatment.

So in 1951, my little pilot program at Mitchel Air Force Base had to be closed down, but it had nevertheless been successful enough that I was able to talk the Air Force into letting me try it again in 1953. And at Lackland Air Force Base in San Antonio, Texas, building on what I had learned at Mitchel, I was able to get a smoothly functioning and sophisticated alcoholism treatment program up and running, with enough personnel being sent in for treatment to justify our staff salaries, and a fifty percent success rate with those whom we accepted into the program. So in retrospect, looking back on it now, I think the Mitchel program has to be regarded as a very successful initial experimental program.

At the time, of course, I could not know any of these things. I was not happy at all when the program was closed down. The only thing that kept me from being extremely depressed over it, was the thrill of being asked to teach college students at Kent State University as my next assignment. As I mentioned, I was going to be sent to join the staff which ran the Air Force ROTC program there, a reserve officer training unit which taught specialized military courses which enabled students to earn an officer's commission as part of their college studies.

And there were enormous rewards even then from what I was in fact able to accomplish at that small air base on Long Island. We cannot allow ourselves to turn alcoholism treatment into numbers and statistics. It is human lives which we are trying to save, and each of these human beings is a distinct individual. We come to love them and treasure them as people, and rejoice in their return to health.

So let me conclude by telling you just one story. During our time at Mitchel Air Force Base, my wife and I had to get a baby sitter from time to time while we went to meetings. We came to call on one young woman on a regular basis because she was so good with our children. Mary W. was a WAC, a member of the women's Air Force unit at Mitchel. From time to time she would ask me various things, with apparent interest, about my participation in Alcoholics Anonymous, but I did not really think anything about that. A lot of people were curious about the new A.A. movement.

Then late one night she called me on the phone at home, and told me that she was thinking about committing suicide. There was real desperation and despair in her voice. I knew she really meant it. She lived in the women's barracks, which male G.I.'s were absolutely forbidden to enter. I was so concerned about her however, that I went over to the barracks to try to talk with her face to face. I will tell you that my heart was in my throat as I sneaked through the door of that building. Getting caught could well have meant the permanent end of my career as an alcoholism treatment counselor. We talked and talked, and finally she calmed down somewhat, and agreed to go to an A.A. meeting with me.

My co-author and I met for the first time at the 2002 Indiana State A.A. Conference in Columbus, Indiana, and he has told me that he was extraordinarily impressed with the informal counseling sessions that would occur when I would sit and drink coffee in the hospitality center.

People would come up and start talking, and he said he was amazed at the way that they would soon start talking with me about some of their deepest and most painful memories and emotions. And yet, he said, I actually talked very little during these conversations myself. It was the people whom I was counseling who were doing all the talking. So how did I do it, he asked me.

You will remember me mentioning that, during my high school days, I had yearned so much for someone to whom I could just have talked, freely and openly, about all the hurt and anger I was feeling. The people who came to me did not need somebody to talk at them, they needed somebody to genuinely listen to them—someone who would actually hear what they were saying with total acceptance.

I did not go into the women's barracks to talk at Mary the WAC, I went there to listen to Mary the WAC, just to be there for her. And the truth of the matter is, that all the words she said, and the few words I said, were not really the important part anyway. She knew as well as I did that I was taking my military career in my hands going in there where she was. Simply the fact that another human being would be there for her, even in those circumstances, was the important thing that night.

It was just a little over a year later that my orders came through to leave Mitchel and go to Kent State. Mary was still sober and doing wonderfully. She rounded up forty-six people for a surprise party for me at the Officers Club the night before I left. There were officers and enlisted people both, all of them people that I had worked with. At the party, Mary gave me an uncirculated 1921 silver dollar as a little going away present.

For most of the fifty-two years since then I have carried that silver dollar in my pocket every day. Much of the design and letters are worn off, and it is much thinner now than it was then, but you can still discern the outlines of the figures on the coin and the date itself. It is a sign and a symbol and a constant reminder to me of so many things. Alcoholics can be helped and are salvageable. I can personally find a higher meaning in my own life, a sense of spiritual value, by using my own experiences to help other alcoholics. My most important job is not to talk at other people, but to be there for them and listen to them. Each alcoholic whom I meet is an individual human being, unique in his or her problems and experiences—there is no mechanical formula or set of procedures to follow. What is required in each case is me, as one unique individual, getting to know and love another human being as a unique individual, whose life I will care about, whom I will not ever wish to harm or hurt, and whom I will authentically listen to.

And maybe in another way, Mary the WAC, during my last year at Mitchel, was in some shape or form the daughter I lost so many years earlier. Maybe in a tiny way I made a partial, inadequate amends to that little girl. I do not know. The holes will always be in the fence. Perhaps the coin, which was her way of saying "thank you," meant a sign of forgiveness back the other way—a token symbolizing the healing and forgiving power which enters our lives when we come into the program, which will wash away the truly crippling guilts from the past.

I simply do not know. But I still carry the silver dollar in my pocket every day. It stands for something very important to me.

CHAPTER 15

The Effects of Alcohol on Our Emotional Development

Over the many years I have been writing and lecturing on the problem of alcoholism, my own work has been identified as centering on the emotional aspects of its development. Both on the basis of what I have learned from my own personal history, and from observing thousands of alcoholics in recovery over the past half century, I have developed a profile of the alcoholic in which I show the paramount importance of various emotional components in producing compulsive and out-of-control drinking.

I began developing my own philosophy of alcoholism, as I mentioned in the previous chapter, when I attended the Yale School of Alcohol Studies in 1949, and first came in contact with the late Dr. E. M. Jellinek. He was one of the most outstanding alcoholism researchers of his time, and made a number of important contributions to the field. He had originally been trained in the application of the statistical method to biological research, and had an impressive ability to sort through complex data, and spot trends and sequences, and then mathematically prove their statistical validity. As I noted in the previous chapter, one legacy of his work was his development of the Jellinek curve, as it is called, which he drew up by making statistical studies of personal life histories given to him by alcoholics involved in recovery in the Alcoholics Anonymous program. Dr. Jellinek demonstrated that there were clearly defined progressive changes in behavioral patterns as alcoholics continued to drink over months and years, which could be laid out in an easy-to-understand chart. The alcoholic's problems not only grew worse and worse, they did so in fairly predictable ways, in a sort of stepwise fashion. This Jellinek curve is still used worldwide in classrooms, treatment programs, and in public educational programs.

In addition to his development of this statistical curve, he had also determined through his own research that the depressive effect of alcohol on the barrier separating the conscious from the subconscious played a major role in the progressive development of alcoholism. With his permission, I began using diagrams based on this part of his theories about alcoholism in my own work at Mitchel Air Force Base, and have continued using them to this day. They have proven to be effective and convincing in working with alcoholics who deny that they have any real problem. I have also found that others who work in alcoholism treatment programs have found these diagrams very useful in understanding important aspects of the problem.

I continued to develop my own theories after I arrived at Lackland Air Force Base, where I was appointed as Psychiatric Social Worker in the Department of Psychiatry. My supervisor and mentor there was the late Louis Jolyon West, M.D., an eminent psychiatrist and dear friend, who taught me about many aspects of human behavior and the emotional components of alcoholism. Dr. West eventually became head of the Department of Psychiatry and Director of the Neuropsychiatric Institute at the University of California at Los Angeles, where he used me as a Consultant to their Alcohol and Drug Program. During his lifetime, he was considered one of the most eminent psychiatrists in the United States and received many awards and recognitions.

With the charts based on Dr. Jellinek's work, ideas drawn from Dr. West's psychiatric observations, and my own practical experience in running alcoholism treatment programs, I have been able to develop speeches and presentations which seem to give most people who attend my talks valuable insights into the underlying nature of this disease. It is an approach which not only works with high success in counseling individual alcoholics, but helps other people involved in alcoholism treatment gain a better grasp of the nature of the problems they are attempting to treat, with again great success when put to practical application.

These charts illustrate the origin and progression of emotional problems, and the way in which alcohol may ultimately be used to alleviate the anxiety and stress associated with both conscious and subconscious problems. We must remember of course, that as mentioned previously, not all individuals who become alcoholics have this sort of emotional component. There are a variety of causative factors which can be at work in producing alcoholic behavior, including genetic, environmental, and experiential factors, and alcoholism can be produced by any one of these factors even though the others are absent.

I have observed alcoholics who suffer only from a physiological addiction, for example. Regular use of alcoholic beverages (including beer or wine) over an extended period of time can create a physical dependence on alcohol in and of itself. These sorts of alcoholics can frequently be identified because there is no gross behavior change displayed in their actions when they are inebriated.

Genetics is one of the contributors for most alcoholics. A vast majority of those who eventually become alcoholic have a history of alcoholism in their family, particularly when one investigates not only their parents' generation but the previous generation as well.

However, one can have alcoholism with no genetic contributor: those who insist that they have no family history of alcoholism cannot use that as a way of defending their obviously out-of-control alcohol abuse as though it were only harmless "social drinking." A mother who drank during pregnancy, even if she was not an alcoholic, can pass alcohol dependency on to the fetus.[13] The kinds of causal factors which can produce alcoholism are many.

Alcoholism is a complex phenomenon. Each alcoholic is unique. There will be a different mix of factors in each individual, so an individualized treatment program has to be devised for each person whom one is attempting to treat. Nevertheless, the emotional component is so often present, that I have found great success over the past half century in making this the centerpiece of my treatment strategy for the vast majority of cases.

If we look at this most typical sort of case, we will discover that the alcoholics' problems tend to begin appearing in some fashion during their earliest years. In early childhood development, parents have a decided influence on their children. They set the standards for human relationships, and they either provide or fail to provide their children with adequate social skills. The parents' emotional conflicts or their inability to act as functional parents, will have a dynamic negative influence on their children.

One does not need to have parents with major emotional conflicts or psychological problems *per se* in order for the children to develop serious personality problems. In spite of the current trend of talking about "dysfunctional families" in the psychological and emotional sense as a central causal factor, problems can just as easily arise from other sorts of issues. In many parts of the United States, for example, children are expected to be able to read and write to some degree prior to school enrollment. Parents who are unwilling or unable to assist their children in this preschool training—who send their children off to school already behind their peers—can create irreversible psychological damage in the child.

School teachers may not be able to reach some of these children in an effective remedial manner, no matter how hard they try. These children's lifestyles have already been established, and they may refuse to be taught. No amount of external pressure appears to change unmotivated children of this sort, unless they themselves can come to recognize the futility of this kind of negative behavior, and can be encouraged to change their fundamental lifestyle.

Even when individuals have problems which obviously produce negative and destructive interactions with the society in which they live, they will still usually have a strong tendency to deny that these problems exist at all. As Dr. Jellinek said many times, "You must break down the alibi system to get at the real cause of the problem." I have found in practice that the four charts which I am reproducing below can help enormously in breaking through this sort of denial and the systematic set of alibis and excuses which alcoholics use to continue their destructive behavioral patterns.

FIGURE 1. CONSCIOUS CONFLICTS
ASSOCIATED WITH PERSONALITY DEVELOPMENT

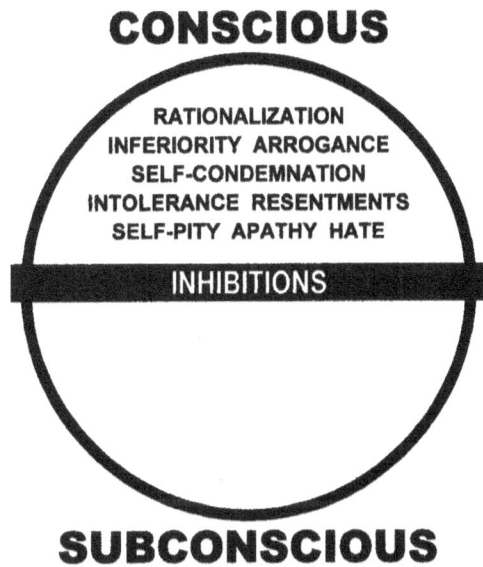

The circle in these charts represents the central nervous system or the brain. It is divided into two separate parts, the conscious and the subconscious. The line through the middle, which divides these two sections, represents the inhibitions, that is, the ability to repress negative personality problems which are painful and anxiety laden. Everything which we perceive consciously (see Fig. 1) is not experienced as negative, but for the purpose of exposing the origin of this sort of alcohol problem, only those which are anxiety provoking are listed above the divider line.

Initially in early childhood the problems listed as subconscious (see Fig. 2) were experienced on a conscious level, but the rejection or punishment received was so painful that they were inhibited. When these emotions were forced down into the subconscious in this fashion, alternative behavior patterns emerged to compensate for these traumatic problems. Inhibited negative conflicts cause tension, for example, which in turn produces emotional unrest. The arrows in Figure 2 represent this internal psychological tension. The person then must develop alternative methods for easing this anxiety. In the alcoholic, that beverage is used as a means for coping with problems which produce this sort of anxiety, and as a way to try to deal with the person's inability to live in an acceptable lifestyle.

FIGURE 2. SUBCONSCIOUS CONFLICTS
ASSOCIATED WITH PERSONALITY DEVELOPMENT

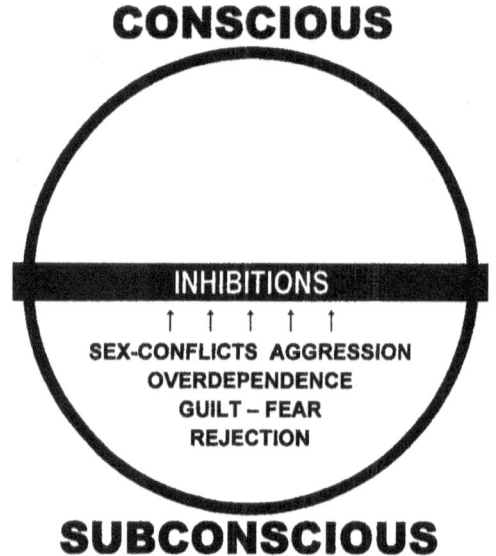

The kinds of inhibited conflicts listed on the diagram down below the line, are buried in the subconscious where the individual is no longer in conscious knowledge of their existence, but they will nevertheless still be manifested on the conscious level in a variety of ways. People with subconscious emotional problems feel inadequate, lonely, inferior, self-condemning, and full of self-pity at the conscious level (Fig. 1). And there are other conditions as well which make the person unable to experience good feelings from his or her interpersonal relationships. The entire process produces anxiety and tension which either interferes with or totally precludes normal behavioral responses.

Again I must issue the warning that not all alcoholics drink to try to self-medicate emotional conflicts and problems of this sort. Alcoholism is a complex phenomenon. Many alcoholics do not exhibit a gross behavior change under the influence of alcohol, which may indicate a primarily physiological addiction. Their bodies demand the alcohol because they begin undergoing painful and unpleasant physical symptoms when there is no alcohol in their bloodstreams. It is often difficult to convince people that they are alcoholics when they display little or no behavior changes of the sort we are describing here, that is, the acting out of subconscious emotional conflicts in a destructive or antisocial fashion. Nevertheless the irresistible compulsion to drink, and the negative effects of constant inebriation on their ability to function, means that they too need help in overcoming their alcohol dependency.

One of the most powerful motivations for continuing to act in a certain kind of way arises from the results these behaviors produce. Basically healthy individuals who are looking for positive paybacks will display behavior which is socially and legally appropriate, emotionally rewarding, and within the guidelines of their culture. The successes they achieve by acting that way motivate them to continue this sort of positive behavior. This will set up a positive reinforcing cycle.

When people respond in an opposite way, reacting to their own negative inner drives without being influenced or restricted by cultural demands, they will not receive these positive results, and anxiety will be the byproduct. When they then drink alcohol because of their feelings of anxiety, this will increase the effect of those negative inner drives on their behavior, which will in turn drive them into drinking even more alcohol, and set up a negative reinforcing cycle which will feed on itself and produce ever-growing levels of antisocial behavior.

We are a success-oriented society. Our motive often seems to be to teach people more about how to succeed than how to gain pleasure from life, but this kind of success philosophy can nevertheless be a powerful motivational tool. We eulogize those who are successful, and condemn those who give up and end up in hospitals or jails. For people who have the negative outlook on life which I had back in my drinking days, there is little chance that the outcome will be positive. My drinking and my attitudes caused me to be a failure a good deal of the time in achieving meaningful successes in life, and I felt the weight of society's condemnation quite powerfully.

Most parents encourage their offspring to excel in both physical and mental tasks. As young people go through the maturation process, rewards are allocated to those who accomplish such things as achieving a high grade-point average in their scholastic endeavors, winning parts in plays, earning badges and letters for their achievements, and making the starting team in an athletic program. In my own youth, I had little to show for what was in fact only limited effort on my part to reach most of these goals. I withdrew psychologically from the process. I merely existed, and passed most of my time in a totally nonproductive manner.

Achieving some of the accomplishments above requires taking part in group activities. Participation in these provides the individual with a feeling of belonging. Young people who never experienced any positive group relationships within their childhood families enter school with attitudes and behavior patterns already set in such a negative way that there is little likelihood of their responding favorably to group work in the educational setting. One cannot live in any human society without having to function within groups of various sorts. Someone like me, who had such strong barriers against feeling a part of any group, was blocked by that from any sort of greatly rewarding life.

We want to feel good. The quality of our interpersonal relationships has a profound impact on our ability to feel good. When we are forced to function within a group, the response of the other group members will determine whether this need to feel good will be met or denied. In my own case, being disruptive and seeking attention through this disruptive behavior, caused negative responses. I tried to be a part of the group by creating trouble, or by attempting to do things which I thought would be humorous, and amuse people and make people laugh. You will remember my drunken attempt to dance with a dog at the Air Cadet School. I ended up each time being isolated from the group. I came to feel that this was my fate, and I bitterly resented those who were well-adjusted and who were regarded as an acceptable part of the group.

From the time a child is introduced into the competitive aspect of our society, and throughout the maturational process, there are several constant themes. (1) We must compete and be evaluated. (2) We must experience either acceptance or rejection. (3) We must ultimately confront either success or failure. How well we do is based on our ability to perform under these highly stressful circumstances. Given that I began the process of socialization and maturation by falling into consistently negative responses to these societal demands, it is not difficult to see why I failed to negotiate that initial period of my life successfully. Some of the obstacles that I believed blocked me from success were figments of my imagination, but whether these obstacles were real or imagined, they created an unbreakable barrier blocking me from growing up into a stable, mature adult.

Societal demands are extremely different now than when I was a teenager, but the basic dynamic has not changed. There still remains the need to feel good about oneself, to function effectively in our competitive society, and to experience love from others. When our inappropriate responses to these external pressures fail to supply these needs, many young people seek alternative routes to temporarily "feeling good." They attempt to alleviate the anxiety produced by their failure to meet societal demands by various substitute methods, but alcohol can become a major component in this game.

Over the past thirty-five years, increasing numbers of American teenagers have also been tempted to use narcotics and other mind-altering and mood-altering drugs for the same kind of purpose. We have become a drug-oriented society, and although opposed to *addiction* to these drugs, we provide all the conditions which are conducive to going down that destructive route. Nearly every ache and pain can be treated with a non-prescription drug. This includes drugs which can be taken which we believe will help us to fall asleep, to stay awake, or to block out all sorts of symptomatic physical pain.

People in our society can be, and often are, deluded even at that level. Taking aspirin for a headache will do no good in the long run if a brain tumor is causing the pain, or if what the person really needs is a new pair of eye-glasses. But the belief still persists that if I can figure out the right pill to take, I will automatically start "getting well" and begin to feel good again, with no further effort on my part. So a useless medication can sometimes seem to produce temporary good results, as a sort of psychological illusion. I want so much to believe that it is working, that I delude myself into believing that it is actually working. And so for a certain period of time I can convince myself that I have found the "cure" for what is making me feel so bad.

So adults in our society regularly turn to drugs for all sorts of reasons, and achieve some psychological relief even if these medications are not always all that effective at the purely physical level. Children who observe the attitudinal changes produced in their parents by the use of these drugs, may easily become convinced that they too could overcome any discomfort they were feeling by finding the right type of drug.

Many American teenagers now at least experiment with the effects of narcotics and other drugs, and some become totally addicted to them. Nevertheless beverage alcohol is still the number one substance used in this country by young people who are attempting to gain for themselves some sort of chemically-induced attitudinal change. Young people who have difficulty in communicating with their parents, their siblings, their peers, and authority figures, still usually turn to alcohol as the primary mind-altering chemical they use in the attempt to alleviate their painful feelings. In part their choice of alcohol is aided by every type of advertising, in newspapers, magazines, radio, and television, suggesting (without considering the consequences for many) that the use of alcohol will produce socially acceptable benefits in a way that other drugs clearly will not.

I am therefore going to confine myself in this chapter to discussing the effects of alcohol on the central nervous system. I do not want to make this chapter any more complicated than I can help. Figure 3 illustrates the change in behavior and attitude when alcohol is ingested by someone with subconscious emotional conflicts.

FIGURE 3. DEPRESSANT ACTION OF ALCOHOL ON
CENTRAL NERVOUS SYSTEM AND ALTERED ATTITUDE

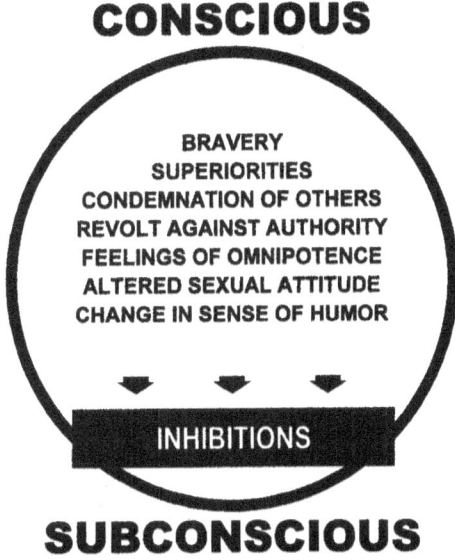

CONSCIOUS

**BRAVERY
SUPERIORITIES
CONDEMNATION OF OTHERS
REVOLT AGAINST AUTHORITY
FEELINGS OF OMNIPOTENCE
ALTERED SEXUAL ATTITUDE
CHANGE IN SENSE OF HUMOR**

INHIBITIONS

SUBCONSCIOUS

The excessive use of alcoholic beverages in our society becomes a trap for the person with emotional problems, as well as for those with a genetic or physical predisposition to becoming addicted to this drug. Alcohol is a socially acceptable beverage in our culture, and most individuals do not intentionally drink compulsively. For vast numbers of people, becoming trapped occurs as a gradual process of falling into greater and greater physical and psychological dependence. However, a small portion of those who drink exhibit extremely negative behavior traits from the onset, as one can see from my own case. Even then, however, the problems progress and the consequences continue to grow worse and worse as the person continues to drink. Those who become trapped in compulsive drinking ultimately become rehabilitated, or descend into a useless life of total alcohol dependence, or die.

As the alcohol problem progresses, the demand for alcohol increasingly overwhelms the ability to control and abstain. Those in an early stage of alcoholism will usually still have some sense of responsibility, but this progressively erodes away. As the dependency grows, they become more and more preoccupied with the need to procure alcohol to sustain their habit at any cost.

Figure 4 illustrates the emotional picture when alcohol is withdrawn. An even greater emotional instability is created. This emotional state becomes increasingly too painful to tolerate. Now the alcoholic feels the compulsion to drink, not just because of the preexisting subconscious emotional conflicts, but also because of the new anxieties and guilt produced by the last drinking bout, which impose an additional burden of pain. The conscious thought processes have also become even more confused and filled with negative and self-destructive attitudes.

Social drinkers (as opposed to alcoholics) have other interests, and are not continually preoccupied with the thought of drinking or obtaining alcohol to drink. Problem drinkers however increasingly come to have no other interests. They rely on alcohol for social involvement, and to ease stress situations, and then in progressive fashion become dependent on alcohol in order to deal with any kind of life circumstance: weddings, funerals, job promotions or job losses, or in any kind of situation involving responsibilities. For those budding alcoholics who begin young, dealing with the pressures of school and school activities becomes increasingly impossible without drinking.

FIGURE 4. CONSCIOUS AND SUBCONSCIOUS
FEELINGS AFTER WITHDRAWAL OF ALCOHOL

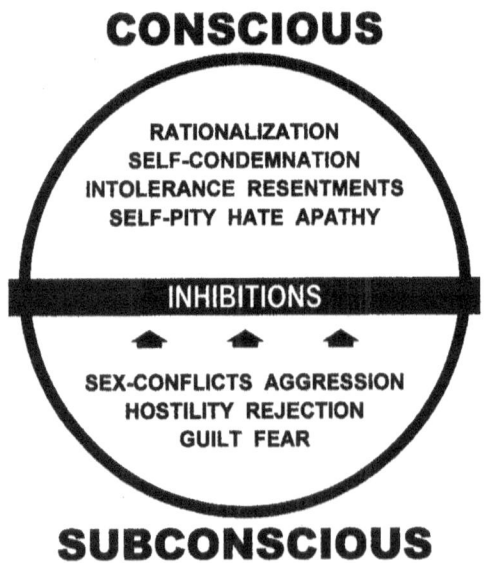

CONSCIOUS

RATIONALIZATION
SELF-CONDEMNATION
INTOLERANCE RESENTMENTS
SELF-PITY HATE APATHY

INHIBITIONS

SEX-CONFLICTS AGGRESSION
HOSTILITY REJECTION
GUILT FEAR

SUBCONSCIOUS

After alcoholism has progressed to a great enough degree, some individuals are unable to recall events that occurred while drinking. This is called having a "black-out." This is a definite warning sign that this person has become an alcoholic. However, the reader should be warned, some people are able to progress quite far in the development of the disease without having clear and distinct evidence of black-outs. The apparent absence of black-out drinking does not at all mean that a person has not already become an alcoholic.

I did have black-outs myself, with increasing frequency over the years of my drinking. I once traveled from Ohio all the way to Virginia, and was unable to remember anything about how I had gotten there. It is an extraordinary surprise, to say the least, to emerge from a black-out and find oneself in a strange location, with no knowledge of how one got to that place or what is going on.

When I was at Hickam Field in Hawaii, and began drinking again after the Pearl Harbor attack, I lived in a sort of black-out much of the time for many months. There are all kinds and degrees of memory loss. During that period my black-outs were external and applied to my physical surroundings, although it did not affect my emotional recall. I might remember that I had been very angry the night before, for example, but would not be able to recall the physical situation.

Black-outs may increase the guilt produced by excessive drinking, for those who become apprehensive about their inability to recall their actions while they were in that mental state. Some alcoholics worry incessantly afterwards about where they were, who they offended, whether they borrowed money from anyone, whether they physically attacked anyone, and so on, *ad infinitum*. Some experts believe that black-outs are a means of escaping the pressures of reality. A strange phenomenon can occur when people in a black-out are suddenly involved in an accident or confronted by the law, and instantly come out of their black-out. It appears that the increase in the flow of adrenaline produces this effect, and returns the mind's ability to remember.

In the early stages of alcoholism, many do not drink in the morning when they first arise. For them, morning drinking begins only in a later stage of the disease, after the physical suffering from withdrawal has progressed to unacceptable levels. When alcoholics begin drinking in the morning, it is to overcome the emotional discomfort of the hangover, or to satisfy the physical craving of their bodies. This first drink in turn seems to trigger a physical or psychological compulsion to continue drinking for all the rest of that day.

Morning drinking of that sort is a clear indication of an alcoholic pattern of drinking, but one should be very careful here. There are some alcoholics whose disease is quite progressed, who do not drink in the morning, and use this as an excuse to rule out the label of alcohol dependency. These are people who either cannot physically tolerate drinking the next morning at all, or who are willing to bear the physical effects of the withdrawal of the alcohol from their systems, no matter how painful it is. Not drinking before noon, or before five p.m., or some other target time, is not ever "proof" that a person is not an alcoholic. It does not at all indicate that the disease has not already progressed to a truly dangerous point.

Prior to the admission of complete defeat, alcoholics use various methods in the attempt to conceal, deny, or minimize their problem. They usually lie about how much they actually drink when they are asked, and they try to "sneak drinks" when no one is watching.

Or they attempt to deal with their alcoholism in ways that never work and never can. Perhaps they begin to realize to a certain degree that alcohol is beginning to interfere in their lives, or that they have developed an unhealthy dependence on alcohol. So they may exclaim, "I'm off the hard stuff, only beer from now on." One of the great American myths is that beer is the beverage of moderation, so alcoholics switch from hard liquor to beer in order to convince others that they really have no alcohol problem. Beer as beverage of moderation is a fairy tale, because it is just as intoxicating as any other beverage containing alcohol. It takes a greater volume of beer because of its lower alcohol content, and a slightly longer time to become inebriated because of its slower absorption rate. But one can produce all the alcoholic symptoms on beer alone, as many people have found to their dismay. It does not slow or reverse the progression of the disease in the slightest.

The same warning applies to wine. The progression of the disease will continue the same way as it would while consuming any alcohol-containing beverage. One need only glance at a wino lying in the gutter, clutching a bottle of wine in a brown paper bag, to dispel the myth that one can stop the progress of alcoholism by switching from hard liquor to wine.

I recently saw a program on television in which the old claim was again being raised that drinking *slight* amounts of alcohol (wine was being recommended in this case) can help people avoid heart attacks. I immediately cringed to think of what this advice could do to undermine someone who was drinking excessively, and who also had a weak heart, but was trying to quit. The television presentation also ignored the fact that any slight statistical gain achieved in avoiding heart attacks by *moderate* alcohol ingestion would be more than offset by the greater statistical chance of dying of cancer (and many other diseases) instead, for consuming even small amounts of alcohol affects those statistics negatively. Those are so many more effective methods of coping with heart problems, which are not risks to those who are already on the edge of becoming alcoholics, such as eating healthier food or walking for exercise. But bending your elbow every day is not what is meant by "taking regular exercise."

And alcoholics use many other tactics to try to talk themselves into believing that some kind of "controlled" drinking would be possible for them, whether it is the type of beverage, or the amount drunk, or the time of day that they take their first drink. The Rand Report that came out in the mid 1970's suggested that some alcoholics, with proper therapy, could return to social drinking with no ill effects.[14] That particular claim has continued to emerge occasionally from time to time. The actual statistics in each instance—when serious controls were applied, truly objective long term follow-up methods were used, and all of the eventual effects were included as part of the data—never bore out any of these assertions, but the claims continue to appear periodically, for they appeal to a certain kind of wishful thinking.

In all my own years of working with alcoholics, I have never known of even one person who was able to accomplish the feat of returning to normal social drinking successfully. The ones whom I know who tried it, returned to the same dysfunctional lifestyle and began exhibiting the same kinds of destructive behaviors that they had shown when they drank previously. Alcoholics do not drink for social reasons in the first place, they drink to escape the pains of reality. That is why the majority of alcoholics, once solidly established in recovery, find that they would not want to drink again at all even if some technique were developed which would allow them to do so without returning to their old compulsive excess—they simply do not desire even a small amount of that kind of sensation or mental state any more.

These comments are based upon observations I have made of other alcoholics who were still in denial. In my own case, unlike many alcoholics, I only rarely attempted to minimize the amount I was actually drinking, and regularly admitted that I drank excessively. I made little or no attempt to deny that. What I did instead was to recite the problems I was having, and complain about the circumstances which I insisted were causing me to drink. It was always the fault of other people and circumstances, and I rarely acknowledged that it was my drinking itself which was causing most of the problems in the first place. I turned to self-pity in order to eliminate self-blame for my alcoholic behavior. So I had my own strategies for evading facing the full truth.

The important thing to note is that in one way or another, alcoholics who have not yet acknowledged their defeat use alibis, lies, and concealment tactics to attempt to hide their excessive drinking or make excuses for it. And they cannot learn how to deal with their problem until they first admit that it exists.

In summary, there are three basic kinds of causal factors which can produce alcoholism, either by themselves or in combination. The most prevalent contributing factor is the genetic background of the victim. Alcoholism as physical addiction can be produced simply by drinking too much alcohol too regularly over too long a period of time. But for most people I have treated over the past half century, the use of alcohol in an attempt to medicate the stress of dealing with reality was what led to the excessive dependence, and serious internal emotional problems and failure in adequate socialization were responsible for the majority of the pain and distress.

The goal of treatment is not only the removal of the irresistible compulsion to drink, but also teaching alcoholics how to feel good. That is what human beings desire more than almost anything else, and that is what the kind of treatment I am describing in this book can produce. If you the reader are an alcoholic who is locked in enormous misery and pain, do please hear me when I tell you that there is an answer. You can be freed from that, and can learn how to feel good about yourself again. This is the most priceless gift anyone could ever be given.

CHAPTER 16

Kent State University and Sister Ignatia

In 1951, the time came when my little one-man alcoholism treatment program at Mitchel Air Force Base had to be closed down. People who entered my program got sober: I had demonstrated clearly that even the simple system I was using at that point would get results which were effective enough to be worth the effort. But my referrals were drying up. Men and women who needed the program were reluctant to come into the Chaplain's Office, which sounded too "religious" in orientation, and too many officers and senior noncoms were hesitant to refer people to me, either because they remained dubious about whether alcoholism could be treated effectively by this new approach, or because they were afraid that admitting that they had alcoholics in their units would be a black mark on their own military records.

But I had in fact helped people, and I had also made some interesting discoveries about myself. During the two years when my little pilot program was operating, I had found that I enjoyed teaching people. I who had been so self-conscious and fearful in group situations, had discovered a new principle of self-worth within myself, thanks to the A.A. program. I had found that I actually enjoyed standing up in front of a group of people and talking.

So I decided that, if I could not continue to work with alcoholics full-time at this point, I would pursue this new love instead, the love of teaching, to earn my bread and butter. I applied for an ROTC assignment. A Reserve Officers' Training Corps unit was based at a college or university. In the process of earning a four-year undergraduate degree, students would also take courses each semester from the military personnel assigned to that university, and (with a small amount of additional training) would be commissioned as second lieutenants at the same time that they received their academic degrees.

The Air Force sent me off for some additional teachers' training first, where I learned some very helpful things which I have been able to use ever since. This special training was conducted at the Academic Instructors School in Montgomery, Alabama, at Maxwell Air Force Base.

I have a fish story to tell from my stay there, which I would not tell, I promise you, if I did not in fact have a witness and written proof. When I arrived in Montgomery, I learned that the bass fishing in that area was considered exceptionally good. Fishing had always been one of my great loves, and by this point in my life, a few hours spent peacefully enjoying the water and the repetitive action of gently casting out the line and reeling it back in, had become one way of carrying out an eleventh-step time for quietness and inner relaxation. The local residents recommended Suggs Pond, which was not far from Montgomery, and since no one else wanted to go with me, I set out alone. I rented a small boat and rowed out to an area that seemed ideal for black bass. After several casts I got my first strike, but that bass was too small, so I released it.

I kept on casting in that same area, and soon thereafter, a really nice bass hit my plug, and the action I had been looking for was on. After a struggle, I finally got him in my boat. Precisely at the point when I was freeing the hook from that bass's mouth, another bass jumped high out of the water right beside my vessel, and came back down in such a way that he landed right in my boat alongside my first bass.

I could hardly believe my own eyes, but a fellow standing on the shore had seen it too, and hollered to me, "I can't even get a strike, and you got them jumping in the boat!" As it turned out, he was a reporter for the Montgomery newspaper, and called me to shore to interview me. They were large bass too, both around four and a half pounds. He wrote a little article for the newspaper about it, so I do have, not only another witness, but also written proof.

So whatever anyone might think about my ideas on alcoholism and its treatment, let no one ever challenge my abilities as a fisherman! There are nevertheless similarities. Just as fish do not normally just jump into your boat, no matter how nice a boat it is, so alcoholics do not normally just jump into treatment programs of their own free will. To catch alcoholics and save their lives, you need things which function like bait and hooks and lines and nets, and you have to row your boat to the right places. The alcoholic will struggle to avoid some of the necessary healing process, so you have to learn how to pull hard enough. On the other hand, you must not become frantic or overbearing and pull too hard, or your line will break. It requires a balance of firmness and gentleness, and knowing when to pull hard, and when to ease the pressure off. And you are not going to catch a fish each time you cast out your plug: becoming a good fisherman also requires learning patience and quiet persistence.

I was given some choice of ROTC assignments, so I selected the one at Kent State University in northeastern Ohio. It was only thirty miles or so from my childhood hometown of Niles, so I considered this a choice location. Kent was also a kind of distant suburb of Akron, Ohio—it was only ten miles from Kent to downtown Akron—so I was also going to discover that this was an excellent opportunity to get to know Sister Ignatia, along with Bill Dotson (the third person to get sober in A.A.) and some other good old-timers there in Akron, where A.A. had first begun sixteen years earlier.

I know that many people still react instantly to the mention of Kent State, because of their memories of that terrible day when the National Guard fired on protesting students and shot and killed four of them, during the anti-Vietnam war protests of a later era. But that was almost twenty years later, and was not part of the world I lived in during my stay on that campus. The Kent State campus that I went to remains in my memory as a very beautiful place, with many beautiful trees shading its grassy lawns, and fine modern buildings. It is still difficult for me to associate such a serene and peaceful setting with the angry, aggressive students of 1970, the rifles of the National Guardsmen, and the national outrage which erupted over that bloody day.

I prefer my original memories of the campus. As an official instructor, I was given the same status as the other teachers and professors at the university. I was provided a rent-free home opposite the university: an older house, on a farm which the university owned, but quite adequate. The town of Kent itself was small and friendly. During the two years we lived there, we also established many friendships with the non-university people who lived in town.

My fellow members of the ROTC staff were cooperative and most of them of very high quality, both the officers and enlisted personnel. As a unit, we had bowling teams, picnics, and many other social events. The Commanding Officer of the unit was especially nice to me and my family. He had been a young second lieutenant at Hickam Field when the Japanese attacked Pearl Harbor, so he and I had a common bond.

I loved to teach. Sometimes it seemed like a dream, that someone like me who had graduated from high school only with extreme difficulty, was now teaching college students. I worked hard and spent a good deal of time preparing my lectures, because I wanted to do the best job I could. I enjoyed the students themselves, and their youth and enthusiasm, and getting the opportunity to see them grow and learn.

A few of my students were from parts of Ohio close to my old home town, which made me feel very much at home. In fact, one of my students was the son of the very doctor who had delivered me when I was born, thirty-three years earlier. An especially strange coincidence there. Who could ever have predicted back then in 1918 that I would be where I was now?

Since Kent State was only a short distance from Akron, I traveled in to St. Thomas Hospital on many occasions, either to take alcoholics in to be hospitalized, or to visit the patients and talk with Sister Ignatia. This was an incredible experience, and I also learned many things about well-run treatment programs which I was able to make use of later.

The alcoholic ward at St. Thomas Hospital in Akron, which had begun in a tiny room used for preparing flower arrangements in 1939, was one of the more important parents of subsequent A.A.-related alcoholism treatment programs. Under the supervision of Dr. Bob and Sister Ignatia, it began to grow and expand, and achieved an incredible record of success in restoring alcoholics to long-term sobriety. Dr. Bob had died on November 16, 1950, almost a year before I received this ROTC teaching assignment, so I never got to know him, but Sister Ignatia was still there at the hospital. Her order did not move her to Cleveland until August 1952, so during my first year at Kent State, I drove into Akron frequently to visit her at St. Thomas, and had many heart-to-heart conversations with her, and was able to observe the alcoholic ward in action.

The ward which I visited was basically just a large room with eight beds set up at one end.[15] An alcoholism treatment center does not require large investments in space and equipment. At the other end of the room was a lounge area for the patients with comfortable chairs and a couch. There was an ice box, a large coffee urn kept continually filled with hot coffee twenty-four hours a day, and a small sink. The ice box was kept well-stocked with food, and especially milk and citrus juice. Patients were encouraged to eat whenever they felt like it, because all too many alcoholics were in fact malnourished, from too many years of drinking instead of eating. There was also a lavatory and shower for the patients in a small room just beyond this lounge area. The patients themselves were responsible for tasks like making the coffee, washing the coffee cups, and emptying ash trays. An A.A. employee did the heavy cleaning, so the only service which the hospital had to provide was a nurses' aide who came in to change the sheets and pillow cases on the beds.

The A.A. employee, a recovered alcoholic himself, worked in the ward eight hours a day, and served as an unofficial counselor. One way or another, the patients were exposed to A.A. continually during their stay in the hospital, and the A.A. sponsors and the unofficial A.A. counselor were given a good deal of input into the treatment of each individual patient, which was, in my estimation, one of the most important reasons why the St. Thomas program achieved such a high success rate.

The lounge area was used by a continual string of A.A. visitors, people who already had gained some sobriety in the program, who would sit and chat with the newcomers, and sometimes give informal talks. The corridor outside the ward room served as an additional lounge space, so two different conversations could be going on simultaneously. The five-day treatment program was a sort of "total immersion" experience in A.A., carried on twenty-four hours a day, where almost everything else was secondary to this continual exposure to A.A. principles and the spirit of the A.A. way of life, with its emphasis upon service and unselfishness and tolerance.

A line of chairs in the outside corridor area gave patients and visitors a place to sit down, and also separated this little nook from the entrance to the balcony of the hospital's chapel, which one entered by going through a door on the other side of the hall. The chapel, with its thirty-foot-high ceiling and stained glass windows, and the Stations of the Cross placed on the walls, is still there today. Patients in the alcoholic ward were allowed to attend daily mass sitting in this balcony while still in their hospital attire, and were also permitted to go over there to pray any time they wished.

Sister Ignatia was a nun, and this ward was located in a Catholic hospital, so the approach was much more religiously oriented than the one I used in my military treatment programs. When the patient was released from the ward, Sister Ignatia gave each one a little Sacred Heart badge to put in his pocket, and a small copy of Thomas à Kempis' *Imitation of Christ*, a well-known traditional Catholic meditational book which was often used by Protestants too.[16] Sister Ignatia was well aware that the majority of the patients in the alcoholic ward came from Protestant backgrounds, and she respected their different beliefs. She also had one Jewish patient in the ward at one point. Her normal practice was to take each patient over to the chapel, ask him to kneel there, and then she would kneel beside the man and they would recite the Third Step Prayer together. The Jewish patient told her that he could not in good conscience go into a Christian chapel, so Sister Ignatia told him that was fine, and made him kneel beside her in the hallway instead, and repeat the Third Step Prayer with her there.

That was her approach. You did not have to believe what she believed on various matters of religious doctrine and dogma, but you had to quit fighting against God, and you had to make a formal surrender, and tell your higher power, in whatever form you construed him, that you wanted to make peace and end the war. And her own deep faith had a profound effect on those who went into her ward for treatment, whether they were Catholics or not.

I went about it quite differently with my own patients on the military bases, but I too tried to make it clear to them that as long as they were hostile and contemptuous toward anything and everything having anything at all to do with a God or higher power of the universe, this was a clear and unmistakable symptom of something going on inside them which still needed a good deal of healing.

The program at St. Thomas had two important things which I had not had access to at Mitchel, but was going to have at Lackland: physicians to help with the patients' medical problems and return them to physical health, as well as psychiatrists to treat any major mental problems. Some alcoholics drink compulsively in a futile attempt to self-medicate what are in fact major psychiatric problems: they may in fact be schizophrenic or bipolar (manic depressive, we called it in those days) or have some other major mental problem. Until this is treated, the A.A. program by itself will do them no good. So when a patient who was admitted to the ward showed signs of serious psychological disturbance, such as continuing serious suicidal thoughts, one of the hospital's resident psychiatrists could be called in.

Dr. Bob had supervised the patients' physical treatment at the beginning of the St. Thomas program. When he fell into his final illness, one of the staff doctors who had worked with him had taken over, and was handling that side of the treatment program there in 1951. Books on the history of A.A. like to speak rather romantically of the extremely primitive detoxification methods used by Dr. Bob back in the 1930's, where the patients were fed on sauerkraut and Karo corn syrup, and given paraldehyde floating on top of a glass of orange juice. But medical science had made significant progress since that point, and St. Thomas now used far more sophisticated techniques and medications.

An article which Sister Ignatia wrote for a hospital journal described all the medical details of what they were doing in 1951 when I was there visiting and observing.[17] Some patients, who were in extremely bad shape from their alcoholic excesses, were given fluids intravenously. Patients were given vitamin B complex, spirits of frumenti, and might be given chloral hydrate if their withdrawal symptoms were especially severe. Patients who needed especially heavy sedation during the first day or two were given sodium luminol, although Sister Ignatia warned that this was a barbiturate, and that one should be very cautious about its use, because alcoholics could easily become addicted to barbiturates as a substitute addiction. An extremely unruly patient might be given one administration of HMC No. 1, and tolserol might be given a patient who was still experiencing severe nervous symptoms even though they had had several days of abstinence from alcohol and were receiving an adequate fluid intake, and an adequate diet. Sister Ignatia and the physicians at St. Thomas were also experimenting with the use of adrenal cortex to help restore the patients' sense of well-being.

———————————

Medical science continued to make progress in this area during the years following. The discovery of medications which would act as better tranquillizers was of great help to those of us who were running alcoholism treatment programs. I co-authored an article in 1958, along with Neville Murray, M.D., a psychiatrist in San Antonio, entitled "To Tranquillize or Not to Tranquillize." It appeared in the *Quarterly Journal of Studies on Alcohol*, and received such wide notice that excerpts from it were reprinted in the 1958 yearbook put out by a popular American encyclopedia.[18]

I wrote the article because I had become unhappy with a small but often highly vocal minority within Alcoholics Anonymous who totally rejected the use of any kind of medication by alcoholics in recovery. When they discovered that a newcomer was taking medication prescribed by a psychiatrist or physician, they would snarl at meetings,

"You might as well change your sobriety date then. You aren't sober until you have quit using drugs in any form at all."

The fact was that large doses of the paraldehyde used by Dr. Bob in the 1930's could further excite and nauseate patients in delirium. Barbiturates like the sodium luminol which Sister Ignatia was sometimes using in 1951 could leave a patient dangerously anesthetized and tended to have unpredictable effects. By 1958, we had discovered that the intravenous administration of some of the newly discovered tranquillizers like chlorpromazine, promazine, or triflupromazine could often produce rapid improvement with many individuals, without the same negative side effects. When a serious alcoholic stops drinking, the delirium tremens which results can be extremely dangerous. Some patients go into convulsions, the heart refuses to start beating properly afterwards, and even with prompt medical intervention the patient may die.

Some people seem to believe that alcoholics must suffer enormously during withdrawal to "expiate their sins" of excessive alcohol abuse, but this sort of punitive approach to alcoholism treatment does not seem to improve a treatment center's success rate at all. In fact patients respond better and more positively to the rest of the treatment program if they can, from the beginning of abstaining from alcohol, start to feel a freedom from discomfort never before experienced. It gives them a positive attitude, at a deep psychological level, toward being freed from dependence on alcohol. "I do in fact feel much better without any alcohol in my system" is an excellent starting point for teaching people how to remain abstinent.

I believe that some misinformed laypeople in A.A. are opposed to using such medication for alcoholics in recovery, because they have seen isolated cases where a physician allowed indiscriminate uses of these drugs to develop into psychological or physical dependency in a patient. Over-reliance on medication alone may serve as an "out" for neurotic patients who simply wish to avoid painful reality, who refuse to accept the true meaning of their condition, or who are indolent or unwilling to put forth sufficient effort in their overall treatment program. Patients of this sort may attempt to use medication as a "crutch," but this is usually eventually self-limiting, because there will be no long-lasting effectiveness when medication is misused in that fashion: the person's external problems and internal discomfort will quickly begin to grow even worse.

"Use *exactly as prescribed* and continue to work your A.A. program thoroughly and honestly" is the secret to using medications of this sort properly. My mentor Marty Mann began suffering from chronic depression toward the end of her life. In the late 1960's, her physician found that Elavil (amitriptyline) was effective in relieving this, and she began taking it. By using antidepressant medication and increasing her attendance at A.A. meetings, she was able to keep her depression from crippling her, and continued to play an effective role in alcoholism education at the national level as well as being better able to deal with the private problem of a partner who was becoming more and more irrational from the onslaught of Alzheimer's disease.

At the present time, medications have also been discovered which are of enormous aid to alcoholics who suffer from schizophrenia or bipolar disorder. There is no way that they can obtain any decent quality of life without using these medications. "Use exactly as prescribed" is again the key.

In my 1958 article in the *Quarterly Journal of Studies on Alcohol*, I made some statements about the three distinct stages in the rehabilitation of alcoholics, which I still believe are true today:

> First is the stage of severe intoxication, requiring expert medical emergency supervision to preserve life.
>
> Then the stage of growing awareness by the patient of the nature of his problem as well as of the personality and emotional difficulties which not only have brought about this condition but tend to perpetuate and accentuate it.
>
> Finally, the stage of repatterning of behavioral activity, in which those who formerly built much of their social intercourse around the drinking situation are helped to adopt other behavioral patterns.

During the third stage, they are often beset by extraordinary feelings of inadequacy whenever they have to become involved in groups, they will sometimes feel overpowering anxiety, and they will be tempted by countless messages coming from modern society, telling them that "a social drink" will relieve that anxiety. The problem is that, for chronic alcoholics, even one drink will do enormous harm and will lead them quickly back down the path to where they were before they entered treatment.

So during this third stage, with certain individuals, a temporary period on medication can sometimes be helpful, so that healing can actually take place. As I put it in my 1958 journal article:

> The secondary anxieties emanating from group interrelationships and preexisting personality disturbance make the task of repatterning behavior particularly hard for the well-intentioned alcoholic in process of rehabilitation, and he can be greatly assisted over this difficult period by the judicious prescription of suitable tranquillizing agents. Their function is that of a psychological plaster cast, to be worn only as long as the patient's fractured social relationships remain unmended.

The decision as to how best to prescribe any medication must be left up to skilled therapists who have real professional competence. This is not a decision to be made by misinformed lay "experts," no matter how well-intentioned.

When I began to put together my treatment program at Lackland Air Force Base, I was able to draw upon what I had learned at St. Thomas Hospital in Akron. I had access to physicians who could treat my patients' physical problems, and minimize the chances that anyone would die during alcohol withdrawal. In the person of Dr. Louis Jolyon West, I had a truly excellent psychiatrist working with me at all times. I took the patients to A.A. meetings off-base, to provide a constant immersion in A.A. principles, and the psychological support which the other A.A. members provided to the person who was just sobering up.

I did however leave out the heavily religious emphasis of Sister Ignatia's program at her Catholic hospital in Akron. Her approach probably did help some people, but particularly in a military context, it was going to drive so many other suffering alcoholics away, that we were going to be condemning far more people to an unnecessary doom than we were ever going to help. Any sort of heavily religious language produced such enormous rebellion and hostility among most military personnel that you would find very few suffering alcoholics who would actually allow you to treat them effectively.

But this is in fact a major problem, which my co-author has written about in a book called *The Higher Power of the Twelve-Step Program: For Believers & Non-Believers*. He has described in great detail the sorts of approaches which were used by the A.A. old-timers in bringing hostile and skeptical newcomers to a better understanding of real spirituality, where reading traditional religious books and feeling constrained to use traditional doctrines and dogmas was, more often than not, of little use for beginners.[19]

There was one additional important feature of the treatment program at St. Thomas Hospital which we copied in the Lackland AFB program: prescreening of all patients. In the early days in Akron, Dr. Bob himself did the prescreening, and had a very accurate eye for determining those candidates who had the internal motivation and underlying psychological stability necessary to succeed in the program. As a result, he was able to obtain a 50% success rate in terms of alcoholics who got sober and stayed sober from that point with no slips at all, and an eventual overall 75% success rate gained by doing further work with those who had backslid.

In 1951, with Dr. Bob gone, Sister Ignatia was using the A.A. sponsors as her prescreening personnel. As she explained it in her article in the hospital journal which she wrote in that year:

> Those of us who have anything to do with admitting these patients would do well to have the humility to rely upon the judgment of the sponsor. Let him decide when the patient is ready for the program. We do not accept repeaters! Sponsors know this, hence they are very careful to qualify the person before bringing him into the hospital. Above all, he must have

a sincere desire to stop drinking. Wives, relatives, friends, and well-meaning employers may try to high-pressure the alcoholic into accepting the program.

In other words, those doing the prescreening have to evaluate how much the alcoholic wants to recover, not how much other people want him or her to recover. And above all, she insisted in her article, experience had shown that in treatment centers where the majority of the patients were repeaters, an overall atmosphere of pessimism and discouragement was created, where even a sincere and highly motivated person who was going into treatment for the first time would often fail.

At Lackland Air Force Base, Dr. West and I prescreened all candidates for admission to our treatment program. Those who were not extremely highly motivated, or who had psychiatric problems so severe that they would have to be dismissed from the service anyway, were denied admission. This was part of the way we achieved our carefully documented 50% success rate.

————————————

I got to meet a number of fascinating people during my visits to St. Thomas Hospital that year. I still have warm memories of a colorful Amishman named Mose Yoder, who was a real character and had been sober for quite a while. I also got to meet Bill Dotson, the famous "Man on the Bed" who became A.A. No. 3 when the program first began.[20] I only knew him on a casual basis, but he did say one thing to me which I will always remember. I asked him why he spent so much time working with alcoholics, when he was a lawyer and could be making so much money if he devoted more time to his legal career. He responded very simply and gently to my question. He said that, living his life the way he was living it now, he only made about $400 a month in cash but got about $1,500 a month in gratitude.

Above all though, I will never forget my many heart-to-heart conversations with Sister Ignatia in her office there at the hospital. No one could ever forget the spirit of that feisty little woman. She was an incredibly compassionate person with a soft spot in her heart for us alcoholics, but she would also bring her patients back into line instantly if they started getting up to any of their old shenanigans again. Newly sobered up drunks can do and say amazing and outrageous things, even mystifyingly bizarre things. Their brain cells have not yet truly begun to function properly again.

One time when I came to visit the ward, Sister Ignatia had come into the room too, and we were talking together quietly. Suddenly one of the newcomers who was still in the early stages of detox just walked over to me and pulled my shirt open in front. Sister Ignatia stared at him, and finally asked, "Why did you do that?"

He replied triumphantly, "I know he is an alcoholic, because he doesn't have any hair on his chest."

She snapped back, "You get back to your bed, I am sick of your behavior!" And he slunk back to his bed obediently right on the spot. This tiny little Irishwoman had what we in the military call command presence, where even the largest and unruliest drunk would not try to cross her when she got in his face and started barking orders.

But it was done out of enormous compassion and love. She had dedicated her life totally to this program at St. Thomas, and she did it purely to help others, because she could have had a much easier life simply carrying out the routine hospital administrative tasks to which she had originally been assigned.

About a year after I was assigned to Kent State, Sister Ignatia's order reassigned her, and she was forced to leave St. Thomas in Akron where she had spent so many years, and move to a new post at Charity Hospital in Cleveland. I, along with quite literally thousands of people in the Akron area, was enormously saddened to see her go. She was a truly unforgettable person, a real angel of mercy. Eventually it was going to be time for me to leave also and move to a totally different part of the country, and I too did not wish to go.

I had enjoyed almost two years of this almost idyllic existence at the university, when in 1953 the Air Force decided to change some of its operating policies for ROTC units. It was decreed that only officers were allowed to teach these university courses. My Commanding Officer recommended me for a commission, but we were not able to get this approved. There is a rigid class system in the military, and particularly back in those days, officers were a kind of aristocracy. I was very angry at the time over the way the workings of this system had pushed me out of my teaching position.

But this was in fact the way I got back into alcoholism treatment. It appeared that the only other kind of reassignment I was apt to get, was carrying out some essentially menial administrative responsibility, shuffling paperwork or making sure that the right airplane parts got on the right shelves in a warehouse or something of that sort. During my five short years in the A.A. program, a new world had been opened up for me. I had undergone a radical process of maturation and personal growth. I wanted to work with people, not pieces of paper or airplane parts, and I wanted some real challenges.

Above all, I had worked out a simple spirituality for myself, not one phrased in complicated religious language, which I have never been any good at, but one based on the simple idea of actually helping other people, and doing concrete work to genuinely make their lives better. Mentoring and encouraging young students at the university and teaching them things which would make them better officers had satisfied that spiritual need. Some may think this a strange thing to say, but to my mind, teaching school can be a highly spiritual vocation. It is all in the attitude we bring to it, and the way we can learn to achieve a higher satisfaction and sense of purpose in our daily work and effort.

So in a mood of some desperation, one night I conceived the idea of writing a letter to the Surgeon General of the Air Force, pleading with him to assign me once again to working full time with alcoholics. After the letter was sent off, I was almost immediately overcome with anxiety and apprehension. Would my plea simply be rejected out of hand? Even worse, sergeants did not write directly to generals in this fashion, bypassing all the normal chain of command, and I could in fact end up in some trouble for doing something like that.

Within a matter of two weeks, the answer to my letter arrived, and I could hardly believe my eyes. With the concurrence of both the Surgeon General and the Chief of Air Force Chaplains, I was not only given permission to set up my second treatment program, but even given a choice of three bases: Sampson, Parks, or Lackland Air Force Base in San Antonio, Texas. The letter put heavy emphasis on Lackland, because it was one of the Air Force's major training bases, and this immediately seemed to me also to be the right idea. I was back in the alcoholism treatment field again.

CHAPTER 17

Lackland: the Fully Developed Treatment Program

When proposals are brought to Colonels and Generals to create fully developed alcoholism treatment programs on military bases, a very frequent response is to say that it would cost too much. But this is not true. A good rehabilitation system saves far more money than it costs to run it. With the aid of a cooperative psychiatrist (who was not an alcoholic himself) I put together a program at Lackland which saved the Air Force one million dollars with the first fifty patients alone. And we proved it, with data and controls far more rigid than the overwhelming majority of scientific papers written on alcoholism and its treatment. There was no "soft data" or subjectivism or use of fuzzy definitions of alcoholism and "success." The results were published in the *American Journal of Psychiatry*, the article was reprinted and distributed by the National Council on Alcoholism in every major city, newspapers all over the United States picked it up and wrote articles about what we had accomplished, and our project was even mentioned in the yearbook of a national encyclopedia as one of the noteworthy achievements of that year.[21] Not only that, we worked out a combination of treatment techniques which achieved a fifty percent success rate, which in alcoholism treatment is a winning combination: alcoholism is the only disease where so many of your patients fight you to the bitter end to avoid getting well.

There in the summer of 1953 the Air Force had given me a choice of several places for setting up my second alcoholism treatment program. Lackland Air Force Base in San Antonio, Texas, seemed the obvious one to pick for a number of reasons. The base itself was huge, because every enlisted person in the Air Force went through basic training there, which in turn required an enormous support staff. This meant a large pool of military personnel, permanently assigned to the base, from which I could draw my patients. The 3700th USAF Hospital at Lackland was the largest Air Force hospital in the world, which meant I could count on medical support when necessary, particularly for detoxification and treatment of delirium tremens (the d.t.'s) and other purely physical issues during the first two to four days after the patient entered the program.

And I also hoped to expand my pool of candidates for the treatment program by bringing in personnel for treatment from the other bases which immediately surrounded the city—Randolph AFB, Kelly AFB, and Brooks AFB—plus the numerous other flying fields the Air Force had set up in nearby areas of Texas and New Mexico. There were an exceptional number of Air Force bases in that part of the United States. It was a good part of the country to train pilots, because you could count on blue skies and sunshine—perfect flying weather—most days of the year. I knew I could count on the fact that, with alcoholism affecting at least ten percent of the general American population, there would be a huge number of Air Force people in that general area who had serious drinking problems, and that a certain percentage of these would be at the point in their drinking careers where they would be willing to accept help.

San Antonio itself was a beautiful place. It was still a small, easy-going town back then. Palm trees grew everywhere, along with huge live oak trees with Spanish moss dangling from their enormous branches, which spread out horizontal to the ground and gave a welcome shade beneath them from the tropical sun. The old Spanish governor's palace and the venerable mission churches (including the Alamo of course, where the Texas rebels made their famous last stand) gave you a feeling of a place with real history. The little parks and flower beds and pathways along the River Walk that wound through the downtown gave the city a kind of Old World charm.

Air Force personnel on leave would paddle rented canoes up and down the river, many of them drinking a bit too much, and occasionally falling out of their boats with shouts of terror, until they stood up and sheepishly discovered that the river was no more than waist deep. And they would dare one another to eat one of the rattlesnake sandwiches which vendors sold to the tourists, and try out the strange flavor of the spicy tequila which the Mexicans distilled from the juice of the Agave cactus. If you wanted to be fancy, you drank it from salt-rimmed glasses, with sweetened lime juice from the citrus groves down further south. Or you could do it the old-fashioned way, where you put a pinch of salt on the back of your hand, squirted some juice on it from a slice of lime, licked the back of your hand, and then downed a shot of the fiery liquid. Whichever way you did it, it was a very potent alcoholic beverage indeed, and you could get very drunk very quickly on a bottle of tequila. The parades and parties during Fiesta Week every April were not as well known as Mardi Gras in New Orleans, but the celebration was almost as big. The old Mexican grandees would still come out on parade back in those days, riding on magnificent horses with silver-mounted bridles and saddles glinting in the sun.

Not long after I got to Lackland Air Force Base, I met the man who was going to supply several of the crucial links necessary for setting up a fully functioning treatment program: Louis Jolyon West, M.D. He was around six years younger than I was, so since I was thirty-five he must have been only about twenty-nine years old. From his middle name, he had been nicknamed "Jolly," and that was what everyone on the base called him, "Jolly West." That was the way he signed his letters to me in later years. He had served as an infantryman for three and a half years in World War II and went to medical school after he got out of the service. He had just finished his residency training in psychiatry, and now, in 1953, had just arrived at Lackland with a new set of major's oak leaves on his collar, to become Chief of Psychiatry at the huge base hospital there.

This was the beginning of an enormously successful career for him. By 1956, Dr. West was also Professor and Head of the Department of Psychiatry and Neurology at the University of Oklahoma School of Medicine, Oklahoma City. He also founded an alcoholism research and treatment facility there at that university, which was later named for him.

He eventually became Professor and Chairman of the Department of Psychiatry and Biobehavioral Sciences at the University of California, Los Angeles, at the UCLA School of Medicine, and was also Psychiatrist-in-Chief of the UCLA Hospital and Clinics and Director of the Neuropsychiatric Institute at the UCLA Center for the Health Sciences. He gave me the title of consultant there after he had taken up that position, so he and I could continue to be in contact with one another. He eventually authored seven books and more than 150 journal articles,[22] and became a major nationally recognized expert on alcoholism, serving at one point as a member of the National Advisory Committee on Alcoholism to the Secretary of Health, Education and Welfare, along with other national advisory bodies.

Dr. West was a brilliant psychiatrist at the theoretical level, but he was not just a "skull jockey." He was a warm, caring, human being. I still treasure the friendship I enjoyed with him during those years. His commitment to establishing an alcoholism treatment program at Lackland came from the heart. He wrote a short piece for me in 1981, describing how we first got together at Lackland, where he talked about the horror he felt when he saw all the Air Force personnel on that base who were compulsively drinking themselves to death.[23]

> A newly-minted major in the United States Air Force assigned to the Psychiatry Service at Lackland AFB Hospital near San Antonio, I realized that alcoholism was a far larger problem in the military service than I had ever imagined. Certainly my years as an infantryman in World War II did not prepare me for what I began to see of the ravages of alcohol in my work as a psychiatrist at the Air Force's largest hospital. Nor did anything I had observed or read during my

recently completed residency training in psychiatry provide any inkling of the scope and complexity of the problem of alcoholism among military personnel.

It is important to note that you do not need to be an alcoholic yourself in order to treat alcoholics effectively. Dr. West was one excellent example. The necessary thing to recognize, if you are a non-alcoholic who wishes to set up a treatment program which will obtain real success, is that you simply must team up with a recovered alcoholic who can serve as your A.A. liaison, and use that person continually for your "insider's knowledge" of the disease and how practicing alcoholics actually think and react. Treatment methods and theories which seem to make perfect logical sense to a non-alcoholic looking at the disease from the outside will often fail disastrously in practice. A fully recovered alcoholic who is active in Alcoholics Anonymous can tell you from actual experience how a man or woman who is still drinking destructively will feel emotionally and physically, and the strategies for denial and evasion which that drinker will use to attempt to manipulate you and undercut your efforts at therapy.

Even if you yourself are aware that the patient is using lies and devious underhanded strategies to block you, people who are alcoholics themselves can often confront the patient far more effectively. If you, as a non-alcoholic, tell the patient bluntly, "That's nonsense, what you're actually doing here is such-and-such," the drinker will simply be apt to use that as yet another excuse to fall into further righteous indignation and rebelliousness. A recovered alcoholic who has been active in A.A. knows how to say the same thing, often even more rudely and bluntly, but with an attitude of "Come off it now, I've been where you are, and I used that technique for years to con people. Sometimes I even believed my own cock-and-bull stories myself, which was how I plunged down to the bottom. You can keep on lying to me—I don't care, it's your life, and it's not going to affect what I do, because I know all the tricks as well as you do—but if you want any kind of real help from me, you're going to have to at least start getting honest with yourself."

Dr. Joseph J. Zuska (Capt. USN) was another well-known example of a non-alcoholic, a physician who became interested in setting up an alcoholism program at Long Beach Naval Station in the mid-1960's, and teamed up with retired Navy Commander Dick Jewell, an alcoholic who had recently gotten sober in A.A. Jewell worked at first as an unpaid co-worker while they set up their enormously effective treatment program there. This facility later became quite famous when President Ford's wife Betty Ford and President Carter's brother Billy Carter were sent there for treatment.[24]

When Sister Ignatia, who was of course not an alcoholic herself, first began trying to work with alcoholics at St. Thomas Hospital in Akron, Ohio, in 1928 she had good hospital facilities and eventually in 1934 gained the additional help of a competent non-alcoholic physician, but still had little long-term success during those early years.[25] When she was finally able to team up with Dr. Bob and the other recovered alcoholics in the fledgling A.A. group in Akron in 1939, she used their additional knowledge and input to help her put her own considerable talents to work more effectively. As a result, she ended up saving thousands of human lives during the many years that followed, and if you wanted to see gratitude, you should have seen the scene on August 6, 1952, the evening before she finally left St. Thomas.

Literally thousands of grateful alcoholics and their families, now restored to good and useful lives, flooded in to say good-by and thank you, until their autos created enormous traffic jams on the streets around the hospital in all directions. Traffic came to a complete standstill on the old Akron viaduct which bridged the valley which lay on one side of the hospital, as drivers simply parked their cars wherever they could find a space, leaving their headlights on, while the police looked on in silent acquiescence. You had to ignore the rules for a heroine of her stature. Parades of people filed down the streets and then stood in long lines at the hospital, just so they could shake Sister Ignatia's hand one last time.[26]

So if you are a nurse or physician, a psychotherapist, a social worker or a criminal justice system case worker, and you recognize that many of the other problems affecting your patients, clients, or inmates are insoluble until they first deal with their alcohol and drug abuse, please do not be afraid to start some sort of treatment program at the facility where you are employed. Just be sure to set up some kind of active linkage, whether official or unofficial, with the Alcoholics Anonymous program in your area, and listen to what they have learned from their own experience with the disease and their recovery from it. You will find them hardheaded and practical: they will understand the limitations of what you can and cannot do within your institutional setting, often because some of them have in fact been patients or inmates at similar institutions. But you will also find them willing to go to any lengths to aid you in any way they can, cheerfully and with contagious good humor.

Dr. West was young and just starting out his practice as a psychiatrist when I first met him there at Lackland. But he became enormously respected in his field during the years that followed. At one point he came within just a few votes of being elected president of the American Psychiatric Association. The reason he failed to win involved an unfortunate occurrence. He was asked to tranquillize an elephant, and prepared what he had calculated was a suitable dose of Thorazine to sedate the huge animal, based on its body weight. Either elephants are more susceptible to Thorazine—unlike white rats and monkeys, they are so big and require so much feed and care, that it goes without saying that they are not commonly used as test animals in experimental labs, so there is not a wealth of data on the drug responses of elephants—or this particular elephant was abnormally sensitive to that agent. At any rate, the poor creature died.

Dr. West had been assumed to be a shoo-in for election, but apparently some of the members of the American Psychiatric Association began to have anxiety attacks at that point over the possibility that some tabloid journalist might publish an article with a scandalous headline such as, "Does Your Psychiatrist Prescribe Enough Drugs to Kill an Elephant? The Head of the American Psychiatric Association Does." I was saddened when I learned that he had fallen just short of gaining enough votes to receive the honor he so richly deserved.

Dr. West had come to Lackland in 1952, and had already been trying to devise some way of treating alcohol and drug abusers at Lackland even before I arrived, but had found barriers on every side. As he described his experiences:[27]

> In those days official policy toward alcoholics and drug addicts in the military service was extremely punitive. It took me more than a year to figure out how to create a treatment program for patients whose illness officially was not allowed to exist. This peculiar situation obtained because the diagnosis of alcoholism immediately rendered the patient unacceptable for service, and required his immediate separation from the service (with an "undesirable" discharge).
>
> Finally I obtained permission from the base commander and the hospital commander (with the informal approval of the Surgeon General's office) to undertake an "experimental" program of evaluation and rehabilitation of persons who were incapacitated because of alcoholism, even though the official diagnosis was not inscribed upon their medical record.

But Dr. West could not find anyone in the psychiatry service there at the 3700th USAF hospital to help him. Everyone on staff was already overburdened with huge psychiatric caseloads of military men and women suffering from numerous kinds of problems, who had been sent from various U.S. bases and from Korea. The traumatic Korean war had begun on June 25, 1950, when North Korean forces invaded the south and quickly captured Seoul. That was back when I was still at Mitchel AFB on Long Island. The Air Force was deeply involved of course in that bloody conflict, and fighting was still going on when I arrived at Lackland, because the armistice signed at Panmunjom did not come until six months after Dr. West and I had started our joint alcoholism treatment program.

But the problem ran deeper than just an overload of psychiatric cases suffering from acute posttraumatic stress disorder from their horrifying experiences in Korea. As Dr. West put it,

> Even more important ... was the fact that among my medical colleagues there was nobody with any particular interest in

alcoholism, and among the other health professionals in the hospital there was no expertise whatsoever.

That was the place where I came in. Dr. West kept on asking around the base, trying to find someone who had previous experience treating alcoholism.

> I learned that a Master Sergeant William E. Swegan, who was at the time assigned to the Chaplain's Office on base, was working with alcoholics independently of any other program. Sergeant Swegan, with the concurrence of the Chief of Air Force Chaplains and the Surgeon General of the Air Force was assigned to Lackland AF Base to work specifically with alcoholics.

He also learned that I was experiencing the same kinds of frustrations that he was, and receiving little support in my efforts to make my own fledgling program a viable one.

> I invited Sergeant Swegan to visit my office ... and made him an offer I reckoned he couldn't refuse: to become my partner in a venture to rehabilitate alcoholics. Naturally he responded to this proposition with enthusiasm. But even Bill Swegan as a canny sergeant who thought he had seen everything, was astonished when I looked him in the eye and said, "Sergeant, as of this moment you are a psychiatric social worker."

That supplied me with one of the most vital components I needed to make my program a success: the right kind of title. Psychiatric Social Worker made my help more acceptable to many who would have bluntly refused my assistance when I was defined as a Chaplain's Assistant. Alcoholics and drug addicts simply did not want to come to anyone associated with the Chaplain's Office, no matter how much I reassured them— if they did get pressured into visiting me—that I was not going to be scolding them or threatening them with going to hell or preaching religious doctrine and dogma at them. It is ironic, but as I mentioned earlier, most practicing alcoholics and drug addicts would far rather be regarded as mentally ill than as religious.

So I had a more effective title now—Psychiatric Social Worker—even though I had no letters like MSW or PhD to put after my name. Even years later, I still felt that I was being hampered at many points by my lack of any professional advanced degree in psychology or social work or medicine. But Dr. West was always far less concerned about that than I was. Thirty years later, after he had become Chairman and Director of the Neuropsychiatric Institute at the UCLA School of Medicine in Los Angeles, he wrote me a nice letter in which he told me,[28]

> My own view is that anyone with sense will listen to you on the subject of alcoholism, and that fools won't pay attention no matter how many degrees you have. Many leaders in the field have no advanced degrees. Marty Mann comes to mind. Erik H. Erikson, one of the great contributors to contemporary psychiatry, had no college degree, much less a doctorate, and yet he may be the most influential psychiatric writer since Freud.

I know that what he said here is fully true—Marty, that wonderful woman, who knew so much about so many subjects, including literature and art, was entirely self-educated in terms of her advanced knowledge of alcoholism and its treatment[29]—but Dr. West's M.D. degree and gold major's oak leaves were also necessary at that point to give us the kind of clout to get our program established in spite of the forces of opposition, apathy, and disinterest which opposed us.

We got our joint endeavor started, and within just three years had enough clinical data to start bragging publicly in national circles about what we had accomplished. As Dr. West summed up our success:[30]

> For the next three years Sergeant Swegan and I worked together in a locally approved but officially non-existent program to identify, treat, rehabilitate, and if possible, retain for the Air Force a significant number of valuable military personnel. The results of this approach were finally published in 1956. Between us, Sergeant Swegan and I were saving the government approximately $1 million a year in salvaged personnel. Unfortunately, it took another generation

and another war [the Vietnam conflict c. 1963-75] before government policy sufficiently changed to make programs like ours official.

———————————

So in January 1953, our small experimental program was initiated at the 3700th USAF Hospital with the approval of the Hospital and Base Commanders and the Office of the Surgeon General. Treatment was offered to a selected group of alcoholics. They had to meet three essential criteria: (1) proved value to the Air Force through a record of achievement, (2) knowledge and approval of the patient's commander, and (3) the economy that could be effected through successful rehabilitation, without military risk.[31] Our official definition of chronic alcoholism was that used by a scholar named Diethelm in an article written in 1951, which had proven widely acceptable in professional circles and was extremely appropriate to the diagnostic standards we knew we could prove by military records:[32]

> A patient suffers from chronic alcoholism if he uses alcohol to such an extent that it interferes with a successful life (including physical, personality, and social aspects), and he is either not able to recognize this effect, or is not able to control his alcohol consumption although he knows its disastrous results.

Alcoholism is a complex illness which is usually the result of multiple causation. So our treatment plan for each patient attempted to take into account all the factors which might be involved in that particular person's case: genetic, hormonal, neurological, psychological, and social.

We employed both individual counseling and small group sessions. With my new title, I was now in a position where I could carry out a certain amount of deeper psychoanalysis on my patients when it was necessary, without being accused of overstepping my assignment. Some sort of marriage counseling was nearly always required: alcoholics— and the people who marry them as well—have difficulty setting up healthy relationships. Our job was to improve the quality of our patients' lives at every possible level, not only when they were carrying out their assigned duties on base, but also when they were at home. As the psychiatric social worker, I also investigated the administrative difficulties in which the patient was usually involved, and negotiated realistic solutions with the command structure.

A small percentage of the patients were able to benefit from more intensive individual psychotherapy. Most of these were individuals who were above average in intelligence and able to be effective in their jobs as long as they stayed sober, but oversensitive. In our sessions with them, we sought to strengthen the ego defenses they already had available. Our psychotherapeutic techniques varied from simple supportive methods to analysis and interpretation of previously unconscious material. In a few cases hypnotherapy was employed. Since alcoholism is such a complex disease and each individual alcoholic will be to some degree unique, we had to use a wide variety of different methods. There is no "one" treatment for alcoholics, and in spite of the fact that many books have been written claiming that there is one single, simple theory which will account for alcoholism and enable it to be treated successfully, in practice these "single theory" approaches do not help most alcoholics at all.

We made use of the excellent hospital facilities to include in our treatment program, when appropriate, a high vitamin regime, adrenal cortical extract, chlorpromazine (Thorazine), and reserpine (Serpasil).[33] Because that was almost fifty years ago, I should say that there are many other medications which have been developed over the intervening years which are sometimes safer or have fewer side-effects or are more specific in their application: serotonin re-uptake inhibitors and other antidepressants that target specific areas of the brain chemistry, antipsychotics, lithium and other helpful medications for patients who are bipolar, specific medications for hyperactive attention deficit disorder, and so on.

Tetraethylthiuram disulfide (Antabuse) was administered to patients who requested it during their early period in the treatment program. Most individuals will have an extremely uncomfortable physical reaction if they try to drink alcohol as long as this is already in their system. The daily dose of Antabuse was discontinued if the patient requested it, if the physician judged it no longer useful, or if the A.A. worker indicated that the patient was now so deeply immersed in the A.A. program that he or she would no longer need this additional precaution.

I should say that Antabuse is no longer used in present day alcoholism treatment programs as frequently as we did back then, because too many of the alcoholics to whom it was administered assumed that taking this medication by itself provided a sufficient protective shield against any possible relapse. It became "the adhesive tape that held together a broken crutch." They developed a false sense of security, and so had a greater tendency to dismiss the need for any significant change in their basic thinking and emotional approach to life. They wrongly assumed that they had been totally freed from any compulsive desire to drink, until some major catastrophe occurred in their lives. Then, when the chips were down, they discovered too late that they had developed very few tools for coping with the stress caused by the emotional upheaval which was now overwhelming them. Some surreptitiously evaded taking their prescribed daily Antabuse dosage (sometimes even if administered by staff, because if the staff were not careful, patients would tuck the tablet under their tongues and spit it out later). Others would become so emotionally desperate that they would drink in spite of knowing what the Antabuse was going to do to them physically after it was combined with the alcohol. This reaction was not only extraordinarily distressing, but was dangerous enough that it could produce fatalities on occasion.

The absolutely vital and necessary component in the treatment program however, was to get the patient actively involved on a long term basis in attending Alcoholics Anonymous meetings conducted by civilians off of the military base. These were the people (all unpaid volunteers) whom we counted on to do the bulk of the therapeutic work. Some of our patients did not become involved in A.A. with any great fervor or commitment—they would go to the minimum number of A.A. meetings which they felt they could get away with, and would just sit passively in the meetings and refuse to become deeply or personally engaged with the twelve-step program or the other members of the A.A. group—but there were very few who failed to derive some definite and measurable benefit from attending these meetings even when they did so grudgingly.

Only about a third of our cases had to receive any individual psychotherapy at all after they had made the return to a more stable pattern of living. This is important to note: we were not asking the U.S. government to take on the enormous expense of creating a huge staff of psychiatrists and psychotherapists to carry on long term individual treatment of numerous military personnel.

The key factor in achieving success in this aspect of our treatment program was found to lie in the commitment and dedication of the military A.A. worker. This needed to be someone with long military experience who had gotten sober himself or herself in A.A. These sorts of individuals were found to be highly effective in dealing with the majority of the patients involved. Their particular usefulness came from their availability and their familiarity with the peculiar stresses of military life, together with their ability to talk about their own life stories. When the patients wanted to talk about some particular anxiety-laden issue or circumstance in their own lives—overpowering resentments against other base personnel or family members, or perhaps circumstances in which they had been traumatically victimized or consistently made to feel inferior and inadequate, or sometimes degrading and humiliating experiences they had had while drunk (experiences which still haunted their memories)—the A.A. workers could respond by telling about similar experiences in their own past histories.

As was pointed out by Dr. Harry Tiebout, the first psychiatrist who became deeply involved in investigating A.A. methods, the therapeutic success of Alcoholics Anonymous is of particular interest in view of the large number of "rules" of psychotherapy which it breaks with impunity.[34] My suggestion is that non-alcoholic mental health professionals simply take advantage of the help which A.A. meetings give their patients, without attempting to overanalyze why this help is working so effectively.

On the other hand, as the military A.A. worker in the Lackland treatment facility, I also found that my close association with a psychiatric unit definitely increased my own effectiveness. Many alcoholics have "problems other than alcohol," as it is said in the A.A. program, and it can take considerable professional expertise to turn these individuals into happy and successful people who can enjoy life to the fullest.

The military A.A. worker was the one designated to carry out alcohol education on the base. In our case, I visited a large number of surrounding Air Force facilities in Texas and New Mexico as well. This work included giving both informal talks and regular formal lectures, showing films, distributing pamphlets and leaflets, and being available after presentations to give individual advice. The arrangements for these visits were made through training officers, chaplains, line officers, traffic safety project officers and the like. The object was not only to talk about our treatment program to the ten percent or so of the military personnel in each group who were likely to be already well on their way to falling into serious trouble with their excessive drinking, but also to make noncommissioned officers and command staff more aware of the help we could give them if they had personnel under their command who was obviously producing more and more disciplinary and efficiency problems by their abuse of alcohol.

This was a time-consuming but vital and necessary part of the military A.A. worker's job. When I worked hard at setting up and making these outreach visits to various units and training groups, I found that referrals to our program shot up dramatically. Some military personnel would be referred to us by their commanders after I had made my presentation or distributed my materials, while others would come in as self-referrals. The core of the message which I delivered was adapted from the three basic principles which had been stressed so strongly by Mrs. Marty Mann all across the country in her role as head of the National Council on Alcoholism, which I have already referred to earlier in this book because of the importance of changing the public perception of this issue: "(1) Alcoholism is a disease and the alcoholic is a sick person. (2) The alcoholic can be helped and is worth helping. (3) This is a public health problem and is therefore a public responsibility." The only change I made was to make the third principle more specific. I stressed that alcoholism was also a basic problem in the U.S. military, and that the military itself therefore had to start taking effective responsibility for recognizing alcoholic personnel and providing the kind of treatment which would return them to full duty.

At least ten percent of the general American public is somewhere along the path in the progressive development of the disease called alcoholism. If the U.S. military attempts to deny that this problem exists, and attempts to brush it under the carpet, our armed forces will pay an enormous price in dollars and cents, and an even greater cost in terms of human lives destroyed unnecessarily.

———————

Our patients formed a quite heterogeneous population, with marked cultural and constitutional differences, and displaying a good deal of variability in terms of the relative influence of different psychodynamic factors. So some patients rejected A.A. but were helped by psychotherapy. Others responded poorly to one medication but were helped by another, or by the appropriate combination of medication and the right kind of talk therapy. Some were not helped by either medicine or psychiatry, but had their lives remade by becoming deeply involved in the spiritual aspects of the A.A. program.

All the cases who came into our program had this in common however, which became our "working definition" of alcoholism at the practical level: They had been experiencing a mounting *feeling* of discomfort and a need for alcohol to relieve this feeling. This need had become so strong that the knowledge of the inevitable negative consequences of drinking so much no longer sufficed as a deterrent. The overwhelming negative feeling itself might be anxiety, boredom, depression, tension, resentment, anger, or feeling used or victimized. There was often very little insight among these incoming patients regarding the real causes of these painful emotions. The precipitating factors which would plunge them back into this intolerable internal emotional state might originate in their family situation, on the job, or when certain memories or fantasies arose in their minds.

No single approach could therefore rationally be expected to meet the needs of every patient. "Single theory" alcoholism treatment programs do not ever achieve significant long term successful results when rigorous and objective follow-ups are carried out one year, two years, three years, and five years later. So Dr. West and I had to try out various treatment methods on each new patient until we found the ones that worked, although we did get much better, with experience, at noting increasingly reliable groups of indicators which would allow us to prescribe a specific treatment program for a given individual without having to go through so much trial and error at the beginning.

I mentioned that our patients formed a heterogeneous population. This sometimes produced tensions, because in San Antonio at that period in our history (this was back in the 1950's we must remember) there was still great resistance toward any social mixing of different races and cultures. On several occasions early on, when I took minority personnel to A.A. meetings off of the base, it created some hostility, and I just had to ignore the negative responses to my breaking of their segregationist assumptions. I will say though, that as I continued to insist on bringing all of my people to the San Antonio meetings and defending them against any attacks, that some of the ones I sponsored ended up having a truly dynamic impact on the city's A.A. groups after they had gotten some sobriety under their belts.

The San Antonio A.A.'s actually held a vote on one occasion, when a local minority businessman with an alcohol problem came to them and sought assistance. Thank God the vote was positive, because among other things, this person not only became a very productive member of that city's A.A. program, but was personally responsible for many other people of minority backgrounds getting sober through the program later on. I wanted to insert these particular comments here in this chapter, because I feel so strongly that the principles I was fighting for back then were so important, and still are today: we practice tolerance, and we do not discriminate against people in A.A., regardless of race, sex, culture, educational level, religious background, or any of the other issues which can sometimes be so divisive outside of the program in the larger society. We must form the model for a new and higher level of human relationships, where those who have been made to feel "less than" and despised can learn to feel good about themselves and begin achieving their full potential as human beings.

But to return to our activities there on the base: what was truly amazing was the enormous success rate we achieved in our pilot program. We analyzed the first 50 consecutive cases who came into our treatment center, and found that a full 50% of these military personnel (25 cases) were much improved, with maintenance of total sobriety from the beginning, and continuously successful performance of their duties. This was a fully objective evaluation: we did not ask the personnel themselves in a telephone call whether they "thought their drinking had been brought back under control?" or "are you doing O.K. now?" There was one notorious report by a major research corporation in the 1970's which based some highly controversial theories about the ability of alcoholics to successfully return to "controlled drinking" on this sort of subjective data. We were in contact with our patients' commanders, looked at their official performance reports, watched out for any recurrence of disciplinary problems (including being sent for court martial for any kind of breach or being arrested by civilian police when off base), and we also conferred with the A.A. people who had worked with them most closely for their evaluation of how well these newly sober people were coping.

26% of these cases (13 of the 50) we considered as outright failures. Five of these never accepted themselves as alcoholics and refused to follow any advice that might lead to rehabilitation. Three of the ones whom we had listed as "failures" got into civilian A.A. programs after they had left the service, and were able at that point to get sober and adjust successfully to life, and obtain stable, long term employment. Those three reported to us that we had planted the seed. As their lives had continued to grow worse and worse, they had finally realized that we were telling them the truth about their condition and what they had to do to avoid death or prison or permanent incarceration in a mental institution.

14% (7 cases) we considered improved. When we did our evaluation, we found that they were doing much better at staying out of trouble, despite one or more episodes of drinking again after they had first entered our rehabilitation program.

We only had 10% (5 cases) whom we could not follow up on because of transfers overseas, so we felt that we had an unusually thorough system for looking at the vast majority of the patients whom we had worked with.

We calculated that we had saved the Air Force at least a million dollars by working with these first fifty patients. There was no question that nearly all of these personnel were on the verge of disaster in their military careers. Most of them would certainly have been lost to the service. We had chosen as our subjects, not raw new recruits, but seasoned veterans. The published figures in 1954 and 1955 for the price of replacing an individual with four years of service showed that this cost the Air Force a minimum of nearly $15,000. For an enlisted person with advanced training, such as an electronics technician, the figure was $75,000. That was what the government had to pay for the classes and course work which would be required to teach someone else to carry out that job. Officers were even more expensive to replace, and the training of a jet bomber pilot cost the Air Force half a million dollars.[35] That was in 1950's prices. Now, half a century later, the lives of trained pilots are literally worth millions.

Is this a valid way to calculate the value of a successful alcohol and drug treatment program, in terms of personnel replacement costs? The present-day military devotes substantial amounts of money to efforts to encourage highly-trained personnel to reenlist, and the military's top financial planners not only insist that this is money well spent, but that the retention of trained and experienced personnel is vital to the maintenance of a topflight military. When a major conflict forces the U.S. military to flood its ranks with inexperienced people, everyone with military experience knows the kinds of difficulties this produces. If the military services are willing to spend enormous amounts of time and money encouraging good people to re-enlist, they ought to be willing to spend a few dollars making sure that some of their most competent people are in adequate physical and mental shape to continue their duties.

The conservative estimate we made of the cost of replacement of the individual patients in our successfully treated group averaged out to $40,000 per person. Twenty-five times that figure comes out to $1 million.

We did not even count in the cost to the Air Force of paying a full salary for personnel who were only doing half their job because of their heavy drinking when off duty, or the equipment damaged by men and women who were bleary-eyed, jittery, and unable to concentrate well because of the aftereffects of their binges. I could give a host of examples, like the Navy pilot I heard about later on, who admitted during treatment at a naval alcoholism rehabilitation center that he had crashed *three* high-performance military aircraft because of his alcohol abuse and its effects on his reflexes.

Nor did we count in the time we saved the command staff, who no longer had to waste hours dealing with the alcoholic escapades of these drinkers, or trying to help them sort out the difficulties they had gotten into in their home life because of their excessive drinking. A general court martial cost the Air Force $4,320 to conduct back in those days. Confining alcoholics in the stockade cost a large amount of money. Hospitalizing people who had injured themselves while on binges cost the government many dollars. When Captain Joseph Zuska, the senior medical officer at the Naval Station at Long Beach, California, started the famous alcoholism treatment center there in 1965, his medical personnel noticed after a while that they were no longer treating so many broken jaws at the hospital.

And there were other positive effects of our program, due to the emphasis placed on alcohol education among all the base personnel. This was preventive psychiatry at its best. Dr. Zuska and his A.A. worker, retired Navy Commander Dick Jewell, noticed the same helpful consequences emerging due to their educational work at their Long Beach facility. From my links with the people in the Alcoholics Anonymous program in San Antonio, I discovered that, as a result of my educational presentations on base, greatly increased numbers of Air Force personnel were joining A.A. groups and getting sober without going through the program on base which Dr. West and I were running. So our official figures said that we saved twenty-five people during the first two years we were operating our two-man program, but in fact during that period quite a few more personnel got sober as the indirect result of our efforts.

So we could have justifiably expanded our claims had we chosen to. We in fact saved more than twenty-five lives during that period, counting the indirect effects of our program, and we in fact saved the Air Force far more than a million dollars by our work over that short period.

We showed what could be done, and we demonstrated it resoundingly well. Our pilot program created a model of a truly successful alcoholism treatment program. In the years that followed, the Navy in particular showed how well this type of effort paid off. If you the reader are assigned to a military base, or are involved in any other kind of institution in which some of your people have gotten in trouble due to alcohol or drugs—including large commercial businesses as well as penal institutions and their associated rehabilitative centers—I hope you will look at this model and see how effective educational and treatment programs can be set up easily and economically. There is no excuse not to fix something which is undermining your operation.

Remember that ten percent of the American public is either in trouble with alcohol already or is well on the way, and that in the penal system (including the juvenile justice system) the majority of your inmates either had alcohol and/or drugs in their systems at the time they committed the offense for which they were incarcerated, or were imprisoned for illegal transactions involving these substances. This is everyone's problem in the long run. Dr. West and I showed a way to help solve that problem, and we showed that it worked.

CHAPTER 18

Recovery through the Twelve Steps

One of the most important things to note about our alcoholism treatment program at Lackland, was that the psychiatric and medical members of the treatment team worked in full collaboration with the Alcoholics Anonymous groups in the vicinity of the base. That was why we were able to obtain such a high success rate. Sister Ignatia ran her program at St. Thomas Hospital in Akron the same way, making full use of the psychiatric staff at the hospital whenever necessary, but bringing the A.A. volunteers directly into the ward, and she also obtained an extremely high success rate.

In the fifty years since those days back in San Antonio, I have never seen a treatment program work very well at all when the principles of the A.A. twelve steps were not introduced to the patients—no signs of significant success in particular when truly rigorous follow-ups were done two, three, and five years after treatment. And the less these programs involved direct participation by Alcoholics Anonymous workers, and the less they had their patients going to A.A. meetings outside the treatment facility, the lower the success rate. In the case of prison A.A. groups, where allowing the prisoners outside the walls is not feasible, the programs that have worked well had committed A.A. members from the surrounding area who came within the walls to conduct meetings on a regular basis, and gave the inmates regular contact with the outside world and its standards and values.

For those who are not too deeply familiar with Alcoholics Anonymous, the heart of its program centers on the twelve steps. Their application must become continual, because successful membership in A.A. requires a commitment to constant self-improvement and growth. It involves a way of life which is in fact healthy and healing for anyone who applies these principles. The word alcohol itself only shows up in the first half of the first step. All the rest of the steps deal with universal spiritual principles. The basic principles can in fact be applied to a whole host of human problems, ranging from out-of-control overeating to destructive sexual compulsions. Narcotics Anonymous replaces the word "alcohol" in the first step with "our addiction," Gamblers Anonymous uses "gambling" instead, and other twelve step groups make similar appropriate modifications.

All the twelve step programs have certain similarities, but the principle of "singleness of purpose" means that a group will only succeed if all the members focus on a single core problem which they all share. In A.A. meetings, people talk only about alcoholism; in N.A. groups, the members discuss their addiction to other chemical substances; in meetings of Overeaters Anonymous, people only try to deal with their eating disorders, and so on. It makes no sense to take my broken television set to a washing machine repair shop, and then grow outraged when the people there refuse to try to repair it. And it does not matter that "they both work on electricity." Repairing television sets is a different kind of job from repairing washing machines, and requires a different kind of tool kit and body of knowledge gained from long experience in repairing those particular items.

The twelve steps lead people through a therapeutic sequence involving (1) insight, (2) surrender, (3) establishing positive goals, (4) introspection, (5) confession, (6) a more complete submission to the positive power of the healing process, (7) humility, (8) amendment, (9) restitution, (10) reorganization, (11) spirituality, and (12) learning to love others in a fuller and less selfish way. It is not psychotherapy, and in places seems to violate some of the normal principles used by professionals in the mental health field, but in fact it works extremely well in the context of regular attendance at twelve-step meetings and identification with the other group members there. It can produce a total transformation in the way people think and act, which psychologists and psychiatrists often marvel at, because the kinds of positive changes which it produces are the same ones which they too have desired for their patients.

The Twelve Steps

I would like to describe briefly how the twelve steps are carried out in good A.A. and N.A. meetings, to make it clearer how these groups supply necessary parts of the overall treatment program:

1. INSIGHT

We admitted we were powerless over alcohol—that our lives had become unmanageable.

Prior to entry into A.A., most alcoholics were unable to assume the responsibility for their alcoholism. They blamed others for the way their lives had deteriorated. The turning point in the lives of these alcoholics came when they could no longer tolerate their own behavior and became willing to go to any length to seek an answer to the crisis. This insight—into what they had become, and the role alcohol played in that—was essential to recovery.

Finally recognizing their powerlessness when it came to managing their own affairs was also one of the few revelations of truth these alcoholics had experienced in many years. This was truly a step in the right direction, for the eleven following steps could not be carried out successfully if this first admission was not unequivocally realized. This deflation of the ego was necessary before the alcoholic could become teachable.

In order to work the twelve step program, drug addicts had to make the same admission about their drug usage, for in their case, whatever drug they were using was certainly destroying their lives: cocaine, heroin, amphetamines, hallucinogens such as LSD (lysergic acid diethylamide), or whatever else it might be. The attitude of "I can handle it" had to be overturned, because an honest observation of the way their lives were continuing to go downhill demonstrated that they were not "handling it" satisfactorily.

2. SURRENDER

Came to believe that a Power greater than ourselves could restore us to sanity.

The admission that the actual course of our lives is in the hands of some omnipotent power is the basis for real surrender. I cannot fight universal laws and principles and succeed. The basis of these principles is all-powerful, and everything in the universe is subject to them. What is sought here is not making people merely compliant—"I will follow these rules because I am being forced to, in this particular circumstance"—but rather a total surrender emotionally and intellectually to the belief that there is a Higher Power governing this universe.

Some who come into the twelve step program object that if something cannot be touched or felt, it cannot exist. The law of gravity also cannot be touched or felt. But no human being can throw a baseball up into the air so hard that it will float up there in the air and never come spinning back down. As a baseball player, I had to learn how to throw a baseball with the right velocity to make it come down at the right place and the right level, and this required learning to work with the law of gravity instead of thinking I could just ignore that rule of nature. We are surrounded by powers and forces greater than ourselves at all times.

The power we are searching for here cannot be touched or felt directly, but it is a Healing Power which is capable of restoring our sanity, which we can see at work in the lives of those who have already been working the twelve step program. It is the power of truth and honesty itself, but it is also the power of compassion and understanding. If this step is carried out properly, those who work it first begin to incorporate within their internal makeup the positive feeling that they are not alone any more. Fear then begins to subside.

3. POSITIVE GOALS

Made a decision to turn our will and our lives over to the care of God *as we understood Him*.

During the active phase of their disease, alcoholics (and drug addicts as well) have a tendency to be engulfed in their own egos. Egocentric people's contempt for anything spiritual makes them seem all-powerful in their own eyes. We could use the word ego—E.G.O.—as an acronym for Easing God Out. When I decide to finally surrender and turn my will over to another, this brings a termination or settling of the controversy in which I had been engaging with the other person. Once this decision is made, not superficially but through a genuine soul-searching process, the battle is beginning to be won. Controversy is one thing that alcoholics and drug addicts do not need.

All is not cured overnight. Each journey starts with the first step, but as people continue on their way, they may still run into road blocks further along in their path. Those who come into the twelve step program need to be warned that just stopping drinking (or drugging) is not the instant solution to all controversy. But as each subsequent obstacle is eventually overcome, each of these victories will provide additional strength in conquering new anxiety-laden situations.

The important thing is to begin the journey. And we must notice the phrase "as we *understood* Him," which means that if traditional religious language makes no sense to me, I am free to think of this Healing Power of truth, honesty, compassion, and personal transformation in ways that do make sense to me. Even now, well over fifty years after I first got sober, I do not feel comfortable with heavily religious language, because I still do not *understand* it (even though I gladly allow those in the program who do understand it to talk about their higher power in that way). You will notice that when I first came into the A.A. program, my own spirituality centered around the spirit of helping and caring for others and saving human lives, which I used to replace my old spirit of egocentrism, anger, and selfishness. That simple *decision* (another key word which appears in this step) allowed me to get sober and stay sober, and begin living harmoniously with the universal principles of nature.

4. INTROSPECTION

Made a searching and fearless moral inventory of ourselves.

The ability to recognize the real nature of the conflicts we are involved in, with the world and with other people, helps to resolve the problems which the alcoholic had developed in his or her attitudes toward the world. When I see what is really causing the conflicts to occur, this "clears the air" and enables me to start dealing more effectively with the issues which actually need resolving. To keep this inventory up to date, periodic revisions of it should be written as the person progresses in sobriety.

Having made this inventory, the stage is set for an objective assessment of assets and liabilities. The façade we erect in which we blame others for our own personal failings, begins to diminish when we start making an honest appraisal of our own personal deficiencies.

Beginners to the program who have a poor record of past behavior and were not good at living harmoniously within the bounds of normal moral and social demands, may be prone at this point to write a fourth step in which they simply defame themselves, and ignore all the strengths of character which they also possess. In fact, with most people who come into the program, there is a tendency to list negative personality characteristics almost exclusively while overlooking their most positive characteristics. This practice produces an inaccurate inventory.

What people want is to feel good. With alcohol (or drugs) we attempted to produce this feeling artificially, and in the long run we only felt worse about ourselves. The twelve step program is designed to teach us how to act and think so that we will feel good realistically as a consequence. Neglecting positive attributes when writing a fourth step inventory blocks this, because it only further perpetuates guilt feelings. Alcoholics need to work on eliminating or reducing feelings of guilt in order to feel good about themselves again.

5. CONFESSION

Admitted to God, to ourselves, and to another human being the exact nature of our wrongs.

Great pain is experienced in admitting that a controversy or conflict exists, and it is particularly painful to have to admit to being at fault ourselves. This action however is part of a mental cleansing of these personality defects, and is a positive step toward a more productive life.

It is an arduous task indeed to establish positive communications with another person when I have in fact been feeling guilty about the harm I caused that other person. But defective communications cause continual frustrations, and are the source of continuing conflicts, particularly in the immediate family. It is traumatic for alcoholics to talk over some of the events in which they have been involved with their own families. Some alcoholics seek a "geographical cure" by walking out and fleeing from their families, rather than attempt a positive resolution of the differences which exist in their homes. The hurt done by fleeing becomes more acute, the closer the ties are in the family.

It is an important benefit having a sponsor in A.A. (or N.A. as the case may be) to talk things over with when newcomers are working on restoring positive communications and resolving conflicts within the family. In fact, obtaining a good A.A. or N.A. sponsor is vital to working the program well and rebuilding our lives successfully.

6. SUBMISSION

Were entirely ready to have God remove all these defects of character.

Coming to terms with the power of God, as we understand Him, and becoming aware of God's ability to act in our behalf, is an aid to achieving greater honesty and objectivity. Trust in the divine wisdom of God is another step in the process of relinquishing our own selfish attempts to control our own environment totally and absolutely.

7. HUMILITY

Humbly asked Him to remove our shortcomings.

During the process of their addiction, individuals become more and more self-centered and unwilling to admit their own intellectual limitations. Alcoholics and drug addicts come into treatment convinced that they already know all the answers, and that they know more than the other people around them, whom they look upon as misguided and fools—as stupid people who need to be corrected and brought into line. And if these other people refuse to be "corrected," alcoholics and drug addicts are convinced that they are fully justified in rebelling against that stupidity.

But one of the major forms of true humility is the willingness to learn. Admitting that one does not have all the answers in fact provides an enormous feeling of new freedom, and dissolves away our pride and arrogance. Humility is not a sign of weakness but a source of great strength.

Furthermore, developing a willingness to start overcoming our own shortcomings is a sign of emotional growth. In this step we become willing to embrace change and positive growth at deeper and deeper levels of our lives.

8. AMENDMENT

Made a list of all persons we had harmed, and became willing to make amends to them all.

Alcoholics (and drug addicts) have difficulty in facing many of the people they had harmed while they were drinking or using. There is a tendency to try to ignore or avoid any contact with these people, at least at any truly intimate and close level. The longer this condition exists, the more difficult it is to make amends to them. This in turn creates even more subconscious anxiety, that will seldom be resolved until the issue is faced directly.

This list of amends we need to make is based upon what we discovered about ourselves in our fourth step personal inventory. As was stressed earlier, a fourth step inventory that implies that all one's actions in the past have been negative, and that all one's personal characteristics were flawed, has not been fully completed yet. That fourth step list should have contained positive elements of personality as well as negative ones.

You will remember me talking in one of the first chapters about the way I was asked to help out in my father's little grocery store when I was a child. Good business people have a knowledge of their stock, and can only succeed in business by keeping account of those items which sell and need to be continually replenished, as opposed to those which have not been selling and should not be reordered. If no one in the neighborhood wished to buy a particular brand of catsup—if in fact the neighbors said that they had tried it and did not like the way that kind of catsup tasted—then my father did not continue to reorder cases of that brand to stock his shelves. Instead he ordered more of the better-tasting variety which people actually wanted.

We must keep this principle in mind while making our list of amends we need to make. To bring about real changes in their lives, people must identify all their behavioral actions, and seek to change those which cause tension. Making amends simply means endeavoring to mend relationships which have been torn and damaged, but to do this effectively, we must also identify the positive things in our personal makeup which we could contribute to human relationships. It is not just a matter of apologizing for past misdeeds, for we must now substitute consistent positive behavioral patterns for all the negative ones we exhibited in the past. Working hard at creating new positive ways of acting is the most important way we mend the fabric of our lives.

9. RESTITUTION

Made direct amends to such people wherever possible, except when to do so would injure them or others.

Rehabilitation means to restore something to its former state of usefulness. In most cases, alcoholics and drug addicts once had some useful characteristics at one time in their lives, and these positive abilities are now in need of restoration. The ability to love and establish friendships with other people was usually present in their lives at some point back in the past. In order to reestablish this ability, it is necessary to make peace now with people whom we once loved, and with whom we were formerly friends, whom we had harmed by our negative behaviors. This is often painful, but is essential to regaining a sense of tranquility.

Newcomers to the twelve step program are at first prone to regard restoration in terms only of material things. If I drove your automobile while I was drunk and dented the fender, then I need to pay for repairing it now. If I borrowed money from you to spend on alcohol (or drugs) and never repaid it, then I need to pay you what I owe you now. This is part of making amends, and must be done wherever necessary, but it is usually not the most important part. Making moral restitution can be traumatic, but is more rewarding than merely replacing material things. When I make moral restitution, I begin making real spiritual growth, and will quickly start to realize the rewards in my life of the program's Twelve Promises of a new kind of "feeling good."

> If we are painstaking about this phase of our development, we will be amazed before we are half way through. We are going to know a new freedom and a new happiness. We will not regret the past nor wish to shut the door on it. We will comprehend the word serenity and we will know peace. No matter how far down the scale we have gone, we will see how our experience can benefit others. That feeling of uselessness and self-pity will disappear. We will lose interest in selfish things and gain interest in our fellows. Self-seeking will slip away. Our whole attitude and outlook upon life will change. Fear of people and of economic insecurity will leave us. We will intuitively know how to handle situations which used to baffle us. We will suddenly realize that God is doing for us what we could not do for ourselves. Are these extravagant promises? We think not. They are being fulfilled among us—sometimes quickly, sometimes slowly. They will always materialize if we work for them.[36]

In making amends, I take the first step toward forgiving others, by making restitution for my own part in the confrontation and conflict. In the process, I at least hope that these other people will eventually forgive me. This does not always happen, but that does not matter. Even if my apologies are not accepted, my making the attempt at restitution helps heal the guilt I had been feeling over my past actions.

Self-forgiveness is also essential, and alcoholics (and addicts) must be able to forgive themselves. Our common human desire is to feel good. Having a large burden of guilt to carry does not allow people to feel good.

10. REORGANIZATION

Continued to take personal inventory and when we were wrong promptly admitted it.

The inventory process is not a one-time endeavor. It must be continual, because as we live our lives, our own attitudes and actions, as well as those of the people around us, are in a constant process of change. Life itself is full of changes, so that even years after obtaining sobriety, alcoholics (and drug addicts obviously too) still find themselves encountering new kinds of adversities. In the process of learning to meet them properly, however, they gain the rewards of further spiritual growth. The changes are in fact going to take place anyway. We can never prevent them from taking place; our only choice is to regard them as opportunities to grow and become more flexible, or to be ground down by them.

As we work to adjust to these new challenges, it is important to remember that if we become ensnared again in continual resentment, hate, intolerance, pettiness, envy, and anger, we will fail to adapt successfully. But if we remain constantly on guard against these kinds of emotional unrest, which warn us that we are beginning to walk down the wrong path, it will help ease the pain and frustration of the new adjustments we are going to have to make.

In the beginning of this new way of life, we find ourselves having to think consciously about making these adjustments. We can fail to notice that the resentment or anger has grown too great until we have been acutely miserable for many days. At this point we then have to remind ourselves that this is a sign that we are heading down the road to defeat instead of victory, and we have to begin the work of methodically healing the obsessive, continually repeated thoughts of resentment or anger, so that we can get ourselves out of this losing life-strategy. All this requires a good deal of conscious thought at the beginning. But with maturity and length of time in the program, this process becomes almost automatic. Being continuously flexible and adaptive has become a way of life.

11. SPIRITUALITY

Sought through prayer and meditation to improve our conscious contact with God *as we understood Him*, praying only for knowledge of His will for us and the power to carry that out.

The right kind of prayer and meditation brings true humility. The ability to relate to a Higher Power does not make one appear weaker in the eyes of others, but is a great source of real strength. Active alcoholics (and drug addicts) often fall into an adversary relationship with this Higher Power, which prevents them from having faith in any kind of spiritual concepts. *It seems easier for alcoholics and addicts to fight God than to fight their illness.* What is more, they usually fail to recognize that they even have an illness and assume its nonexistence, which makes it doubly impossible to combat the real source of their unhappiness and misery.

Faith and trust in oneself is also essential to progress in the program. Because they have had so many past failures, and no longer trust themselves either, there is a reluctance to believe that coming to any kind of trust in a Higher Power will produce any kind of valid help. Many alcoholics feel programmed for failure, and I believe that with drug addicts this is often even more severe. Many are unwilling to try any kind of real change in their way of dealing with life, because of the failures that resulted from their own previous attempts at self-administered rehabilitation.

12. LOVE

Having had a spiritual awakening as the result of these steps, we tried to carry this message to alcoholics, and to practice these principles in all our affairs.

This step is not only the one which perpetuates the twelve step program and keeps it growing and spreading, it also provides the opportunity for a new kind of happy and pleasant experience. Alcoholics (and drug addicts also) find that there is no greater reward than to not only get their own house in order, but also to be able to share the joy of their recovery with others.

There is in addition a hidden personal therapeutic benefit from sharing our recovery with people who are still drinking or drugging themselves to ruin and destruction. When we see others using the same excuses and rationalizations which we ourselves used to use, we see even more clearly how hollow and empty our own attempts were to justify our excessive drinking (or our use of obviously destructive narcotics and other drugs). It is marvelous how powerfully our own thoughts of ever drinking or using again are obliterated by working with others who have brought themselves to the brink of total destruction with these substances. It brings the message home to us in a way that nothing else can.

"Practicing these principles in all our affairs" is not easy for alcoholics and addicts. Negative thoughts and actions were so prevalent in our lives back in the past, that we sometimes have to work hard now at maintaining a positive attitude toward our affairs. Nevertheless, length of time in A.A. or N.A. and the regular application of the positive principles contained in the twelve steps is an assurance that our sobriety and peace of mind will continue. As the basic A.A. text puts it, "rarely have we seen a person fail who has thoroughly followed our path," which means living by these twelve principles, and learning to practice them on a daily basis.

It is a good way of life, and a psychologically healthy way of life. Countless people who had been spreading paths of destruction through the world have learned how to be positively contributing members of society through practicing these principles. Any number of men and women who had been quietly miserable inside their own heads to the point of total desperation, and even afflicted by serious suicidal thoughts on many occasions, have found a new peace and new happiness by following this route. All over the world—for numerous local twelve step groups now rescue lives all over the globe—we can see the living proof right before our eyes. These are not mere theories, they are established facts.

There should be rewards experienced for abstinence. Few will give up the use of alcohol if the result is to continue to feel more miserable even than when they drank. But if the alternative to drinking is eventually far more rewarding, those who were once compulsive drinkers will in most instances remain sober. A.A. provides that more pleasurable alternative, if alcoholics are willing to work through the twelve steps. Quality sobriety can end up becoming as addictive in its own way as drinking, so that there are any number of dedicated people in Alcoholics Anonymous who literally eat, sleep, and work the program twenty-four hours a day. But to become "addicted" (if we can use that word slightly inappropriately) to feeling good, finding real satisfaction in performing our jobs well, helping other people in genuinely useful ways, and feeling an authentic sense of self-worth, leads to the healthiest of all kinds of human life.

Although I only know the N.A. program "from the outside," once we got to the Vietnam war period (1963 to 1975 and afterwards) I had drug addicts as well as alcoholics in the treatment programs I ran, and addicts achieve exactly the same positive way of life through their involvement in N.A.

The belief among some that only a recovered alcoholic or addict can help those who have drinking or drug abuse problems is a myth. Dr. Louis Jolyon West at Lackland was neither an alcoholic nor an addict, nor was Dr. Joseph J. Zuska, who founded the famous and highly successful alcoholism program at Long Beach Naval Station in the mid-1960's. Professional people can help the alcoholic and the addict provided they have real empathy, can create a spirit of mutual honesty, and have at least some specialized skill and training in treating alcohol and drug abuse. But they will usually send their patients to Alcoholics Anonymous (or Narcotics Anonymous) as part of the process. A large number of A.A. members today originally started coming to meetings at the suggestion of a therapist, often via a treatment program.

A.A. also works for some who cannot relate to a professional therapist at all. Some of these alcoholics may simply be unable to trust a therapist. If a large educational difference exists, alcoholics may feel that they are being talked down to by the professional. The therapist, on the other side, may not be fully aware of how much suffering the alcoholic has been experiencing, or may in some other way lack empathy with the alcoholic's problems. There may also be the problem of the therapist's inaccessibility in times other than regular scheduled visits. Sometimes these problems exist more in the mind of the patient than they do in reality, but as long as the alcoholic feels this way, any help he or she can receive from that therapist is going to be minimal.

Nevertheless, professionals who are not alcoholics or addicts themselves, but who are truly caring people, can and do accomplish marvelously successful work in treatment centers. The most important thing for them to remember though, is that in all the treatment programs which I have seen which had any great degree of success, great emphasis has also been put on patients attending A.A. meetings (and/or N.A. meetings) outside the treatment facility.

Good treatment programs get good results. But why, our detractors have sometimes complained, do even good treatment programs never achieve anything close to a one hundred percent success rate? For that matter, A.A. itself has never been able to save all the alcoholics who walked through its doors. If you have something genuinely workable, some are apt to say, there should be few or no failures at all.

The great problem is resistance on the part of the alcoholic. Many alcoholics are unaware that they are ill. They blame their problems totally on the other people around them, and their position in the world, and what they like to believe was simply "bad luck." Or they are aware at some level that they have a serious drinking problem, but they still have no deep-seated desire to stop drinking. They cannot identify with A.A., and when sent to meetings, treat the program in such an adversarial way that they get little or nothing from attending. They spend their time criticizing the meetings, and insisting that A.A. is only for people whose drinking is much more severe than theirs, or some other excuse of that sort.

There has to be a decision to recover from alcoholism on the part of the drinker, one that must of necessity always be an internal personal decision. True motivation must always arise from within. The A.A. philosophy insists that a person has to ask for help, and mean it. Family or friends may sometimes call A.A., recognizing that a serious problem exists, but unless the alcoholic himself or herself is receptive, the A.A. members will not pursue this call any further.

Professional therapists and Employee Assistance Programs will sometimes set up "interventions," where other people surround the problem drinker and force him or her to start looking at the problem seriously, but even well-orchestrated interventions of this sort do not always work. And the A.A. groups themselves resolutely refuse to use any coercive measures of that sort, or any kind at all. Their attitude is that individuals must be responsible for their own decisions, and that those who wish to continue drinking must be allowed to go on their way.

One of the biggest problems in alcoholism treatment is that alcoholics will invariably begin by struggling as hard as they can to avoid acknowledging their disease, or to evade taking any serious action to regain their health. This resistance is misdirected, for it is the alcoholism that must be fought and doubted. But many find it easier to fight something tangible, like the A.A. program, than it would be to fight the intangibles that actually cause these people to remain locked in their alcoholism. Commitment to the program may only come after a long period of doubts and resistance toward A.A. One never knows when that glimmer of light will illuminate the newcomer and suddenly remove the blockage, revealing a whole new world to his or her eyes. But some alcoholics never get to the point of internalizing this vision of hope to a great enough degree to become actually willing to change.

No real healing begins to take place until alcoholics finally recognize their need for help, and become willing to go to any lengths to stop drinking permanently. Up to that point, alcoholics are invariably fighting for the right to continue drinking, even if some of them are doing this covertly and silently inside their minds, while pretending on the outside to be complying with the requirements of the treatment program.

"Oh, I'm not that bad," is a familiar statement among those who are still battling for the right to continue drinking. Their own ego is often preventing them from having much success in the search for a new way of life. Too much false pride keeps them from recognizing their need for massive assistance. So we can ask the interesting question, "How bad does your life have to get before accepting A.A.?" The truth of the matter is that *if people are worrying about their drinking, their condition is bad enough to need help.*

Great harm can sometimes be done when people talk about the need to "hit bottom" before anyone can be helped in A.A., because a good many people who are in fact in serious trouble because of their drinking believe that "hitting bottom" means that individuals must sink to such a depth that they have become ineffective, unemployed, divorced, and totally defeated before they need to cry for help. If this were the case, the death rate due to alcoholism would be staggering. Many people get sober today long before they reach this point, due in part to increased public education regarding alcoholism.

Nevertheless, until alcoholics are willing to "surrender," little can be accomplished in the way of effective treatment Surrender is often viewed as a mysterious phenomenon, but in reality it is simply coming to an acknowledgment that help is needed, which then opens the door to the recovery process.

Once people are willing to seek help, membership in Alcoholics Anonymous provides all sorts of necessary assistance. Crisis intervention is one important area where A.A. keeps the new member from sinking. Help and emotional support is available at all times of the day or night, and is usually only a telephone call away. The majority of alcoholics have established a record of failure. They have lost confidence in their ability to succeed. They are familiar with the consequences of drinking but are fearful of facing the unknown world of sobriety. The other A.A. members give them constant encouragement and hope, particularly when they are under exceptional stress.

One of the biggest helps which A.A. can give a new member is a good sponsor. This is a person in the program who has already been sober for a while, who provides advice and counsel. The rule in the old days was that a sponsor had to have been sober for at least six months minimum. But in general, the longer they have been in the program, the better these sponsors will understand how to be of greatest help—this is the only instance in which length of sobriety has any real significance in A.A. The sponsor's role continues even after the newcomer has been in the program for a while. The sponsor has a heavy personal responsibility in fact, because the new members need to be provided support even after they have begun to feel more self-sufficient.

The new members are usually lonely, experiencing pain, and full of apprehension, doubts, and remorse. When they reach a point where they need real help to overcome their overpowering feelings of rejection, guilt, shame, and hopelessness, their sponsors can be invaluable to them. They need to identify with someone who can relate to them with empathy and care. Being available whenever help is needed is especially essential to good sponsorship.

A good sponsor will not attempt to solve all the new member's problems. The poorest support a sponsor can provide is financial. Many alcoholics come into the program in severe financial difficulties, and will take advantage of anyone who offers them money as an "instant cure" for their woes. In fact, suffering some pain for a while is usually more productive in terms of building long term sobriety and responsibility.

Newcomers who find the right kind of sponsor will eventually come to regard that person as one of the greatest heroes and wisest men or women they have ever known. Even years after a person's dearly beloved sponsor has died, he or she will speak of that sponsor with love and awe and respect, and a kind of enduring loyalty that I have seen in few other contexts. This alone can sustain sobriety over many troublesome times. Even though possessed of an insatiable desire to drink, the person simply does not want to let the sponsor down. It would be a betrayal of that good sponsor's love and hope.

If you yourself have ever wanted to become a real hero in other people's eyes, then become the best A.A. sponsor you possibly can. There are no other experiences so rewarding.

Sometimes people make a start in the A.A. program and then have a relapse. This is another reason why neither alcoholism treatment programs nor A.A. itself can produce a one hundred percent success rate. Sometimes in fact these people came into the program seeking only a temporary reprieve from the consequences of their drinking. The crisis which created the call for help will have dissipated after a period of time, and they then feel free to return back to drinking once again. No amount of urging by a sponsor seems to correct the condition, because the stage was already set for a relapse from the beginning.

The desire to recover is an individual one; even the best sponsors are helpless to do anything once people make up their minds to return to drinking. Neither A.A. nor any of its members can insure the will to become well. It is a personal matter and the new member must weigh the differences between the misery of intoxication and the rewards of sobriety. If a relapse does occur, hopefully the experiment will be short-lived, but some do not come back, or if they do, it is only after incredibly much more needless suffering.

Recovery is a process. Newcomers searching for a new life want the restoration of their self-dignity, self-respect, honor, and the ability to care about themselves and others. It takes a long struggle to achieve these goals. The battle is never easy. Initially the efforts to ward off the disease can be painful and intense, and the lack of immediate results can be what causes the person to have a relapse. The conditions which brought about the alcoholism did not occur overnight, which means that they also cannot be resolved overnight.

The dynamics of recovery from alcoholism is often misunderstood. For instance, when a person recovers from surgery, there is a long process of healing afterwards which involves pain. People are willing to endure this pain to correct the condition. But many alcoholics want an immediate relief from their emotional pain and they want relief right now. It is vitally important for them to realize that recovery is not an event, it is a process. This process can take months or years, but the adventure associated with recovery, and the thrill of discovering who I myself actually am, and learning to love and appreciate myself, is well worth the effort.

There is a warning I should give however. There is one important way in which recovery from alcoholism is not at all like going to a hospital and having surgery. Often in medical procedures we are more or less the passive recipients of someone else's ministrations, and healing from the surgery is a matter of just lying around recuperating in bed and not overtaxing ourselves too soon. In recovery from alcoholism, no matter how fortunate problem drinkers might be in finding the best treatment center or sponsor, they still have to rely on their own skills and motivation to recover instead of the skills of a physician or any other external authority figure or expert. It becomes their own responsibility at bottom, and theirs alone. People who expect recovery in A.A. to take place automatically, just by passively attending meetings, will also end up among those unhappy souls who do not make it.

A.A. offers any alcoholic the opportunity to create a new lifestyle. Alcoholism causes emotional, physical, spiritual, and material losses, but it is possible to recoup these losses and end up better off than one has ever been in one's life. A.A. in fact forces the new members to adopt a different lifestyle, but these changes are essential to maintaining sobriety. Negative thoughts and actions are replaced with positive alternatives. The challenge of building a more productive and meaningful life without alcohol is an exciting journey, which leads to a life freed from all the misery and discomfort caused by their old excessive drinking.

Alcoholics Anonymous is a very personal program of people sharing and caring for one another. It offers a reprieve from the misery of alcoholism. People find a new desire and ability to care for other people, which is a complete turnabout from the days when their only real goal in life was to be able to procure and ingest enough alcohol to escape the pains of reality for another few hours, or to function in an anesthetized state. A.A. is a "prescription for a new life" which provides alcoholics with faith, hope, love, and a spiritual approach to living. We who have been afflicted by this disease are offered membership in a community where love and fellowship abound. We are given an opportunity to become some of the most blessed of all human beings on this earth. Those unfortunates who do not make it—those who either do not or cannot feel that togetherness and love—end up as the greatest losers of all. Physically, psychologically, and spiritually; in terms of career, family, and home, they are doomed to a miserable and inexorable fate. Untreated, the disease only gets worse with time. My heartfelt hope for you, if you the reader are an alcoholic, is that today you will choose life instead of death.

CHAPTER 19

Another Generation and Another War

Once I had demonstrated that alcoholics in the military could be successfully treated and restored to full duty by this sort of quite inexpensive treatment program, my next major concerns were to attempt to train other personnel to carry on this work, to turn the Lackland program from an experimental "pilot project" into a permanent treatment center which would continue to receive full official Air Force support after Dr. West and I had gone on to other assignments at other locations, and to establish similar centers on other Air Force bases.

Unfortunately, as Dr. West commented later on, it was going to take "another generation and another war" before our society and our government policies had sufficiently changed to allow this sort of thing to be done on any large scale. When we started our coordinated treatment program at Lackland in 1953, Eisenhower was just starting his first term as President, and the Korean War was still going on, although it was in its last few months of active hostilities. The majority of Americans were fairly conservative during the Eisenhower era, and on most issues did not like changes in the traditional ways of doing things. The new generation and new war of which Dr. West spoke was the Vietnam conflict which began roughly ten years later and so dominated Americans' concerns from around 1963 down to 1975. The many new alcoholism treatment programs which were instituted then were often "piggy-backed" to a certain degree on widespread concern with the epidemic of drug addiction which began appearing in the military at that time, and eventually within the civilian population as well. But it was during this Vietnam period that we were finally able to start setting up large numbers of fully functioning alcoholism treatment centers all over the United States.

It was also not until then, in the mid 1960's, that the patient work which Mrs. Marty Mann had begun back during the 1940's to alter general American public attitudes toward alcoholism began sinking in deeply enough to allow truly major strides forward. It takes time to change the perceptions of an entire national population. The new concern with social issues in general which was part of the spirit of the 1960's also helped the alcoholism treatment cause. And then it took recovered alcoholics in Congress, like Senator Harold Hughes and Representative Wilbur Mills, to spearhead changes in U.S. laws and conduct investigations of alcoholism in the various branches of the military, beginning in the 1970's, so that some outside pressure could be put on the upper command echelons in the armed services to do something to help and rehabilitate those whose drinking had become destructive, and restore them back to active duty instead of just casting them out. I knew Senator Hughes as someone I could call on for help on occasion, but was much closer to Representative Mills.

So it took the changes of the Vietnam war period, from around 1963 to 1975, to begin turning good alcoholism treatment in this country into more of a reality, not just in the military but also in the civilian world. Nevertheless, when I look back on those events from several decades later, it seems clear that I accomplished something valuable in the late 1940's and early 50's by simply showing conclusively that it could be done: alcoholics whose continual excessive drinking had made them military liabilities could be turned into sober and fully contributing members of the service once again. Someone has to go first. Charles A. Lindbergh flew across the Atlantic by himself in 1927 and demonstrated that such flights were possible; commercial airline journeys from the United States to Europe are now everyday matters which everyone takes for granted. This parallel strikes me especially strongly, because coincidentally, the field from which Lindbergh took off on his historic flight was located on Long Island, right next to Mitchel Air Force Base where I took my own first "flight" into working as a full-time military alcoholism treatment specialist in 1948. He and I started at the same place, geographically speaking.

While I was at Lackland, I did manage to set up successful liaisons with many other Air Force, Army, and Navy installations in the area. Demands came from every source requesting lectures, services, and assistance in coping with alcoholism. Rehabilitation programs were established at Randolph, Kelly, Brooks, Laredo, Cannon, Holoman, and Medina Air Force bases, and also at the Army's Fort Sam Houston and at Corpus Christi Naval Air Base. I crisscrossed Texas from one end to the other on a regular basis. After a while, personnel from Air Force bases throughout the world were being sent to Lackland Air Force Base Hospital for treatment.

When I paid my first visit to Walker Air Force Base in New Mexico, I had an unusual experience. This was a Strategic Air Command base, where military security was extraordinarily high. I showed up at their gates while a practice full alert was going on, and explained to the Air Police there that I had come to give lectures on alcoholism. This seemed to them so preposterous, that they assumed on the spot that I must be a Russian saboteur or spy with an unusually clumsy and unbelievable cover story, and immediately marched me off to the Provost Marshal's Office, where they kept me confined in a holding cell for several hours in fact, until they were able to contact the senior officer who had approved my visit there. He was in the Officers Club drinking, and had left orders that he was not to be disturbed.

He was profusely apologetic however when he finally found out what had happened to me, and supported me in every way during my visit. As a result, in spite of this awkward start, I in fact was able to persuade them to assign a full-time worker on their base, assigned to dealing with alcoholism as his official job responsibility, and this person in turn was able to set up an active continuing program there. I have no detailed statistics on how well this program did, because SAC bases were considered top secret installations and they did not allow outsiders, even within the Air Force itself, to have access to information about personnel who served on their bases. But this base visit where they threw me in the guardhouse turned out clearly to be one of my greatest successes by the time it was over.

The things that I was able to achieve during my time at Lackland at all these other Air Force, Army and Navy bases in Texas and New Mexico showed that what I was doing would work on any sort of military installation. But I was well aware that central command in Washington, D.C., had to be persuaded to back our program more seriously if we were to achieve anything permanent and enduring. Our opportunity seemed to have finally arrived on May 27, 1954. I went to Washington and appeared before a hearing of the Character Guidance Ad Hoc Committee on Alcoholism, which was made up of a brigadier general and various colonels and lieutenant colonels who were on a wide range of staff agencies, including the Provost Marshal, the Air Police, Personnel, and so on. I described what we had accomplished at Lackland and proposed the full-time assignment of one person on each Air Force base as coordinator and director of an alcoholism program, that person to be trained by me.

The response to my testimony seemed to be extremely positive and enthusiastic that day, and I left the hearing room feeling very pleased. But even though I felt that we had demonstrated conclusively that such a person would save the Air Force far more money than his or her salary cost, I was quite dismayed when that committee (or people higher up) eventually came to the conclusion that such a program would be "too expensive" if extended to the entire Air Force. I was too far ahead of the times, even if by only ten or fifteen years.

I explored other avenues, of course, for keeping this new endeavor going. On two different occasions I managed to get another person officially slotted to be trained by me, either to succeed me or to expand the program. The first was promised in 1954, and the second was promised in 1956. But for reasons unknown, both assignments were retracted before the training could actually be carried out.

I also managed to interest Dr. Albert J. Glass, Chief of Psychiatric Services at Brooke Army Hospital, in what we were doing. This was another of the string of military bases which encircled San Antonio.

During 1954 and 1955 he published several articles on how alcoholism treatment in the Army might best be carried out, but no full-time Army treatment personnel ended up being appointed, and it became clear that the Army was going to be even more resistant to change than the Air Force. We simply kept on hitting too many dead ends.

––––––––––––

When Dr. West left in 1957, I was left at Lackland without much in the way of support. As Chief of Psychiatry at the hospital there, he had had a good deal of influence. In September of the next year, 1958, I was suddenly notified that I was being reassigned to Heathrow Air Force Base in England as a Psychiatric Social Worker, where as far as I could see, I would have no freedom to work with alcoholics on any large scale. I went to Col. Gold, the Hospital Commander, and told him I was assigned to my present position by the Surgeon General of the Air Force, and could not be reassigned in this fashion. He knew so little about the terms on which the program had been begun five years earlier, that he demanded I show proof that this was the case. I had the original letter, and finally persuaded him to call Washington to confirm it. Brigadier General Victor A. Byrnes of the Surgeon General's Office fortunately sent back a very nice letter on September 22, 1958:

> Sgt Swegan was assigned to the Lackland Hospital per a special arrangement between the Office of the Surgeon General and the Office of the Chief Chaplain, in order to set up a pilot study on the rehabilitation of chronic alcoholics. Sgt Swegan was sent to Yale to take a special course on rehabilitation of alcoholics and he is the only person in the Air Force so trained. It is our opinion that the alcoholic rehabilitation program which Sgt Swegan is conducting at Lackland is not only of value to the local base, but will have ultimate value in developing the Air Force-wide program. Plans are underway to develop training materials from this program and to disseminate information regarding the techniques on an Air Force-wide scale.
>
> Chronic alcoholism is a serious problem when it exists in any organization and it is important to find a solution. Since

this pilot program is still in an experimental stage, it is our opinion that it is very important to retain Sgt Swegan in the project in order that a worthwhile evaluation can be made. The loss of this man at the present time would make an objective evaluation of the work to date impossible.

So I still had some backing for what I was doing, from people at the higher levels in Washington, enough at least to save my job at this point. But Gen. Byrnes either did not or could not carry through on some of the promises in that letter, and in addition, the psychiatric and hospital personnel at Lackland quickly began undercutting my program in so many ways that it eventually became impossible to carry it out effectively any longer. For example, they suddenly announced that they were moving my office to a dilapidated old building on an isolated part of the base where hardly anyone ever came. I found more and more obstacles continually placed in my way. Anyone who understands politics knows the various ways such covert sabotage can be carried out. I had really needed the gold oak leaves on Dr. West's shoulders to run interference for me. The majority of people in the mental health professions and in the medical professions were still very little interested in alcoholism treatment during the 1950's.

In fact even later, during the 1970's, Nancy Olson's book on the struggle to pass decent alcoholism legislation in Congress during that period, shows that the concerned alcoholism people were still having to battle continuously against some at least of the mental health professionals who wanted to undercut, or take over for their own purposes, any appropriation of funds or personnel which had been designated to deal with the problem of alcoholism.[37] In other words, historically speaking, from the 1950's all the way through the 1970's, the psychiatrists were not always our friends. It is those who did back us and support us whose memories we still cherish and honor so deeply: people like Dr. William Duncan Silkworth who worked with Bill W., Dr. Harry Tiebout who worked with Marty Mann, and Dr. Louis Jolyon West who worked with me. And there were other medical professionals, like Dr. Joseph J. Zuska, who understood how the combination of their knowledge and skills with the experience of the people in Alcoholics Anonymous would produce the highest success rates in the treatment of alcoholism.

But after Dr. West left in 1957, there was no one left at the Lackland base hospital of their stature and knowledge. So finally in 1961, after twenty-one years in the Air Force, having risen to Senior Master Sergeant, almost the top of the noncommissioned officers ranking system, I decided to put in my papers for retirement. I signed a contract to establish a treatment center in Lubbock, Texas, and became the director of the Arnett-Benson Rehabilitation Center as it was called.

I had been too far ahead of the times, but the times were changing rapidly. In February 1965, retired Navy Commander Dick Jewell, who had gotten sober in Alcoholics Anonymous after he left the service, approached Dr. Joseph J. Zuska (Capt. USN) at the Long Beach Naval Station, and persuaded him to start a serious alcoholism treatment program there. Dr. Zuska knew my friend and supporter Dr. West, and I myself got to know Jewell and came to Long Beach to give talks later on, so I have some familiarity with the excellent program they established there. This experiment gained permanence when it was designated as an official Navy alcoholism treatment facility in 1967, and has successfully rehabilitated thousands of alcoholic officers and enlisted personnel since that time.

Long Beach later became famous when Betty Ford, the wife of President Ford, was sent there for successful treatment of her alcoholism. I enjoyed meeting the two of them later on at an alcoholism conference. When I shook hands with the former president, who had once been a good football player I remembered, I was nevertheless amazed because he had the largest hands I have ever seen on a man. Both he and his wife especially were marvelous people. Billy Carter, the brother of President Jimmy Carter, was also sent to Long Beach for treatment later on.

In November 1966, Dr. Donald R. Seidel, Chief of the Psychiatric Service Branch at the Hospital at Wright-Patterson Air Force Base, described a two-phase treatment program for alcoholics, consisting of a "drying out" period with extensive evaluation, plus a recovery process including counseling, therapy, and participation in Alcoholics Anonymous. When he was transferred to Lackland Air Force Base, he re-instituted the alcoholism treatment program there. This one remained operational into the 1980's I know—I checked when I wrote an article for *Alcoholism* in 1981[38]—and functioned as a major regional center for the treatment of alcoholism.

During the Vietnam War, say from around 1964 to 1975, pressure was applied to get the military to come up with a drug program to combat the drug usage both in Vietnam and in the European theater. The major emphasis was placed on illegal drugs, but Senator Harold Hughes of Iowa insisted that alcoholism be given the same attention as the drug problem, and helped spearhead programs through Congress which included alcoholism treatment as well.

All branches of the services were forced to begin weighing options for drug treatment at that time, even if often without enthusiasm, but more and more programs did begin to be established. The Navy expanded its services to include drugs, but still kept the drug and alcohol treatment separate at that point.

The Navy developed a better system for treating alcoholism than any of the other services. Each naval installation was required to develop a program for alcoholism on an outpatient basis, while cases requiring hospitalization were sent to regional centers, which were patterned after the model program which Dr. Zuska and Dick Jewell had set up at Long Beach. But when I was writing that article in 1981, I found that the Air Force had established what they called a Social Actions Program, relying heavily on the industrial model, which now involved the new concept of Employee Assistance Programs. The Army had similar programs in place which were able to help some people with alcohol problems, but had no actual regional treatment centers set up at that time, where a full treatment program could be carried out by a large, organized staff.

All the military programs were by that point similar however, in that they placed a heavy reliance on participation in Alcoholics Anonymous. There were good reasons why this came about. Perhaps the most important one was that A.A. worked for so many alcoholics. Second, by going that route, the military itself did not have to become so deeply involved in policy, financial support, or the group meetings themselves. In addition, military personnel tended to feel that they could best avoid prejudicial treatment by the command structure if they dealt with their problems within an anonymous organization which was totally run by civilians off the base.

To this day, the kind of program which is modeled after the Lackland treatment center which Dr. West and I organized—or programs which follow the example of the Employee Assistance Programs (EAP's), which were originally developed in the business world—still give by far the highest success rates. I ended my career in alcoholism treatment running EAP's, first on an Army and then on a Navy base, from 1971 down to 1983. The latter program in particular, which I set up at Alameda Naval Air Station near San Francisco, was extremely successful. I have already written and published a good deal about EAP's, so I will not include that material in this book.[39]

The main point to make is that these programs do work, when they are given serious backing. Any problems we have with alcoholism in the military at this point do not reflect lack of knowledge about how to treat these problems, but lack of commitment to the application of this knowledge. As the old A.A. slogan goes, "It works if you work it, and it won't if you don't."

CHAPTER 20

The Silver Dollar

As I mentioned, when I left the Air Force in 1961 after twenty-one years, I became Director of the Arnett-Benson Rehabilitation Center in Lubbock, Texas. I was forty-three years old, at the midpoint in my life, and back in the civilian world again. I had to adjust to things like getting to choose what color clothes I was going to put on in the morning when I got ready to go to work. As you can imagine, I had been devastated by the way the Lackland program had been terminated. Instead of giving any kind of recognition for the extraordinary things we had accomplished there, they had just sent over an Airman Second Class to brusquely hand me my discharge papers on my last day.

But at least, or so it seemed to me at that time, I had figured out a way to still be involved in working with alcoholics. This small treatment center, which was in northwest Texas, almost in the Panhandle, was owned by two osteopathic physicians who had little experience in the field of alcoholism, and as the lone therapist, I was being called out at all hours of the night to deal with alcoholics undergoing crises.

Then in early 1962 my father died, and when I went back to Ohio for the funeral, I decided that I wanted to go back home. I was exhausted from fourteen years of having to struggle so hard to aid people in what were often such frustrating circumstances. But I had no money left after moving our things back to Ohio and I soon came to wonder whether this had been the wisest decision in the world. I was broke and feeling totally defeated.

I still had the silver dollar that Mary the WAC had given me ten years earlier, my little token reminding me of the power of faith and hope to triumph over adversity when the final reckoning came. But that faith and hope had worn very thin by now. I had no idea what I was going to do next.

This was the point however when the A.A. program comes to our aid in ways we never would have expected. There was a marvelous woman who lived in Niles, Ann Crawe, who was very active in A.A. and was close friends with all the good old-timers in the Akron area. (We need to remember that Niles is only forty miles or so from Akron, so that our linkages were very strong with the city where A.A. first began.) Ann was also well known to the A.A. leadership in the New York area for that matter. But Ann felt a special compassion for me because I had been brought up in Niles and was a "hometown boy." She gave me strong moral support, and even loaned me one of her cars for about a month while I was looking for a job.

There was a recession going on in that part of the Midwest, and at first the only job I could find was selling cars at a place called Sanzenbacher Motors in nearby Warren, Ohio, four miles north of Niles. My wife and I and the five boys (David, Robert, Bill, Albert, and Alfonso) had been living in Texas for so long that we had forgotten what northern Ohio winters were like, with all the ice and snow. In the winter of 1963 the thermometer dropped to 30 degrees below zero Fahrenheit one day, and my car was the only one in the neighborhood that would start. (I spent the whole morning out in the cold, going around jump-starting other people's automobiles.) We lived in the house I had been brought up in, which had running water now, so that living there was not as primitive as it had been when I was a child, but the house was still not in very good shape.

But Ann Crawe continued to show a deep sense of concern for my welfare, and eventually was able to use her influence to help me obtain a job with the American Red Cross as Director of their blood donation program in Warren. The A.A. program provides help for us in ways we never could have even imagined when we walked through the doors for the first time. If you live long enough, there will always be crises: you can find yourself without a job, or ill, or suffer a devastating death in the immediate family. This can be a difficult emotional crisis, regardless of how many years you have been sober. That is the point when we discover that there will be other people in the program who will instantly come to our aid. It can sometimes be material help of the sort which Ann provided—in this case the temporary loan of a car, and using her connections to find me a job—but even more important is the knowledge that, no matter how bad things get, there are other human beings who will show up instantly, and be there for you, who genuinely care at the deepest possible level about what is going to happen to you.

You can never adequately explain, to non-program people who have never experienced it, the incredible strength to cope which comes from this awareness that you can contact a person who cares, at any hour of the day or night, in any conceivable situation. In fact they are usually there, to your surprise, without your even having to call on them: you may be in a hospital confronting a sudden devastating medical situation, and the next thing you know, two or three A.A. people seem to just walk in, to be with you and support you and comfort you. You don't even know how they knew you needed them.

In fact, the little silver dollar was still working, or rather, what it stood for. My confidence and hope were renewed. It was not the coin itself obviously: there is nothing magical about a piece of metal. But for me, it stood for some important universal spiritual truths: life can be renewed, adversities can be overcome, and there are people who care.

The Red Cross job greatly renewed my spirit, because this was something I felt I could really dedicate myself to, and donations reached an all-time record in that county as I tried various innovative approaches to donor recruitment. I soon began to regard this new vocation as one which also centered around a deeply spiritual mission. My own spirituality is a very simple one, which centers around helping other human beings. There is something especially "pure" about the help one gives to others by donating blood: the donor and the recipient never know one another by name, so you are being asked to help another person who will never be able to thank you personally. You will get no personal credit for it, and yet you are literally saving someone else's life.

When I can learn to help other people simply because it makes me feel good, without requiring any gratitude or appreciation in return, I have begun to understand more deeply the meaning of the part of the St. Francis Prayer which says: "Lord, grant that I may seek rather to comfort than to be comforted—to understand, than to be understood—to love, than to be loved." For as the prayer goes on to say, "it is by self-forgetting that one finds," that is, it is by devoting my life to some meaningful higher purpose—something larger than myself, which is genuinely good and positive—that I finally learn to start truly feeling good about myself. So I undoubtedly needed these years with the Red Cross, to impress that simple truth on myself more deeply.

Strangely enough, it was precisely my dedication to this kind of approach which put me at odds with the local Chapter Manager of the Red Cross there in Warren, who had a different perception of the world, and I only lasted two years in that job. But fortunately there were others in the Red Cross who saw things differently, and I was soon offered a job by the San Jose Chapter of the California Red Cross as head of their Donor Recruitment Program. They offered to pay our moving expenses, so in 1965, the year I turned forty-seven, we packed everything up and headed out west to California. I am still in California now, almost forty years later, living in Sonoma, just ten miles north of San Francisco Bay, and if I should ever have to move, one of my major criteria will be a guarantee of no vast amounts of snow and ice and subzero winters wherever I go next.

Those were six good years there in San Jose, and as I mentioned, I felt that I could live a spiritually satisfying way of life by helping to save other human beings who, without emergency blood transfusions, would otherwise have died. But then in 1971, I was told that due to budget problems, I would have to absorb a twenty percent pay cut. This came as a complete shock, and I decided to resign. I unfortunately began developing some resentment at that point—no matter how many years people have in the twelve step program, situations like this are always painful to some degree—but in fact it turned out to be a blessing in disguise.

There had been only a small number of reasonably successful alcoholism treatment centers in this country when I was at Lackland in the 1950's, and certainly very few which followed the model of coordinating the treatment at the facility with attendance at A.A. meetings outside. Even when I left the Air Force in 1961, there were so few good treatment centers that there were almost no jobs at all for people with my kind of training in alcoholism counseling. That was the major reason I ended up doing Red Cross work.

But the times were rapidly changing. When Senator Harold Hughes, himself a recovered alcoholic, entered the U.S. Senate, he introduced the Comprehensive Alcohol Abuse and Alcoholism Prevention, Treatment and Rehabilitation Act, and by the end of 1970 had successfully gotten it passed. The Hughes Act, as it was called, created the National Institute on Alcohol Abuse and Alcoholism (the NIAAA), one of whose principal missions in its earliest years was to develop an alcoholism treatment network all over the United States. In addition, the Hughes Act required that federal employees who suffered from alcoholism be provided an opportunity for treatment and rehabilitation. And the Senator successfully attached an amendment to the Selective Service Act in 1971 which required that military personnel also be offered treatment and rehabilitation. As a result, by the end of the 70's the number of patients receiving treatment for their alcoholism at any given time in this country had grown around fifty-fold.[40]

So when I left the Red Cross, I was able to find a civil service position as the Chief of the Alcoholism Program at Ford Ord in California. This was in 1971, and after two years I was promoted to Employee Assistance Coordinator. The NIAAA had just begun pushing for this new program model. The older type employee alcoholism programs which the NCA had encouraged businesses to establish in earlier years were designed to deal with abusive drinking alone. The new Employee Assistance

Programs (EAP's) were set up to deal with "the troubled employee" and were designed to reach out to employees with any problem that affected their work performance.[41]

I have already written about these EAP's in various national publications. It was easier to get people to take their drinking problem seriously when you focused, in your initial contact with them, on the totally objective data which showed that their job performance had been suffering grievously, and spoke in terms of the necessity to bring their performance back up to reasonable standards. Alcoholics have a tendency to respond with outrage when their drinking itself is criticized head-on, and are apt to start angrily insisting on "their right to drink," and asserting that "how much I drink is none of anybody else's business." Furthermore, a large number of alcoholics also have other problems, ranging from poor relationships with customers or fellow-employees, to strained marriages, to serious financial difficulties, all of which also have to be dealt with if they are to live successfully without alcohol. By the time they hit the depths of their disease, alcoholics cannot live with the beverage or without it either.

The situation at Fort Ord was not ideal. There were a good many civilian employees at this Army base, and I attempted to consult with all supervisors and commanders on a regular basis. I also provided supervisor training where I explained the symptoms of alcoholism, and told how we had a good chance of restoring these employees back to health and decent job performance once again. But their referrals of employees to my program were few and far between. This was partly due to the fact that too many people in the U.S. Army were still locked into the old punitive mindset, and had little empathy regarding troubled employees in general and problem drinkers in particular. But another major problem came from the hostility toward all alcoholism treatment programs on the part of one of the officers who held a top position on that base.

I eventually noticed something which Dr. Joseph J. Zuska has also commented on. When people in a military organization are extremely and vocally hostile toward programs for rehabilitating alcoholics, it is surprising how often it turns out that the antagonistic officers are either themselves practicing alcoholics or are married to practicing alcoholics. They are still locked in denial about their own personal problems, and respond with great anger toward anyone who threatens their denial system. Dr. Zuska called it the "flush phenomenon."[42]

I have seen this happen repeatedly at a number of different military installations. At one base, one of the greatest foes toward any serious attempt to rehabilitate alcoholics was an officer who was dismissed from the service himself later on because of a series of drunken driving arrests. At another base, one senior officer was adamantly hostile toward my alcoholism treatment program and openly opposed it at every opportunity, making my life miserable in every way he could. He was later transferred to another base, and it finally came out that his wife was an active alcoholic when her drinking drove her into committing suicide. I forgave him for his attitude toward the program when I learned this fact.

I am trying to write this book in a way that might help people in future years to set up good alcoholism treatment programs in their organizations, so I think it is good for me to point out some of the pitfalls into which one can stumble. In order to set up a new alcoholism treatment program in an institution, one may sometimes have to fight on several fronts simultaneously. One can meet opposition from people who are still active alcoholics themselves (or married to them), from those who still cling to the old "get tough" punitive approach, from mental health professionals who want to put the funds you are requesting into their own pet projects instead, from people who are so frightened by drugs and narcotics that they do not realize that alcoholism is still a much greater problem in the United States by almost any criteria invoked, and from other quarters as well. It can be surprisingly difficult even to get people to understand that good alcoholism treatment programs are a form of "preventive maintenance," where a few dollars spent now will save you from having to lay out much larger sums later on. All they tend to see are the dollar signs in the small amount you are requesting. Human psychology is sometimes quite mysterious in its outcomes.

Nevertheless, the stakes are so high, in terms of the number of human lives which can be saved, and in terms also of the personal satisfaction that you yourself will be able to feel when you first start seeing alcoholics and addicts restored to health, that I know you will find it worth your strongest efforts. The first few times they experience it, treatment personnel find it difficult to believe that the happy, cheerful, cooperative, enthusiastic, relaxed people they see after a few months, are even the same people as the miserable alcoholics and addicts whom they met at the beginning. But this is what does happen, and I have been seeing it take place over and over again for well over fifty years now.

The good old-timers in A.A. nevertheless feel it important to warn newcomers continually that the twelve step program is not a magical device which eliminates all struggle, frustration, and opposition from life. The difference in my latter years was that I never felt the urge to drink over any of these things. And not only that, back when I was still drinking, I was always doomed ultimately to be one of life's losers. When I stopped drinking and began to work the program, I started to really win some games for the first time, sometimes some big ones. Looking back over my life at this point, I realize that in all the things that are truly important in the long run, I am a winner.

———————————

The program teaches us flexibility and adaptability, and I often needed that. Those who were opposed to serious alcoholism treatment at Fort Ord eventually managed to get my position abolished, but I quickly learned that there was a position open at the Naval Air Rework Facility at Alameda Naval Air Station. So I decided to actually visit the base and talk personally to the individual who was in charge of the hiring decision. This was not supposed to be part of the hiring process, but as it turned out, this person was also a recovered alcoholic, and as we discussed what was needed at Alameda, it quickly became clear that the two of us were both on the same wavelength. We had both recovered ourselves, and knew what was necessary.

This was in 1978, the year I turned sixty, and it turned out to be the most delightful and productive and enjoyable experience in my whole career in alcoholism treatment. There had been no Employee Assistance

Program already established at the base, so I had to create and assemble the entire operation from the ground up, but I found complete support and cooperation at all levels of command. They seemed to be aware from the beginning that my program was going to help them and make their jobs easier, by taking a lot of worrisome personnel problems off their hands and giving them more time to concentrate on other parts of their own assignments.

In this and many other ways, the attitude of the Navy personnel at this base was entirely different from what I had encountered from the Army. There was a feeling of relaxation among the Navy people, and a sense that you were actually appreciated for your contributions. The prevailing attitude in the Army at that time had been more that any alcoholism program was at best a necessary evil, and probably counter-productive to what should have been the military mission. So there among "the sailors," I finally felt as though I belonged to a team, and that we were all working together on a real team effort. When I played baseball, I may have been a pitcher, but I never believed that a baseball game could be won by the pitcher alone, no matter how good he was. The pitcher, the catcher, the basemen, and the outfielders had to learn how to work together smoothly as a unit in order to keep the other side from gaining bases on you.

It was at this point that I began to publish some of my ideas about alcoholism and Employee Assistance Programs in national trade journals, and started being invited to travel around the country speaking at conventions and participating in seminars. One of the greatest honors I received at this time, at least in my own eyes, was being invited to be part of the ceremony honoring my dear mentor Mrs. Marty Mann for her forty-five years of dedication in helping others recover from the insidious disease of alcoholism. Her death in 1980, soon afterwards, left a vacuum in my life. She was a pillar of strength in the field, and respected by all who knew her.

It was also during this period that I was asked to speak at the Betty Ford Alcoholism Center, and was able to meet President and Mrs. Ford for the first time. Mrs. Ford, who performed a great service for alcoholism and drug addiction treatment by going public on her own recovery, was a truly gracious lady, whom I was delighted to be able to thank in person. I have known well, or at least met, a host of major Washington figures during the course of my career, including of course Senator Harold Hughes and Representative Wilbur Mills (who was always extremely kind to me), but she was someone whom I was especially pleased to meet, even if just briefly.

In 1983, I finally had to make good on my promise to retire at age sixty-five. The Association of Labor Management Consultants on Alcoholism organized a special meeting where they presented me with a trophy and honored me for my contributions to the Employee Assistance Program movement. I felt as though I had now demonstrated conclusively that Marty Mann's credo had been right, that alcoholism was a disease which could in fact be treated successfully.

But the big surprise came when I was notified that I had been awarded the Meritorious Service Award, the Navy's highest award for a civilian at a duty station. It was presented to me by the Base Commander in a ceremony which made me feel especially good about what I had done there at Alameda. But perhaps the hardest thing to comprehend, was that somehow, over the course of the previous thirty years, I had turned from someone who had to fight as hard as he could to keep even a small alcoholism treatment program in place, into a publicly honored hero. I still find it hard adjusting to that idea sometimes.

When my co-author told me that I was now being described as the Father of Military Alcoholism Treatment, my first response was simply to laugh and say jokingly, "that is all right with me, as long as I am not required to pay child support." But it did in fact make me feel good, even if I am not yet totally used to this sort of acclaim.

During the years that followed, I have continued to be active in Alcoholics Anonymous. In recent years in particular, I have been asked to speak all over the United States. That was the way I met my co-author. I was invited to speak at the Indiana state A.A. convention in Columbus, Indiana, in 2002, and one of the organizers, one of the Hoosier A.A. old-timers named Neil S. (who lives in Fishers, a suburb of Indianapolis), brought Glenn down from South Bend just to meet me, and gave us the use of his home to spend a couple of days before the conference getting acquainted. A.A. people are incredibly generous, and Neil is one of the truly self-giving and dedicated ones. And Frank N. from Syracuse, who has worked closely with Glenn on the Hindsfoot Foundation publishing projects, also came down to take part in all our discussions.

I have almost fifty-five years of sobriety now, and there are only a handful of us around the country left whose involvement in the program goes back that far. At the last Founders Day celebration in Akron, Ohio, there was only one person present in that huge gathering who had more time in the program than I had. But I have found that simply going around and talking to groups and conferences is a service which I can give to my fellow A.A. members now, because it seems that there are many who eagerly want to know about the early years of the movement, and what it was like in the world of "the good old-timers." So I am very pleased to still be able to do something useful, and contribute to others.

I told the story earlier in this book of getting to know Bill Dotson, the third person to get sober in A.A. back at the beginning. When I was stationed at Kent State, outside of Akron, I asked him once why he spent so much time working with alcoholics, when he was a lawyer and could be making so much money if he devoted more time to his legal career. He simply said that, living his life the way he was living it now, he only made about $400 a month in cash but got about $1,500 a month in gratitude.

And you do not even have to have other people's gratitude in order to feel a sense of self-worth, and feel good about yourself. That is one of the major goals, because that is what we human beings really want, to feel good. Alcohol and drugs seem to do that at first, but it is an illusion, and we will destroy ourselves if we do not learn to see through the lies which that artificial chemical euphoria will tell us.

When Mary the WAC gave me that silver dollar when I left Mitchel Air Force Base back in 1951, it was as a small gesture of thanks for what I had done to save her life. I still carry it with me in my pocket at all times, even these many years later, and it has become so worn by now that you can barely see the ghost of the inscription on it. But you must remember that when I went into the WAC barracks after receiving her cry of desperation, I did not do that much; mainly I was just willing to be there, and to listen. I did introduce her to the A.A. program and got her going to meetings. But this is what we most want and need when we have hit the point of terminal despair, someone who will simply be there for us, and genuinely listen. And the twelve step program and the A.A. meetings are the genuine new hope that we have to offer to those who have lost all hope.

So that silver dollar is a symbol of all sorts of things: the possibility of atonement for the past, the memory of a good person whom I really liked, a memento of that period when I found my first real success in treating other alcoholics, and all kinds of other things too. It is above all a symbol of new hope, of a hope which must never be allowed to die.

I am almost 85 now, and am not always happy with the increasing physical limitations of age. My body bears the wear of time. I am very much aware that I am probably playing in the last inning of my life now, and that the game will one day soon be over. But I can still do something like write this book, so that perhaps I may be able to keep on giving, even after I have left this earth. So would you please accept this book as a gift from me, in the same spirit as that worn old silver dollar, which now shows the marks of wear and time but still continues to bear the spirit of new hope for all those who still walk the earth on paths of self-destruction, miserable and frightened, and knowing nowhere to turn. That would make me feel good.

Afterword

Bill Swegan's experience is now enormous. There are few people in the field of alcoholism who have seen as many, or as many different kinds, of alcohol abusers, their families, friends and employers, as he. A genuine professional in a field that the traditional health professions have consistently neglected, he has labored diligently and unceasingly for more than a quarter of a century among the alcoholics. Against the ominous background of alcoholism, his thoughtful observations and plain talk shine like a candle in the dark. He is a hero in the war against alcohol, the great destroyer.

—Dr. Louis Jolyon West, M.D., Professor and Chairman, Department of Psychiatry & Biobehavioral Sciences, University of California, Los Angeles; Psychiatrist-in-Chief, UCLA Hospital & Clinics; Director, the Neuropsychiatric Institute, UCLA Center for the Health Sciences. April 1981

It is now one thirty in the morning but sleep evades me. I know that I need to be creative and constructive to help those who are still suffering escape from the damning process of addiction. Also, I was thinking of all the problems that I had while growing up and the way I processed those memories for so many years in almost total negativity. But now, I am not only grateful for my life but consider myself fortunate, because I can talk about these things from a changed perception. I now realize that I have been uniquely privileged. I was given the tools for recovering from the insidious disease of alcoholism, and the knowledge and means for passing this on to others. It was Alcoholics Anonymous which gave me those gifts.

I received a call the other day from San Antonio. It was from a member of the fellowship who was seeking my advice on some marital problems he was having. Greater love hath no alcoholic than to lay down the bottle for a loved one. I tried to help him as much as I could, but also warned him that I would have to know his wife's interpretation of the circumstances in order to go much further. But perhaps I helped him some. This man is a Congressional Medal of Honor recipient. I thought, here is a man who is a great hero to his country, who has an alcohol problem and is seeking my counsel. Boy, do I owe A.A. much? You bet I do, and I hope I never forget the enormous change that has come into my life because of what I have learned from the A.A. program.

I pray that those who are still suffering from pain and the inability to lead a truly productive life, can learn how to repair and heal the defects in their way of living, by learning how to use the Twelve Steps of Alcoholics Anonymous appropriately. We must surrender to the fact that we can no longer rely on alcohol or drugs to resolve our problems. We need the new and therapeutic approach to life which results from utilizing these twelve fundamental principles of spiritual and psychological healing to learn to feel good and to become all that we can become.

—Bill S., April 2003

Notes

1. Sally Brown and David R. Brown, *A Biography of Mrs. Marty Mann: The First Lady of Alcoholics Anonymous* (Center City MN: Hazelden, 2001), tells the story of this notable woman. They describe how she acted as my mentor and major backer as I was setting up my first treatment programs, and used her influence to help ensure that this "ground-breaking example spread to the other armed forces" (pp. 170-1). Marty was especially aided in the latter "when Harold Hughes offered an amendment to the Selective Service Act requiring the military to offer treatment and rehabilitation to alcoholics" (p. 341 n. 2). Senator Hughes wrote his own autobiography later on after he had retired from politics: Harold E. Hughes, with Dick Schneider, *The Man From Ida Grove* (Waco, TX: Word Books/Chosen Books, 1979). But the enormous amount of work he did in the United States Congress to help alcoholics at the national level has now been described in far greater detail in a book which has just been published: Nancy Olson, *With a Lot of Help from Our Friends: The Politics of Alcoholism*, Hindsfoot Foundation Series on the History of Alcoholism Treatment, ed. Glenn F. Chesnut (Lincoln NE: iUniverse/Writers Club Press, 2003); see pp. 144, 146-7, and 487 nn. 136 and 140, for Olson's description of my work at Mitchel and Lackland and its place in the overall development of military alcoholism treatment.

2. Sally and David Brown, *Biography of Mrs. Marty Mann*, and Nancy Olson, *With a Lot of Help from Our Friends*, see previous note.

3. Co-author's note: it is important to remember that this was what the term "religion" continued to mean to Bill Swegan all his life. Even when he was in his eighties, it was something that made no sense to him, and just made him uncomfortable. And in his experience, as he stated to me on more than one occasion, when people attempted to use this kind

of reliosity as the base of their Alcoholics Anonymous program, it often seemed to keep them locked into anger, resentment, lack of compassion for other people, continual attacks on those around them, and the almost complete absence of any real love or serenity in their hearts.

The evangelist E. Howard Cadle, from his base at the Cadle Tabernacle, a huge Spanish-mission-style building in Indianapolis which seated 10,000 worshipers and had a choir of over 1,400 singers, broadcast his fire and brimstone message over radio station WLW in Cincinnati to all the surrounding states. At the height of his popularity, his Sunday sermons were heard at 330 radio-equipped churches in Kentucky, Indiana, Ohio and West Virginia. After E. Howard Cadle's death in 1942, the tabernacle's operations were run by his wife Ola, his son Buford, and his daughters Helen and Virginia Ann. In his autobiography—*How I Came Back: Life Story of E. Howard Cadle, Founder and Builder of the Cadle Tabernacle* (Indianapolis: Cadle Tablernacle, 1932)—E. Howard Cadle explains how he turned from the life of a drunkard and gambler by accepting Christ as his savior and returning to the simple religion of his sainted mother, whose favorite hymn was the old frontier revivalist standard, "There is a fountain filled with blood drawn from Emmanuel's veins; and sinners plunged beneath that flood lose all their guilty stains." This hymn, whose words were originally written by William Cowper, 1731-1800, went on to proclaim, "The dying thief rejoiced to see that fountain in his day; and there may I, though vile as he, wash all my sins away."

4.   Co-author's note: one can see the influence on Bill S., direct or indirect, of the Neo-Freudians Erich Fromm, Karen Horney, and Erik H. Erikson, who emigrated from Germany to the United States in the 1930's, and emphasized the importance of social and cultural influences on psychological development. Excessive feelings of isolation, they found, can play a major role in psychological disorders. The Austrian physician Alfred Adler also stressed developing interest in others and participation in society as an important goal of therapy, along with learning better ways of interacting with other family members. Like many therapists in the United States, Bill S. has always utilized an eclectic approach, combining techniques from a number of theoretical systems and tailoring his treatment to the particular psychological problems of the patient. He learned most of this, he says, from his work with psychiatrist Louis Jolyon West and with medical researcher E. M. Jellinek, who had

studied psychiatric principles and practice in great depth in order to better understand the workings of the human nervous system.

5.   Nancy Olson, *With a Lot of Help from Our Friends*, refers to these two programs on pages 146-7, as a preface to her more detailed study of developments afterwards.

6.   *Ibid.*, see espec. chapts. 15-17 and (on veterans and the Veterans Administration) chapt. 19. Nancy's book tells the inside story of the way many of these major governmental policy shifts were brought about during the 1960's and 70's, made the more interesting because she played a personal role in these events herself, serving as a key senatorial aide in Washington D.C. from 1968 to 1980, with alcoholism issues as her special assignment. In fact, I remember her well from that time. Her volume supplies an excellent background to the story of my own work with alcoholism treatment on individual military bases. The struggles to shape national alcohol policies in Washington were emotionally loaded and highly complex, and the pressures she was under were of a sort which I hope I never have to contend with.

7.   Marty Mann, *Marty Mann Answers Your Questions About Drinking and Alcoholism* (New York: Holt, Rinehart and Winston, 1970), xi. Compare Marty Mann, *Marty Mann's New Primer on Alcoholism: How People Drink, How to Recognize Alcoholics, and What to Do About Them* (New York: Holt, Rinehart and Winston, 1958), 3, 17, 116-7, and 189-91.

8.   Sally and David Brown, *Biography of Mrs. Marty Mann*, 94-108. Marty's story was added to the A.A. Big Book in the second edition under the title "Women Suffer Too," see *Alcoholics Anonymous*, 2nd ed. (New York: Alcoholics Anonymous World Services, 1955), 222-9. In the present fourth edition (2001) it is on pp. 200-07.

9.   *Dr. Bob and the Good Oldtimers* (New York: Alcoholics Anonymous World Services), 74.

10.   Yvelin "Yev" Gardner, an important and influential early leader in the activist wing of the A.A. movement, see Sally and David Brown, *Biography of Mrs. Marty Mann*, 203, 219, 231-3, 246-7, 293 (after Bill W.'s death, he presided over the memorial service at St. John the Divine in New York City in 1971), and 319 (delivered the eulogy at the memorial service at St. Bartholomew's Episcopal Church in New York City after Marty Mann's death in 1980).

11. As detailed in Sally and David Brown's biography of her.

12. The basic psychiatric theories which I assume in this book in my discussions of the way the human mind works, are based heavily on what I learned from Dr. Jellinek and, later on, from the psychiatrist Dr. Louis Jolyon West (see the next chapter, and also Chapter 17, "Lackland: the Fully Developed Program").

13. This is in addition to the abnormalities produced by the fetal alcohol syndrome and may be present even if that is absent. In the same way, a mother who smokes crack cocaine during pregnancy may give birth to a baby who is already physiologically addicted to crack cocaine: those poor newborns whom we call "crack babies."

14. See William L. White, *Slaying the Dragon: The History of Addiction Treatment and Recovery in America* (Bloomington, IL: Chestnut Health Systems/Lighthouse Institute, 1998), 293-295; and Nancy Olson, *With a Lot of Help from Our Friends*, ch. 27, "The Controlled Drinking Controversy."

15. For more details, see the article which Sister Ignatia wrote the year I was there, describing the entire operation: Sister M. Ignatia, C.S.A., "The Care of Alcoholics: St. Thomas Hospital and A.A. Started a Movement which Swept the Country," *Hospital Progress* (the journal of the Catholic Hospital), October 1951. See also Mary C. Darrah, *Sister Ignatia: Angel of Alcoholics Anonymous* (Chicago: Loyola University Press, 1992), 104-8.

16. In the article in *Hospital Progress*, Sister Ignatia referred to this work as *The Following of Christ*, but she was clearly referring to the traditional meditational work which is called the *Imitatio Christi* in its original Latin version. See Mary C. Darrah, *Sister Ignatia*, 24, 36, 109, and 276 n. 72. The basis of Sister Ignatia's own spiritual formation lay in years of constant disciplined meditation on two books: *The Spiritual Exercises* of St. Ignatius Loyola (which was used as a basic foundation for the spiritual life by many Roman Catholic priests and nuns in the United States during that period, and not just the Jesuits) and also Thomas à Kempis's *Imitatio Christi* or "Imitation of Christ" (as the title is usually translated). She carried in her pocket well-worn copies of the *Imitation of Christ* (with special passages pencil-marked and dated) and a small book of selections from Loyola called *A Thought from Saint Ignatius for Each Day of the Year*, published in 1887. In the early years she sometimes gave

her alcoholic patients a copy of this latter book instead of the *Imitation*, but it became increasingly difficult to find copies because of its date of publication.

17. Sister Ignatia, "The Care of Alcoholics," *Hospital Progress*.

18. Neville Murray, M.D., and M/Sgt William Swegan, USAF, "To Tranquillize or Not to Tranquillize," *Quarterly Journal of Studies on Alcohol* 19, no. 3 (September 1958): 509-510. Excerpts reprinted in the 1958 yearbook of the *American Peoples Encyclopedia* (a popular set of volumes distributed by Sears Roebuck).

19. Glenn F. Chesnut, *The Higher Power of the Twelve-Step Program: For Believers & Non-Believers*, Hindsfoot Foundation Series on Spirituality and Theology (Lincoln NE: iUniverse/Authors Choice Press, 2001). This book was designed to gently lead people who are antagonistic toward traditional religious language into a deeper understanding of what those spiritual concepts are actually about, and how they help the everyday working of a good twelve-step program. It is built on traditional A.A. teachings, and is especially useful for the way in which he put down in writing, for the first time, a good deal of oral A.A. tradition passed down from the good old-timers of my own younger days.

20. <http://www.barefootsworld.net/graphics/billdotsonobit2.jpg> reproduces his obituary, an Associated Press newspaper release dated September 19, 1954. William I. Dotson was born on a Kentucky farm in 1892 and did most of his college work at the University of Kentucky before enlisting in the Army in 1917, when the United States entered the First World War. After the war he went to Akron, Ohio, and studied law at night at Akron Law School. He was admitted to the Ohio bar in 1926. The obituary tells how Bill W. and Dr. Bob found him in Akron City Hospital, the famous "Man on the Bed": he had been admitted to the hospital on June 26, 1935, only forty-three years old but regarded as a hopeless alcoholic doomed to an early death. He became the third person to get sober in the newly founded A.A. program. The obituary speaks of his recovery as "the turning point of Alcoholics Anonymous," and describes how "in his later years he spent much of his time traveling about the United States and Canada, speaking at A.A. meetings." Something Bill W. said to Bill Dotson's wife Henrietta stuck in his mind and became the central motto of his own work in the program: "The Lord has been so wonderful to me, curing me of this terrible disease, that I just want

to keep telling people about it." He died on Friday night, September 17, 1954, at Crile Veterans Hospital in Cleveland, at the age of 62. He had been in ill health since a heart attack the previous October. His story first appeared in the second edition of the A.A. Big Book, which was published the year after his death—see *Alcoholics Anonymous*, 2nd ed. (1955)—entitled "Alcoholic Anonymous Number Three" and placed at the very beginning of the story section, right after Dr. Bob's story (pp. 182-192).

21. Louis Jolyon West, M.D., and William H. [*sic*] Swegan, "An Approach to Alcoholism in the Military Service," *American Journal of Psychiatry* 112, no. 12 (June 1956).

22. See for example Louis Jolyon West, M.D., ed., *Alcoholism and Related Problems: Issues for the American Public*, Spectrum Books.

23. Louis Jolyon West, M.D., "I Couldn't—We Did," written to accompany an article written on military alcoholism treatment in that year: William E. Swegan, "Our Country's Largest EAP: Military Alcoholism," *Alcoholism* (July-August 1981), 36-39.

24. For the full story, see Nancy Olson, *With a Lot of Help from Our Friends*, ch. 16, "Twelfth Stepping the Military."

25. She seems to have begun sneaking alcoholics who were in especially bad shape into isolated nooks and crannies of the hospital to sleep it off, not long after her arrival at St. Thomas on September 28, 1928. In 1934, she convinced an intern in the emergency room, Dr. Thomas P. Scuderi, to work with her on these unofficial alcoholic patients, giving them shots to calm them down and trying to keep them from going into convulsions. They worked together to treat an enormous number of alcoholics, beginning their project in fact before A.A. was born in 1935. August 16, 1939, was the date the first A.A.-sponsored patient was admitted to St. Thomas with her aid, not the beginning of Sister Ignatia's work with alcoholics. See Mary C. Darrah, *Sister Ignatia*, 8-11 and 79-80. Mary Darrah interviewed Dr. Scuderi on September 26, 1985, to obtain some of the details of the earliest work at St. Thomas.

26. Mary C. Darrah, *Sister Ignatia*, end of chapter four, p. 150.

27. This and the following passages are excerpted from Louis Jolyon West, M.D., introduction to William E. Swegan, *From Intoxication to Emancipation*. This short account of his and Sgt. Bill's work was originally

written by Dr. West in April 1981, and later also distributed separately as a bifold leaflet.

28. Letter to William E. Swegan from Louis Jolyon West (signed "Jolly"), December 22, 1982.

29. Marty had of course gone to the best private schools when she was young, including the Chicago Latin School for Girls, Santa Barbara Girls' School, Montemare School in Lake Placid, New York, and a year at Miss Nixon's School in Florence, Italy, where she finished her studies the year she turned twenty-one. It was a superb education of the highest quality, but gave her no formal college degree where she could put a B.A. after her name. In 1944, the year she became a member of the Yale Center of Alcohol Studies, she spent six months living with the Jellinek's in New Haven, where "Bunky" (as the doctor was called by those close to him) became her close personal friend and mentor. She spent that time voraciously reading on her own every scholarly book and article he gave her on alcoholism, and turned herself into a nationally recognized expert on the subject. See Sally and David Brown, *Biography of Mrs. Marty Mann*, 22, 36-7, 50, 52-3, and 160.

30. West, introduction to *From Intoxication to Emancipation*.

31. The account which follows is based upon the original one given in Louis Jolyon West, M.D., and William H. [*sic*] Swegan, "An Approach to Alcoholism in the Military Service," *American Journal of Psychiatry* 112, no. 12 (June 1956). Subsequently printed and distributed nationally under the imprint of the National Council on Alcoholism, 2 Park Avenue, New York, which was headed by my old friend and mentor, Mrs. Marty Mann.

32. O. Diethelm, *Bulletin of the New York Academy of Medicine* 27 (April 1951): 232.

33. All patients were initially given high daily doses of basic vitamins. A number of them continued to receive those supplements because it was found that their cravings for alcohol returned when we stopped giving them the vitamins. Patients showing evidence of hypoadrenocorticism were treated with aqueous adrenal cortex extract (ACE), or in a few cases with Lipoadrenal Cortex. Chlorpromazine (Thorazine) proved to be very useful in treating the acute symptoms of newly-hospitalized patients. In some cases, it also helped them manage the tension-laden periods while they were in the process of reorganizing their way of life in the period

immediately after they left the hospital. After a stable period back on the job, these patients were told to discontinue the regular dosage, but to keep a supply on hand. When they felt marked tension and anxiety as a result of some stressful life situation, these patients were instructed to use the chlorpromazine until they were able to confer with the doctor or an A.A. worker, to diminish the risk of turning to alcohol. We were also able to use reserpine (Serpasil) with some benefit in the same fashion.

34. H. M. Tiebout, *Quart. J. Stud. Alcohol.* 12 (March 1951): 52.

35. H. E. Talbott, *Air Force Information Letters*, September 1954 and January 1955.

36. From the A.A. Big Book: *Alcoholics Anonymous*, 4th ed. (2001), 83-84. "Before we are half way through" refers to carrying out the ninth step. As we work progressively through the steps, it is at this point that the greatest promises begin to be fulfilled: the stage where we begin to seriously amend our lives, make restitution for the harm we did in the past, and rehabilitate ourselves so that our positive personality characteristics will re-emerge.

37. Nancy Olson, *With a Lot of Help from Our Friends.*

38. William E. Swegan, "Our Country's Largest EAP: Military Alcoholism," *Alcoholism* (July-August 1981), 36-39.

39. *Ibid.*

40. Nancy Olson, *With a Lot of Help from Our Friends*, ch. 45, "Third Look in the Rear View Mirror."

41. *Ibid.*

42. *Ibid.* 151-2, quoting from Joseph J. Zuska, M.D., "Beginnings of the Navy Program," *Alcoholism: Clinical and Experimental Research* 2, no. 4 (October 1978): 353.

Index

A

Adler, Alfred 312
Akron 3, 131, 147, 161, 207, 232, 233, 234, 240, 241, 243, 251, 267, 298, 307, 315
American Medical Association 157, 170

B

Bacon, Seldon 204
blame 14, 87, 89, 103, 185, 187, 228, 272, 281
Brown, David R. 7, 311, 313, 314, 317
Brown, Sally 7, 311, 313, 314, 317

C

Cadle 33, 312
character defects 188, 190, 194
character disorders 188, 189

D

Darrah, Mary C. 314, 316
depressant 180
depressed 85, 130, 209
depresses 108
depressive 214, 236

disease 6, 9, 10, 11, 13, 14, 18, 52, 67, 71, 81, 83, 88, 117, 118, 121, 127, 128, 129, 132, 134, 135, 136, 139, 146, 153, 162, 168, 170, 171, 193, 200, 206, 207, 208, 214, 225, 226, 227, 239, 246, 250, 252, 257, 260, 261, 270, 282, 285, 286, 302, 305, 306, 310, 315
Dotson, Bill 232, 242, 307, 315

E

ego defenses 165, 189, 190, 257
Employee Assistance Program (EAP) 153, 162, 164, 282, 295, 296, 302, 305, 306, 316, 318
Erikson, Erik H. 255, 312

F

Ford, Betty 251, 294, 305
Freud 169, 255
Freudian 179
Fromm, Erich 312

G

Gardner, Yev *(see also Yev)* 196, 197, 198, 199, 203, 313
genetic 9, 13, 87, 138, 158, 170, 171, 215, 223, 228, 256

Greenberg, Leon 204
guilt 14, 15, 18, 19, 20, 24, 35, 37, 43,
　44, 51, 52, 63, 71, 74, 89, 101, 102,
　124, 132, 133, 136, 137, 139, 141,
　146, 152, 153, 161, 163, 182, 195,
　212, 224, 225, 272, 273, 276, 284, 312

H

healing 15, 21, 42, 88, 102, 130, 134,
　136, 157, 173, 174, 178, 186, 187,
　188, 189, 212, 232, 236, 240, 268,
　277, 282, 285, 286, 310
healing power 270, 271
Hickam v, 1, 46, 82, 83, 90, 92, 93,
　97, 99, 104, 106, 107, 225, 233
Horney, Karen 312
Hughes 4, 5, 6, 7, 38, 129, 202, 209,
　289, 295, 301, 306, 311
Hughes Act 301
Hughes Amendment 129

I

Ignatia 206, 230, 232, 233, 234, 235,
　237, 238, 240, 241, 242, 243, 251,
　267, 314, 315, 316, 323
inhibited 51, 52, 185, 189, 217, 218
inhibitions 50, 51, 53, 55, 85, 108, 217

J

Jellinek 3, 5, 12, 132, 204, 213, 214,
　216, 312, 314, 317, 323
Jewell, Dick 251, 265, 294, 295, 323

L

Lackland 5, 128, 156, 193, 199, 207,
　208, 209, 214, 236, 240, 241, 242,
　244, 245, 246, 247, 248, 249, 252,
　253, 254, 259, 267, 280, 288, 290,
　291, 292, 293, 294, 296, 297, 301,
　311, 314, 323

Long Island 3, 4, 151, 153, 155, 160,
　166, 167, 196, 197, 210, 253, 289,
　323

M

malaria 1, 121, 124, 127, 128, 131
Mann, Marty *(see also Marty)* 4, 5, 6,
　7, 38, 135, 156, 161, 162, 196, 197,
　198, 199, 200, 202, 203, 204, 209,
　239, 255, 260, 289, 293, 305, 306,
　311, 313, 317, 323
Marty *(see also Mann)*
maturation 170, 173, 175, 177, 179,
　220, 221, 244
Mature Behavior, Fifteen Guidelines to 179
Mills, Wilbur 289, 306
Minnesota Model 323
Mitchel 3, 4, 34, 128, 130, 135, 151,
　156, 160, 167, 187, 193, 198, 200,
　202, 203, 205, 207, 208, 209, 210,
　211, 212, 214, 230, 236, 253, 289,
　307, 311, 323

N

National Council on Alcoholism 5,
　162, 170, 197, 246, 260, 317, 323
Neo-Freudians 312

O

Olson, Nancy 7, 293, 311, 313, 314,
　316, 318, 324

P

Pearl Harbor v, 1, 46, 90, 93, 97, 99,
　106, 107, 109, 119, 205, 225, 233,
　323
personalities 49, 190
personality 26, 74, 172, 173, 174, 184,
　185, 188, 189, 190, 192, 216, 217,
　239, 240, 256, 272, 274, 318

psychosocial 158, 166, 170, 172

R

Rand Report 227
religion 33, 161, 311, 312
religious 33, 34, 35, 89, 134, 156, 176,
    196, 199, 208, 230, 236, 240, 241,
    244, 254, 262, 271, 315
repatterning 239, 240

S

Seidel, Donald R. 294
Silkworth, William Duncan 293
Snake Ranch v, 84, 85, 86, 91, 98,
    105, 126
social drinker 13, 88, 108, 122
social drinking 65, 119, 215, 227, 228,
spiritual 34, 35, 134, 156, 158, 188,
    190, 196, 199, 205, 211, 244, 261,
    268, 271, 276, 277, 278, 286, 299,
    310, 314, 315, 323
spirituality 33, 34, 134, 161, 188, 241,
    244, 268, 271, 278, 299, 315, 324
St. Thomas 157, 206, 233, 234, 235,
    236, 237, 240, 241, 242, 243, 251,
    267, 314, 316
subconscious 50, 51, 52, 53, 54, 55,
    57, 63, 64, 65, 66, 71, 72, 74, 82,
    89, 101, 102, 105, 106, 107, 108,
    111, 112, 120, 132, 133, 137, 138,
    139, 152, 153, 161, 172, 177, 179,
    180, 182, 189, 191, 214, 215, 217,
    218, 219, 222, 224, 274
superegos 137

T

Tiebout 156, 259, 293, 318
Tools for Personal Freedom 179
tranquillize 237, 252, 315
tranquillizers 237, 238

Twelve Steps 6, 267, 269, 310
Twelve Traditions 6

V

V.A. 1, 128, 129
Veterans Hospital 1, 2, 3, 316

W

West, Dr. *(see also Louis Jolyon West)*
West, Louis Jolyon *(see also Dr. West)* 5,
    128, 207, 214, 240, 242, 248, 249,
    250, 252, 253, 254, 255, 261, 265,
    266, 280, 288, 292, 293, 294, 296,
    309, 312, 314, 316, 317, 323
White, William L. 314
will-power 50

Y

Yale 5, 18, 132, 135, 167, 193, 196,
    197, 203, 204, 205, 206, 213, 317,
    323
Yale School of Alcohol Studies *(see also
    Yale)*
Yev *(see also Gardner)*

Z

Zuska, Joseph J. 251, 265, 280, 293,
    294, 295, 302, 303, 318, 323

About the Authors

William E. Swegan (1918–2008)

"Sgt. Bill" was the major spokesman for the psychological wing of early Alcoholics Anonymous—that group within the A.A. movement of the 1930s, 40s and 50s which stressed the psychotherapeutic side of the twelve step program instead of the spiritual side.

Swegan was born in Niles, Ohio, on June 29, 1918, and enlisted in the Army Air Corps in 1939, on the eve of World War II. He served in the Pacific theater in that war, narrowly escaping death in the attack on Pearl Harbor. He had become a self-destructive alcoholic by the end of the 1930s, and did not gain sobriety until 1948, when he threw himself wholeheartedly into the newly founded Alcoholics Anonymous movement.

Later that year, the famous early A.A. leader and American social reformer Mrs. Marty Mann (founder of the National Council on Alcoholism) got the Air Force to assign Swegan full time to creating the first military alcoholism treatment program in the world at Mitchel Air Force Base on Long Island, where he was able to put into practice all the many things he learned from his studies in 1949 with his great hero E. M. Jellinek at the Yale School of Alcohol Studies.

In 1953 Bill went on to team up with famous American psychiatrist Louis Jolyon "Jolly" West at Lackland Air Force Base in San Antonio, Texas, to expand these ideas even further, designing a method of alcoholism treatment now called the Lackland-Long Beach Model (the basic methodology was given further development at Long Beach Naval Station in the mid 1960s by Dr. Joseph J. Zuska and Navy Cmdr. Dick Jewell). It became one of the three basic types of A.A.-oriented alcoholism treatment program, along with the Minnesota Model and Sister Ignatia's more spiritually oriented approach.

Swegan went on to expand this program to include a number of other air bases in Texas and New Mexico. He then retired from the Air Force in 1961, but during the latter part of his life worked with the U.S. military as a civilian specialist on the problem of alcoholism, serving from 1971 to 1978 as Chief of the Alcoholism Program at Fort Ord in California, and then running a treatment program at Alameda Naval Air Station in California until his retirement in 1983, when he was given the Meritorious Service Award, the Navy's highest award for a civilian at a duty station, for what seemed to be his almost miraculous successes with the alcoholics and drug addicts whom he had treated there. President George W. Bush sent him a presidential citation in April 23, 2007.

Sgt. Bill died August 17, 2008 at the age of ninety, with sixty years of sobriety, survived by his five sons, as well as by his new wife Mary (theirs was a marvelous love), and remembered with undying gratitude by all of the thousands and thousands of alcoholics whose lives he had saved.

Glenn F. Chesnut

Brought up in San Antonio, Texas, and Louisville, Kentucky, he earned his doctorate at Oxford University in England in 1971. During his three decade long professional career he taught at the University of Virginia, Boston University, and Indiana University, where he retired as Professor of History in 2003. He is now Director and Senior Editor at the Hindsfoot Foundation.

He is the author of several books on A.A. history and ideas, including *The Higher Power of the Twelve-Step Program: For Believers & Non-Believers* (2001), *God and Spirituality: Philosophical Essays* (2010), and *Changed by Grace: V. C. Kitchen, the Oxford Group, and A.A.* (2006). This latter volume has been listed as one of the fifty best books tracing A.A.'s history, written over the past century.

He has also edited and published several classic books in that field, including Nancy Olson, *With a Lot of Help from Our Friends: The Politics of Alcoholism* (2003), Richard M. Dubiel, *The Road to Fellowship: The Role of the Emmanuel Movement and the Jacoby Club in the Development of Alcoholics Anonymous* (2004), and Annette R. Smith, Ph.D., *The Social World of Alcoholics Anonymous: How It Works* (2007).

www.ingramcontent.com/pod-product-compliance
Lightning Source LLC
Chambersburg PA
CBHW030249290526
45785CB00001B/23